DATE DUE

ENCYCLOPEDIA
of
SOCIAL ISSUES

ENCYCLOPEDIA
of
SOCIAL ISSUES

Volume 6

Support groups – Zoos and wildlife refuges

Index

Editor
JOHN K. ROTH

Marshall Cavendish
New York • London • Toronto

Project Editor: Robert McClenaghan
Research Supervisor: Jeffry Jensen
Acquisitions Editor: Mark Rehn
Photograph Editor: Valerie Krein
Production Editor: Cynthia Breslin Beres
Proofreading Supervisor: Yasmine A. Cordoba
Layout: James Hutson

Published By
Marshall Cavendish Corporation
99 White Plains Road
Tarrytown, New York 10591-9001
United States of America

Library of Congress Cataloging-in-Publication Data

Encyclopedia of social issues / editor, John K. Roth
    p. cm.
  Includes bibliographical references and index.
  1. United States—Social conditions—Encyclopedias. 2. United States—Economic conditions—Encyclopedias. 3. United States—Politics and government—Encyclopedias. 4. Canada—Social conditions—Encyclopedias. 5. Canada—Economic conditions—Encyclopedias.—6. Canada—Politics and government—Encyclopedias.—I. Roth, John K.
HN57.E59   1997
306′.0973—dc20   96-38361
ISBN 0-7614-0568-2 (set)   CIP
ISBN 0-7614-0574-7 (volume 6)

First Printing

PRINTED IN THE UNITED STATES OF AMERICA

Contents

CONTENTS

ENCYCLOPEDIA
of
SOCIAL ISSUES

Support groups: Mental-health programs utilizing group interaction as a key helping ingredient. Support groups usually involve two or more individuals who meet for the purpose of assisting each other with common problems via the sharing of intimate feelings, ideas, and experiences. The problems addressed may be very specific, such as alcohol dependence or sexual-abuse recovery, or more general, such psychological growth. Groups can be facilitated by degreed profes-sionals or by trained paraprofessionals. While most support groups meet in real-life settings, they also are forming on the Internet via the exchange of electronic communication.

Supreme Court, U.S.: Highest legal authority in the United States, established by the Constitution in 1787. During the twentieth century, the Supreme Court

Members of a support group for cancer patients. (UPI/Corbis-Bettmann)

involved itself in a variety of social issues, including ABORTION, school DESEGREGATION, AFFIRMATIVE ACTION, SCHOOL PRAYER, and criminal defendants' rights, through decisions interpreting the Constitution.

History. In outlining the design of the nation's governing system, the Constitution gives the Supreme Court the authority to interpret laws and decide legal cases. The Court's authority includes the power to interpret the BILL OF RIGHTS, the Constitution's first ten amendments, which specify the protections possessed by the people that cannot be infringed by government. For most of U.S. history, the Court did not use this interpretive power to involve itself in social issues. In the 1833 decision *Barron v. Baltimore*, the Court decided that the Bill of Rights applied only with respect to the federal government and not with respect to state governments.

The ratification of the Fourteenth Amendment in 1868 gave the Supreme Court new tools to use in affecting social issues. The new amendment was specifically intended to limit the activities of state and local governments, and it gave the Court the authority to enforce rights to "EQUAL PROTECTION" and "DUE PROCESS of law." Although the Court was slow to employ the Fourteenth Amendment to affect social issues, by the middle of the twentieth century, the nine-member Court contained a majority of life-tenure justices who were eager to use their power to achieve their sense of fairness—even if such action meant clashing with Congress, the president, and public opinion on controversial issues.

The Warren Court Era. Earl Warren, a former governor of California, was appointed by President Dwight D. Eisenhower to become the Court's chief justice in 1953. Under Warren's leadership, the Court became increasingly active in asserting its authority to influence controversial social issues. Warren made the Court the focus of controversy and political opposition by writing an opinion for the unanimous Court in *BROWN V. BOARD OF EDUCATION OF TOPEKA, KANSAS* (1954), which declared that racial SEGREGATION in the nation's public schools violated the Fourteenth Amendment's right to equal protection. Under the Court's direction and in the face of fierce public opposition, federal judges throughout the country began ordering local school districts to dismantle their segregated school systems. Local districts were thereby required to mix white, African American, and Hispanic children together through the use of BUSING plans, magnet schools, and redrawn school-district boundaries. Although members of Congress and various governors and state legislators sought to amend the Constitution to prevent the Supreme Court from affecting the desegregation issue, their efforts were unsuccessful, and the Court continued to make decisions affecting education and other controversial issues.

Under Warren's leadership, the Court made decisions expanding the rights of criminal defendants by interpreting the Fourth Amendment's right against unreasonable SEARCHES AND SEIZURES, the Fifth Amendment's right against self-incrimination, and the Sixth Amendment's right to counsel. Among the Court's most controversial decisions was *MAPP V. OHIO* (1961), which declared that state and local police officers were barred from using any evidence against a suspect if that evidence was not obtained through proper procedures. In *MIRANDA V. ARIZONA* (1966), the Court ruled that police officers must inform suspects of their constitutional rights upon arrest, before initiating any questioning. Many police chiefs and legislators complained bitterly about these decisions, arguing that the Court was favoring the rights of criminals over the needs of law-enforcement officials. The Court's decisions sparked various efforts by elected officials, who tried—generally with little success—to write new laws, amend the Constitution, and obtain new judicial decisions that would undo the Warren Court's actions.

In 1963, the Court ignited another national controversy when it declared in *ENGEL V. VITALE* that public schools could not sponsor prayers or require students to pray. The Court's decision was based on the First Amendment's prohibition of an establishment of religion and the Warren-era justices' belief that such prayers involved the government in religious activity. Once again, the Court's decision produced continuing efforts by politicians and interest groups to reduce the Court's influence over specific issues.

The Burger Court Era. When Warren retired in 1969, President Richard M. Nixon appointed Warren Burger to be the new chief justice. Nixon openly stated that he hoped Burger would lead the Court to make new decisions that would reverse some of the Warren Court's rulings; he also wanted Burger to reduce the Court's involvement in controversial issues. By 1972, Nixon had appointed three additional newcomers to replace retiring justices from the Warren era. President Gerald Ford's appointment of John Paul Stevens in 1975 produced a new five-member majority that had not participated in the controversial decisions of the Warren Court. Although the new majority issued some

CHIEF JUSTICES OF THE UNITED STATES

Chief Justice	Years Served	Appointed by
John Jay	1789-1795	George Washington
Oliver Ellsworth	1796-1800	George Washington
John Marshall	1801-1835	John Adams
Roger B. Taney	1836-1864	Andrew Jackson
Salmon P. Chase	1864-1873	Abraham Lincoln
Morrison R. Waite	1874-1888	Ulysses S. Grant
Melville W. Fuller	1888-1910	Grover Cleveland
Edward D. White	1910-1921	William Howard Taft
William Howard Taft	1921-1930	Warren G. Harding
Charles Evans Hughes	1930-1941	Herbert Hoover
Harlan Fiske Stone	1941-1946	Franklin D. Roosevelt
Fred M. Vinson	1946-1953	Harry S Truman
Earl Warren	1953-1969	Dwight D. Eisenhower
Warren E. Burger	1969-1986	Richard M. Nixon
William Rehnquist	1986-	Ronald Reagan

decisions that reduced the scope of criminal defendants' rights, it did not fulfill Nixon's goal of withdrawing the Court from participation in controversial issues. In fact, the Burger Court itself soon began to make additional controversial decisions.

In 1973, the Court issued one of its most controversial rulings in ROE V. WADE, which declared that women possess a constitutional right to make their own choices about abortion as part of the Constitution's right to privacy. The Court subsequently decided a dozen additional cases during the 1970's, 1980's, and 1990's that reconfirmed its position on the existence of this right. Although the word "privacy" does not appear in the Constitution, the justices interpreted the document as containing an implicit right to make personal choices about contraception. The Court's decision mobilized antiabortion interest groups and generated decades of political conflict between "pro-choice" and "pro-life" groups.

The Burger Court spawned a similar controversy when it endorsed the concept of affirmative action in REGENTS OF THE UNIVERSITY OF CALIFORNIA V. BAKKE (1978). In the *Bakke* case and other decisions, the Court approved the granting of preferences to historically disadvantaged racial minorities, women, and military veterans in specific contexts of employment, admission to educational institutions, and government contracts. The Court also initiated a series of decisions

that interpreted the Fourteenth Amendment's right to equal protection as including restrictions on gender discrimination—even though historians generally agreed that the Fourteenth Amendment was originally intended to protect African Americans against racial discrimination by government. In *Craig v. Boren* (1976), for example, the Court declared that states cannot have different legal drinking ages for men and women. In addition, the Court in FURMAN V. GEORGIA (1972) temporarily halted the use of capital punishment before requiring judges and juries in GREGG V. GEORGIA (1976) to apply more careful standards in making decisions about the application of the death penalty.

The Rehnquist Court Era. During the 1980's and early 1990's, Presidents Ronald Reagan and George Bush both believed that the Supreme Court had become too involved in controversial social issues. As Nixon had done before them, both Reagan and Bush sought to use their power to appoint new justices as a means to reverse many of the controversial decisions of the Warren and Burger eras. When Burger retired in 1986, Reagan promoted William Rehnquist, the most conservative of Nixon's appointees, to be chief justice. As holdover justices from the Warren and Burger eras retired, Reagan appointed three new justices from 1981 to 1987; Bush appointed two new justices in 1990 and 1991, thus creating a new five-member ma-

The U.S. Supreme Court in 1990. From left, back row: Anthony M. Kennedy, Sandra Day O'Connor, Antonin Scalia, David Souter; front row: Harry A. Blackmun, Byron White, William Rehnquist, Thurgood Marshall, John Paul Stevens. (AP/Wide World Photos)

jority under Rehnquist's leadership. Although President Bill Clinton subsequently appointed two more liberal justices in 1993 and 1994, Rehnquist's conservative majority remained intact.

The new justices acted to reduce the extent of rights for criminal defendants by, for example, rejecting the use of statistical evidence to prove racial discrimination in death-penalty cases in *McCleskey v. Kemp* (1987). The Court also limited the use of affirmative action in government contracts in *City of Richmond v. J. A. Croson Co.* (1989) and *Adarand Constructors v. Peña* (1995). The justices, however, surprised many experts who had expected sudden changes by issuing decisions that reconfirmed the right of choice for ABORTION in *Planned Parenthood of Southeastern Pennsylvania v. Casey* (1992) and expanded the prohibition of SCHOOL PRAYER by extending the ban to high-school graduation ceremonies in *Lee v. Weisman* (1992).

Despite continuing changes in the Supreme Court's composition, including appointments explicitly intended to reduce its social activism, during the twenti-

eth century, the Court became an active and enduring participant in the formulation of policies concerning a wide range of social issues.   —*Christopher E. Smith*

SUGGESTED READINGS: Comprehensive presentations of the Court's history, procedures, and involvement in social issues appear in Lawrence Baum's *The Supreme Court*, 4th ed. (Washington, D.C.: CQ Press, 1992), David M. O'Brien's *Storm Center: The Supreme Court in American Politics*, 3d ed. (New York: W. W. Norton, 1993), and Stephen Wasby's *The Supreme Court in the Federal Judicial System*, 4th ed. (Chicago: Nelson-Hall, 1993). A detailed history of the Court's involvement in controversial issues is presented in Henry J. Abraham's *Freedom and the Court*, 5th ed. (New York: Oxford University Press, 1988).

Supreme Court of Canada: Highest court in Canada. The Canadian Supreme Court has undergone substantial transformation since its 1875 creation.

History and Structure. The plan for such a court

originated with the first Canadian prime minister, John A. Macdonald. Although the groundwork was laid in the years 1867 to 1873, the court did not come into being until Macdonald's government had been defeated. It was then left up to his Liberal successor, Alexander Mackenzie, largely through the efforts of his justice minister, noted legalist Edward Blake, to usher the legislation through the House of Commons and the Senate. The first justices were sworn in October 8, 1875. The court consists of nine justices. One is designated as chief justice; the others as puisne, or junior, justices. All appointments are made by the governor-general from among provincial court judges or lawyers who have been members of a provincial bar for at least ten years. The court meets in January, April, and October. A quorum is five justices, but for constitutional questions, the full court usually hears the case.

Through its first seventy-five years, the Supreme Court faced significant problems. The most significant was that while the 1875 legislation established the institution as the highest court in the land, unlike its U.S. counterpart, it was not the court of last resort. Not only could Canadians appeal to the Judicial Committee of the Privy Council in Great Britain, they could bypass the Supreme Court altogether in doing so. Despite the name, the Supreme Court was really an intermediate court that did not readily gain acceptance from either the government or the public. The subordinate position of the Supreme Court was underlined by the fact that 48 percent of appeals of decisions from the Canadian court were upheld by the committee and that all decisions made there automatically became binding precedents. From time to time, there were calls to remedy the situation, especially in 1931, when the passage of the Statute of Westminster by the British government increased the level of Canadian independence from the mother country. The one concession made came in 1895 when Canada's chief justice, along with those from South Africa and Australia, received automatic appointment to the Judicial Committee. This custom remained in place until 1954. The appointment was more symbolic than real, as the practicalities of distance and time meant attendance was sporadic. Canadian justices were signatories to committee decisions but did not make significant judgments. The right of appeal was revoked only in 1949 with the revision of the Supreme Court Act.

Problems of the Court. The attitude of successive governments was that it was politically inexpedient to spend much money on the court. Initially, it was housed in the parliamentary library. When the first court building was constructed, there were neither enough courtrooms nor offices. Inadequate library facilities were a constant source of concern.

Court personnel also presented ongoing problems. Ideally, the court should have attracted the best legal minds; it did not. Appointments were not necessarily made on the basis of ability. For example, there must always be three justices from both Ontario and Québec, with representation from Atlantic and Western Canada, which meant that geographic origin often superseded other factors. In many cases, appointments were refused because appointees believed more money could be made in private practice. Others complained of the need to move to Ottawa, the northern climate of which they found distasteful. In some cases, those who accepted judgeships resigned within a short time rather than live in the nation's capital. Others were critical of the fact that many of the appointments were of a blatantly political nature.

The court also seems to have been singularly unlucky in the number of justices beset with health problems. The result has been a rapid turnover in personnel and the appointment of justices of less than sterling ability.

There were three other difficulties for the pre-1949 court. First, there was a general distrust of the legal profession as being less than honorable. Second, for those who, at the provincial level, felt that the federal government was overly centrist, the court was seen as simply an instrument to concentrate power in Ottawa. Finally, there was the difficulty of having to deal with a two-tiered legal system in the province of Québec, where both English common law and French civil law are used. Since the justices from the rest of Canada traditionally are versed only in common law, this forced Québec justices into an overly heavy workload.

Changes to the Court. The change in attitude toward the court had much to do with the country's relationship with Great Britain. There were a number of key incidents that precipitated the gradual growth of the desire to raise the stature of the institution. Certainly, the role Canada played in World War I was one factor. So, too, was the King-Byng affair of 1926. In that instance, the English governor general, Julian Byng, refused to grant Prime Minister Mackenzie King an automatic dissolution leading to an election when his government was defeated in 1925. Byng instead called upon the leader of the opposition, Arthur Meighan, to form a government, which was defeated after a very short time in office. Although Byng had acted constitutionally, King made the unwarranted interference of a non-Canadian in national affairs the major issue, leading in turn to the 1931 passage of the Statute of Westminster. After doing little to deal with the negative effects of the Great Depression, the Conservative prime minister, Richard Bedford Bennett, introduced his own version of U.S. president Franklin D. Roosevelt's NEW DEAL just before the election of 1935. When the appeal of the federal legislation was made to London, it was ruled unconstitutional. The ensuing outcry, however, was lost in the preparation for and the prosecution of the war effort. Canada's success led to a new self-confidence. The Liberal government, over some considerable objection, introduced legislation to make the Supreme Court the court of last resort. The bill was passed in 1949. As if to underline the new importance to be accorded the court, the government also built a large, architecturally pleasing courthouse on Parliament Hill. Perhaps the greatest irony was that before the legislation could be proclaimed, the government sent it to the Judicial Committee to ensure its constitutionality.

The court did not go through an immediate transformation. "Judgements," as they were referred to before 1949, tended to be conservative and noncontroversial. There were also some significant changes in the personnel, particularly during the prime ministership of Pierre TRUDEAU, which began in 1968. During the 1950's and 1960's, political appointments continued to be made but became less tolerated. An intellectual who had taught law but never practiced it, Trudeau saw no necessity for a justice to have a practical background. The result was a number of appointments of legal scholars. The greatest departure came in 1970 with the appointment of Bora Laskin as one of the Ontario justices. Laskin was the first appointee who was of neither French nor English Canadian origin; he was also the first non-Christian. Like Trudeau, he was a constitutional expert with a commitment to civil liberties. He also had absolutely no experience in private practice. Although his appointment was reputedly unpopular with the legal profession, he was appointed chief justice in 1973, a post he held until 1984. The Laskin years are noted for bringing a much more intellectual tone to the court.

The other major personnel change came in 1981 with the naming of Ontario judge Bertha Wilson as the first female justice. There were also several pieces of legislation that raised the profile of the court. The first

of these was the passage in 1960 by the Conservative government of John Diefenbaker of the Canadian BILL OF RIGHTS, guaranteeing all Canadians equal treatment under the law. It was expected that the legislation would cause a flurry of activity, but it was not until *Queen v. Drybones* that the court had to rule. In this case, Joseph Drybones, an Indian, was convicted under a section of the Indian Act dealing with intoxication. Since the act put much greater restriction on Indians than on other Canadians, the court ruled that the act was a violation of Drybones' rights.

The next important change came in 1975. The automatic right of appeal to the court was eliminated; henceforth, litigants would have to seek the right of appeal, which would be granted or denied with no reason given for the decision.

The most important development came with the repatriation of the Canadian constitution in 1982 after the court had ruled that the federal government had the right to amend the constitution. In the new legislation, the Supreme Court was entrenched. Also in the new constitution was the CHARTER OF RIGHTS AND FREEDOMS, which delineated the privileges and obligations of Canadian citizenship. The Supreme Court was given the task of deciding upon the interpretation of the charter. There were some complaints that in enacting the legislation, the government had "Americanized" the system, that the court would be put in the position of making laws rather than reviewing them, and that litigation would increase dramatically. Certainly, this latter fear has been realized; between 1982 and 1984, one thousand charter cases were heard. In that time, however, only two decisions were rendered, indicating that while the court would have an enhanced role in the justice system, it was not likely to alter itself readily or rapidly.   —*Gerald J. Stortz*

SUGGESTED READINGS: There is surprisingly little written on the Canadian Supreme Court. The most readable work is James G. Snell and Frederick Vaughan's *The Supreme Court of Canada: History of the Institution* (Toronto: University of Toronto Press, 1985). Also useful is Paul C. Weiler's *In the Last Resort: A Critical Study of the Supreme Court of Canada* (Toronto: Carswell, Methuen, 1974).

Surgery: A triumph of twentieth century health care, surgery cures or improves many previously untreatable maladies. Yet surgery is dangerous, expensive, and sometimes unnecessary or harmful, factors that encourage lawsuits, suspicion among patients, and escalating health-care costs.

Surgery refers to any medical procedure in which doctors use instruments to open a passageway into the body to diagnose or treat a medical condition. Its modern success rate has been so great that every year about 20 percent of Americans have operations. However, not all surgeries are equal. A surgery is necessary if the patient must have it to stay alive or maintain good health and if medical experience suggests that the surgery will succeed. A surgery is elective if it stands a chance of improving a medical problem but is not clearly needed or if, like cosmetic surgery, a patient chooses to have it for nonmedical reasons. Elective surgeries are the ones most likely to be judged unnecessary.

Undeniably effective, necessary surgeries sometimes fail and questionable procedures sometimes benefit patients. Consequently, the distinction between necessary and unnecessary surgery is often difficult to make. Nevertheless, reviews by Congress and professional medical organizations estimate that 2 million to 10 million unnecessary surgeries are performed yearly in the United States, causing well over ten thousand deaths. Various reasons for this excess play a part. The number of surgeons has increased faster than the population, and competition to make money may tempt some surgeons to perform unnecessary procedures. It is also difficult to judge the general worth of a surgical procedure. Clinical trials of the sort used for new drugs are hard to manage and potentially unethical, and no equivalent of the Federal Drug Administration exists to set standards and assess the findings of surgical research. As a result, surgery is subject to fads based upon the experience of famous surgeons, promising yet incomplete data from research, or the preferences of medical schools and hospitals. Surgeons lack a clear means of testing a new technique's worth, other than success in the operating room.

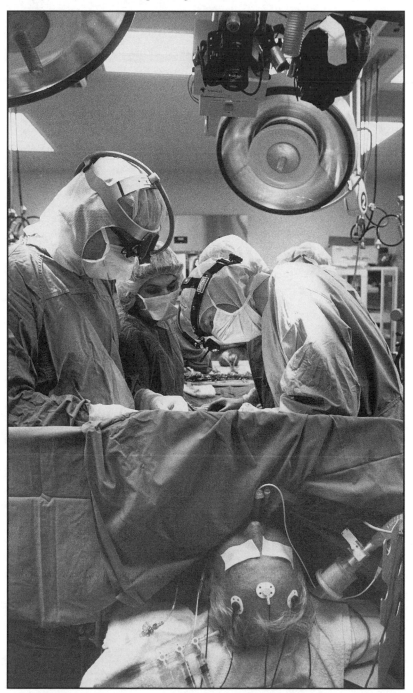

A surgical team implants an artificial heart in 1985. (UPI/Corbis-Bettmann)

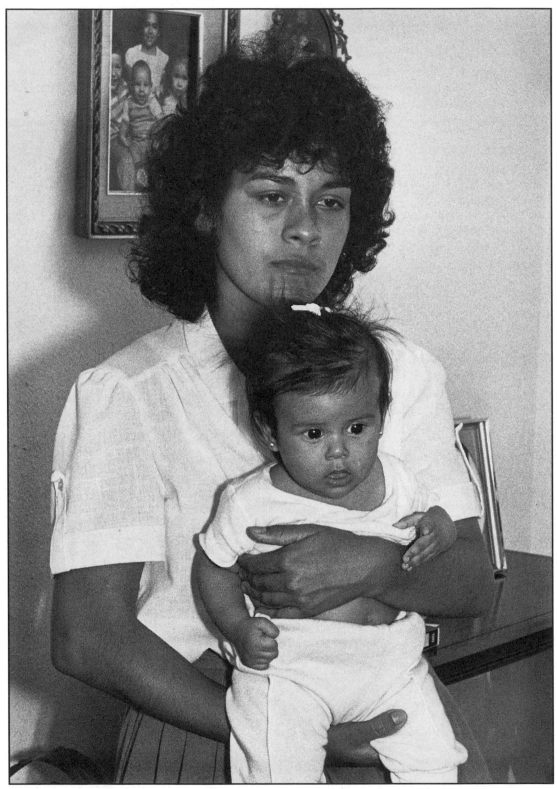

A surrogate mother poses with her child before a 1986 court hearing to determine custody. (UPI/Corbis-Bettmann)

Several surgeries that were once famous and frequently performed have since been denounced and discontinued. The most famous example is the lobotomy, a procedure during which the frontal lobe of the brain is surgically altered in order to change deranged or criminal behavior. Less drastic operations, once routinely done, are now either thought largely unnecessary or are controversial, including removal of tonsils, cesarean section, coronary-artery bypass grafting, hemorrhoid removal, and circumcision.

Surgeries are among the most expensive medical interventions, both to perform and to recover from. That many are unnecessary helps drive up national health-care costs, increase insurance premiums, and, when surgeries cause harm, generate lawsuits for malpractice. Furthermore, unnecessary, harmful surgeries can obscure the great benefit of surgery overall.

SUGGESTED READINGS: Most popular books on surgery recommend ways to ensure good medical care and avoid unnecessary procedures. John Lewis' *So Your Doctor Recommended Surgery* (New York: Dembner Books, 1990) is a surgeon's view of his profession's strengths and weaknesses. Charles B. Inlander is more openly critical in *Good Operations, Bad Operations* (New York: Viking, 1993) as a consumer-protection handbook.

Surrogate mothers: Women who undergo pregnancy for women who cannot, carrying an embryo that was fertilized *in vitro* using the other woman's egg. Through most of history, "surrogate mothers" were wet nurses, nannies, slaves, or kin who served as a substitute mother for a woman who died or for a woman who was wealthy enough to hire someone else to take on her mothering tasks. In the 1990's, the term refers to women who volunteer or who are paid not as nursemaids or caretakers but as childbearers: Today's surrogate mothers are impregnated with an embryo from another woman, carry the embryo through a full pregnancy, and give the baby to the biological mother after birth.

Medically, surrogacy involves a combination of procedures, each of which is sometimes used alone to enhance fertility. The first step is to stimulate the "egg donor" with fertility drugs so that she ovulates several eggs at a time. The eggs are then surgically removed and fertilized in a petri dish with sperm from the sperm donor (usually the husband of the egg donor). Once the eggs are fertilized and have begun to grow, one or two are inserted into the uterus of the surrogate; if more than two or three eggs are collected, the remaining embryos are generally frozen for future use, in case the first surrogacy attempt is unsuccessful. In the meantime, the surrogate takes hormones to ensure that her uterus is in the appropriate condition to maximize the chances that an inserted embryo will implant itself and continue to develop. Because this process is medically complicated and expensive, surrogacy serves as a last resort for the few infertile women who can afford both the emotional and financial investment.

While surrogacy is medically safe, there are many ethical questions about the process that remain unresolved. Some people regard surrogacy as unnatural and improper; others see it as a waste of money and technology in an increasingly overpopulated world full of unwanted children. Still others see it as akin to prostitution or child-selling.

Legal questions also exist. Who is the child's true mother? Who is the legal parent? Does the sperm donor have any legal claim to the child? In the case of a custody battle, who can best represent the child's interests? (In a small but widely publicized set of cases, notably the "Baby M" case, surrogate mothers have decided that they wanted to keep the baby to whom they gave birth. In most cases, the egg donor has been determined to be the legal mother, and the surrogate has been viewed as similar to a wet nurse or nanny who contracted her services.) Governments and members of the legal community have only begun to tackle these issues. Like other topics that mix sex, politics, and religion, they generate continuing controversy.

Swann v. Charlotte-Mecklenburg Board of Education (1971): U.S. Supreme Court case. In *Swann*, the Court affirmed the decision of a North Carolina district court ordering a county school board to adopt plans for DESEGREGATION. The school system had approximately 29 percent African American students and 71 percent white students. Chief Justice Warren Burger held that the application of ratios of white to black students was an appropriate method of attaining an equitable remedy. Pairing and grouping of noncontiguous school zones was ruled permissible; where it appeared that assignment of children to the school nearest their homes would not effectively eliminate SEGREGATION, bus transportation was approved as a desegregating tool.

T

Tabloid journalism: Form of newspaper reporting that sensationalizes events. The advent of inexpensive printing methods in the 1890's, combined with a more literate public, created newspapers with a style and tone aimed at human-interest stories. These papers also contained cartoons and illustrations for the less literate parts of the population. By themselves, however, these ingredients would not have had the lasting impact that tabloid journalism created. The competition between newspaper owners for the most sensational stories created the penny newspaper and the reporter who found stories. The best examples of this type of journalism were Joseph Pulitzer's *New York World* and William Randolph Hearst's *New York Journal*.

Newspapers prior to the late nineteenth century typically contained items of public knowledge, court records, speeches, births, deaths, other vital statistics, and usually a particular political stance. Tabloid journalism changed this. The reasons for the change were a coming together of technology that created lower publishing costs, a mass literate market that wanted to know what was going on, and the profit to be made from advertising.

To create a greater audience, the tabloid press told of great adventures such as Henry Morton Stanley's finding of Dr. David Livingstone in Africa, wars, corruption in the meat and drug industries, political corruption, and the evils of some publicly supported institutions such as insane asylums. Through in-person reporting, the tabloid press informed the public of these events in the most sensational manner possible, often in competition with other papers, to produce the most graphic, exciting stories. Tabloids often used lurid headlines to attract readers, supplementing these headlines with stories containing illustrations and, later, photographs. These methods did not change even though the century did. Through the 1920's, tabloids addressed changes in fashion, lifestyle, and crime.

From the Depression through the 1960's, there was a sharp decline in many of the lurid newspaper accounts, as most metropolitan newspapers gave up the sensational for a more factual style. The tabloid, though, did not disappear; it merely found another format, the supermarket tabloid such as the *National Enquirer* and the *Star*. Here the stories centered on those in the political, athletic, or Hollywood spotlight, as well as on reports of extraterrestrials and medical miracles.

The tabloid moved from print to TELEVISION in the 1970's with the growth of the talk show. Like their print counterparts, TALK SHOWS addressed the sensational aspects of life with a new slant, bringing together individuals or groups of often violently opposing views, or a panel in support of a particular attitude of lifestyle. Further extensions of the tabloid concept include call-in radio talk shows, via which the ordinary person can speak to any subject.

The media and material have expanded, but the bottom line has remained constant—the tabloid with the most outrageous material is the one that creates the largest audience.

SUGGESTED READINGS: Joyce Milton's *The Yellow Kids* (New York: Harper Press, 1989) provides an account of the beginnings of tabloid journalism. *Jazz Journalism: The Story of Tabloid Newspapers*, by Simon Michael Bessie (New York: E. P. Dutton & Co., 1938), gives a rounded review of the medium in the early years, whereas *For Enquiring Minds: A Cultural Study of Supermarket Tabloids*, by S. Elizabeth Bird (Knoxville: University of Tennessee Press, 1992), discusses more recent history.

Tai Chi Chuan: Exercise system and therapeutic technique based on principles of body equilibrium, rhythmic movement, and breathing. The technique was popularized in China by Chang San-Feng, a renowned Taoist boxer who lived during the Sung Dynasty (960-1270 A.D.). Tai Chi Chuan is characterized by slow, continuous movements and countermovements.

Practitioners reach a relaxed state of consciousness by loosening their muscles and releasing their stored nervous tension. Millions of people practice Tai Chi every day in China, and in Western countries its popularity is on the rise, particularly among "NEW AGE"

Chinese women practice Tai Chi Chuan. (UPI/Corbis-Bettmann)

adherents, who claim that the discipline provides a variety of health benefits.

Tailhook scandal (1991): U.S. armed forces controversy that generated widespread criticism of the U.S. Navy and its treatment of women.

The Tailhook Association is a San Diego, California, based organization for military aviators. The association holds an annual convention attended by many naval officers, both retired and active. The group, which was founded in the 1950's, sponsors symposiums on tactics, weapons, and policies during the conferences.

During the 1991 convention in Las Vegas, at least twenty-six women were sexually assaulted or harassed by conventioneers. Women at the convention, including fourteen naval officers, were forced to run a gauntlet of drunken male officers and to drink from a simulated rhinoceros penis. Male officers were accused of shoving their hands into the women's clothes and trying to remove their undergarments as the women ran the gauntlet; the proceedings resulted in more than $23,000 damage to the hotel.

One of the women assaulted was Paula A. Coughlin, a Navy helicopter pilot, who was the first woman to come forward to report the incident. Coughlin won punitive damages from the Las Vegas Hilton, where the convention was held, and received an undisclosed amount of money as a settlement from the Tailhook Association. In the wake of the incident, Coughlin left the Navy, citing related incidents of harassment.

The Navy conducted an initial inquiry into the Tailhook scandal, but critics assailed the inquiry's integrity. A subsequent PENTAGON report found that the Navy investigation was deficient, as Navy officials had attempted to limit the exposure of their officers and their organization to criticism. The naval investigation was found to have had the primary purposes of protecting the senior officers who were involved in the scandal and of avoiding damaging publicity. The Pentagon report specifically cited the two admirals who were in charge of the Navy's investigation as having provided inadequate leadership. Both admirals, Rear Admiral Duvall M. Williams, Jr., the commander of the Naval Investigative Service, and Barbara S. Pope, the Assistant Navy Secretary for Manpower and Reserve Affairs, took early retirements as a result of the controversy surrounding the investigation.

The incident intensified public criticism of the Naval Investigative Service, which was already under scrutiny for its handling of the investigation into an explosion on the battleship *Iowa* in 1989. Following the Tailhook scandal, even more attention was focused on the Navy and on how the organization dealt with issues of SEXUAL HARASSMENT and discrimination.

Takeovers, corporate: Business term. Corporate takeovers are mergers of two or more companies, usually accomplished with less than full cooperation of the company being taken over. These mergers usually involve publicly traded companies and are accomplished by buying up controlling percentages of stock and thereby taking control of the company. Sometimes takeovers are achieved by legal maneuvering done to obtain control of weak or ineffective companies, or by forcing other companies to relinquish clients, territory, or other operational activities. A natural phenomenon of aggressive corporate life, takeovers usually bring vast reorganizations in all companies involved, sometimes costing jobs on many levels. The acquiring company believes it can do a better job of running the company than can current management, but current management may be unwilling to relinquish control.

Takeovers, hostile: Business term. A hostile takeover is the merging of one or more companies into a larger corporate unit. Hostile takeovers, one type of corporate takeover, usually involve extreme maneuvering to achieve the takeover, such as stock buyouts at inflated prices or legal tie-ups. Many companies not part of a conglomerate resist takeovers because they wish to stay independent to retain organizational preferences that may be threatened under such takeovers. Because the victim companies are traded publicly, a hostile takeover may be relatively easy to accomplish. Federal agencies including the SECURITIES AND EXCHANGE COMMISSION and the FEDERAL TRADE COMMISSION oversee such activities to ensure that only legal means are used and that monopolies, which are illegal, are not formed as a result.

Talk shows: Programs on radio and TELEVISION that involve a host talking to an audience or some type of discussion between the host and others, such as a panel of guests, a live audience, or telephone callers.

History of Radio Talk Shows. In the 1920's, as radio broadcasting developed, talk shows became a major feature, making up about 20 percent of programming time. Most of the early radio talk shows were monologues, with experts talking to a radio audience. As early as the 1930's, audience participation became a feature of many talk shows, but it was in the 1960's that radio began to put more emphasis on talk shows, largely because of the need to target specific subgroups from its large and diverse audience and because of competition from television. With the large-scale use of satellite networking and toll-free telephone calls in the 1980's, national AM radio shows received a boost in listeners and audience participants. Talk shows successfully spread to FM radio in the early 1990's.

In the mid-1990's, radio talk shows underwent a resurgence of popularity, reflecting the public's distrust of the government, network news, and large newspapers, and a desire for unfiltered opinions and discussions. The most popular talk shows on radio were politically oriented, often with a conservative orientation, or at least with a position critical of the establishment. "Shock radio," with uninhibited discussions and flamboyant style, also became popular on many music-radio stations in the 1990's.

History of Television Talk Shows. Beginning in the 1950's, different types of radio talk shows crossed over to the new medium of television. In 1952, the profitable news talk show *Today* began. News interview programs such as *Meet the Press* and celebrity-variety talk shows such as *Tonight* also became popular. Reflecting the political protest of the 1960's, political talk shows became popular. A form of talk show referred to as "loud talk" because of its flamboyant and controversial nature moved from radio to television in 1966. The audience-participation talk show became a feature of television in 1967, with Phil Donahue becoming the first well-known host. The first investigative documentary, *Prime Time Live*, began in 1989.

In early 1992, politically oriented talk shows gained popularity when Ross PEROT announced on *Larry King Live* that he might run for president of the United States. Later in the year, Perot and Bill CLINTON appeared on the *Today* and *This Morning* shows, answering questions from hosts and the audience. At first, President George BUSH refused invitations to appear on talk shows, saying that they were beneath the dignity of the office of president, but he changed his position as he saw how effective they were. Television talk shows on political topics became as popular on television as on radio because they were viewed as more direct and less manipulated than much of the news.

The political talk shows, on both radio and television, are criticized for their ideological biases, and the "shock" and "loud talk" shows are criticized for their controversial, combative, and sensationalized styles. Despite the criticisms, by the 1980's, talk shows were not only popular but also were among the most financially successful programs because of their comparatively low production costs. Although political, current events, and celebrity talk shows are popular, the service talk shows such as *The Phil Donahue Show*, *The Oprah Winfrey Show*, *Geraldo*, *Sally Jessy Raphael*, and *The Ricki Lake Show* became the most controversial talk shows in the 1980's and 1990's. These talk shows are frequently criticized for their selection of topics, "shallow" treatment of topics, and their sensationalized approach.

Talk Show Topics. In the early 1990's, the most popular topics on radio talk shows dealt with specific current events such as presidential elections, the Mike Tyson rape trial, and the Rodney King police-beating trial, or with major societal issues such as race relations, the economy, CRIME and the justice system, ABORTION, AIDS, the health-care crisis, and foreign affairs. Talk shows frequently are biased, with radio programs more likely to be conservative and television programs more likely to be liberal.

Topics on television talk shows vary much more than radio topics. The news talk shows (referred to as magazines) such as *Today* and *Good Morning America*, news interview programs such as *Meet the Press*, and investigative documentaries such as *Prime Time Live* generally focus on current events. In 1995, for example, the O. J. SIMPSON trial was the single-largest topic, but even more time was spent on contemporary political issues such as HEALTH CARE, the economy, and foreign affairs. The celebrity-variety talk shows also have a large mix of topics, usually centering around the personal lives of celebrity guests.

The service talk shows have the greatest variety of topics and generate the most attention, controversy, and criticism. The range of topics has been virtually unlimited. Some talk shows announce forthcoming topics and request people to contact the show if they have experienced the personal situation to be discussed (for example, a woman cheating with her husband's best friend or a man deserting his pregnant girlfriend). With many talk shows operating, there is a substantial overlap of topics, with several talk shows covering the same topic with only minor differences.

A fight breaks out between guests on the *Geraldo* talk show in 1988. (UPI/Corbis-Bettmann)

Some guests have been exposed as phonies, making false claims or charges.

Roles in Society. The relatively unstructured format on both radio and television allows "average people" to talk, either as guests, audience members, or telephone callers, to an extent prohibited by more formal media. People can feel that their experiences and opinions are important, and they can hear opinions of others uncensored by formal programs. A sense of an old-fashioned town meeting, where people meet to openly discuss issues, can be experienced, giving people the feeling of a time when they were less controlled by technology.

Another role served by talk shows is empowerment. A specific political agenda has characterized some shows. Donahue, for example, early on became a television crusader for FEMINISM, discussing many issues specifically from the female perspective and being critical of, or negative toward, males in general. Women still are more likely to be the bulk of the audience for daytime television talk shows, another factor that has encouraged presentation of the female per-

spective. A few talk shows on sports are aimed primarily at men.

Talk shows also have increased the heterogeneity of views and topics to which people are exposed and have played a major role in giving a podium to racial, ethnic, and (especially) lifestyle groups that might be overlooked by more formal and staid programming. With increasing sensationalism, however, guests frequently reinforce negative stereotyping of minorities.

Another role of several talk shows is to provide amateur therapy ("psychobabble") on a wide variety of topics. This has become the major feature of the leading service talk shows. People like to hear about other people's problems, sometimes simply to eavesdrop, sometimes to hear about other people having similar problems, and sometimes because they feel they can give or receive helpful advice. Experts give brief advice on some talk shows, although some of the talk shows more critical of "the establishment" challenge the so-called experts as intellectuals out of touch with the real world. Talk shows also give a brief moment of fame to people who do not mind exposing their most intimate lives to public scrutiny in exchange for television exposure.

The service talk shows, with their amateur therapy and emphasis on misery, also help further the strong emphasis on victimization in the United States, the tendency of some people to claim no responsibility for their behavior because of something that might have happened to them in the past. In 1994, Oprah Winfrey began a highly publicized campaign to move away from an emphasis on dysfunctions, conflict, and sensationalism.

Talk shows can also serve informational purposes, such as informing audiences of new findings in medical areas. The political and current-events talk shows serve a major role of informing the public. Talk shows also can be purely entertainment, bringing personal information about top celebrities to their fans.

—Abraham D. Lavender

SUGGESTED READINGS: Wayne Munson's *All Talk: The Talkshow in Media Culture* (Philadelphia: Temple University Press, 1993) gives a general history of, and reactions to, radio and television talk shows. Alan Hirsch, in *Talking Heads: Political Talk Shows and Their Star Pundits* (New York: St. Martin's Press, 1991), gives a detailed discussion of several specific talk shows and of six popular talk show hosts or panelists. Todd Gitlin's *Inside Prime Time* (New York: Pantheon, 1983) argues that talk shows recombine and synthesize standardized and cost-efficient formats. "The Shameless World of Phil, Sally, and Oprah: Television Talk Shows and the Deconstructing of Society" by Vicki Abt and Mel Seesholtz (*Journal of Popular Culture*, Summer, 1994) gives a detailed overview of criticisms of service talk shows. "Tuning into Trouble" by Jeanne Albronda Heaton and Nona Leight Wilson (*Ms.*, September/October, 1995) shows how service talk shows negatively stereotype both women and men.

Tariffs: Taxes on imports. A tariff may be specific, imposed as a fixed sum per unit of the imported item, or *ad valorem*, imposed at a percentage of the value of the imported item. All countries have regulations on their international trade, usually to protect vital or emerging industries and domestic employment. These regulations include controls on imports, among them tariffs and quotas.

Tariffs and Commercial Policy. Tariffs constitute a major tool used by most industrial countries to regulate trade. Because they affect a product's final price, tariffs affect firms' pricing and production decisions. Among the arguments supporting tariffs, only two, regarding movement toward the economic optimum and product dumping, find widespread support in economic analysis. Some analysts contend that nontariff barriers, such as government purchasing policies and safety and technical standards that give advantages to domestic firms over foreign firms, are more effective.

Some economic analyses suggest that free trade policies enhance economic welfare, whereas protectionist policies reduce economic welfare. Free trade, it is argued, increases the opportunities available to consumers and businesses. Problems arise from deliberate attempts by some nations to subvert market processes in order to create or change their international comparative advantage through discriminatory commercial policies. Most analysts agree that a high level of world tariffs reduces economic welfare to all the world's trading nations as a group. One country, however, can sometimes gain a selfish advantage by levying high tariffs. If one country does so, others may retaliate in self-defense, eliminating the advantage. The net result may be rounds of tariffs that end up lowering living standards in all countries.

Tariffs may reduce welfare in countries that use them as tools of commercial policy. For example, a tariff designed to discourage Americans from buying foreign vehicles will increase the price of foreign vehicles for Americans, thereby lowering their real income and standard of living. This policy may slow sales of foreign vehicles, thus increasing profits for U.S. automakers and protecting employment of domestic autoworkers, but it will lead to price increases on foreign cars and probably on domestic cars, as demand switches to them from foreign cars. Likely secondary effects of the tariff include INFLATION, reduced quality of domestic vehicles, lower overall U.S. exports, and lower employment in export-oriented sectors. A policy intended to protect one industry and its workers has widespread repercussions.

Tariff Reduction. There are global agreements, such as the GENERAL AGREEMENT ON TARIFFS AND TRADE (GATT), and regional agreements, such as the NORTH AMERICAN FREE TRADE AGREEMENT (NAFTA), aimed at lowering or eliminating tariffs. These agreements were reached because countries recognized the benefits of cooperating to reduce tariffs.

Tariff structure—the overall pattern of tariff rates—is a source of concern for some economists. Tariffs usually are not imposed at a uniform rate. Some

President Bill Clinton signs a 1994 international agreement on tariffs. (Reuters/Corbis-Bettmann)

structure may allow duty-free entry of raw materials, positive tariffs on CKD ("completely knocked down") parts, and higher rates on finished goods. Some foreign firms seeking to avoid tariffs may establish "tariff factories," moving production facilities from low-cost to higher-cost locations in countries with high tariff barriers.

Tariffs are only a small source of revenue in the United States. Excise taxes, including tariffs, were about 4.2 percent of revenue in 1993.

SUGGESTED READINGS: For a sound economic analysis of tariffs, see Richard G. Lipsey, Paul N. Courant, Douglas D. Purvis, and Peter O. Steiner's *Economics*, 10th ed. (New York: HarperCollins, 1993). For comprehensive data on tariffs, see the U.S. Trade Commission's *Harmonized Tariff Schedule of the United States, 1994, Supplement 1* (Washington, D.C.: Government Printing Office, 1994).

Taub, Edward Arnold (b. 1939): Specialist in physiological psychology, which deals with functional relations between mind and body. His experiments with monkeys, in which the nerves to one limb were severed so as to eliminate sensation in the limb, revealed that the subject animals ceased trying to use the affected limbs but that if the remaining limb were put in a restraining device, the subjects could then be taught some use of the injured limbs. He has transferred this procedure to human victims of stroke and other traumatic brain injuries with significant success, but his experimental techniques have been decried by ANIMAL RIGHTS activists.

Tax deductions: Items that can be subtracted from income before taxes are computed. Examples on personal INCOME TAXES include deductions for children, charitable donations, and work-related expenses. The intent of offering tax deductions is to reward certain behaviors, such as donating to charity, and to recognize higher costs faced by some taxpayers in the course of earning a living. The Tax Reform Act of 1986 phased out the deduction for interest paid on consumer loans, but interest paid on home mortgages remained deductible. Tax deductions differ from tax credits in that credits reduce the amount paid in taxes directly; each dollar of a tax credit reduces taxes by one dollar, whereas each dollar of a tax deduction reduces the amount of income that is subject to tax by one dollar. The value of a deduction therefore depends on the percentage rate of TAXATION applied to income.

Tax loopholes: Irregularities in tax laws that create opportunities for people to reduce their tax payments in ways that were not intended by the laws. In some cases, people will engage in economic transactions that have no purpose other than to exploit a tax loophole. Some of the most commonly abused loopholes relate to credits given to businesses for investing in various technologies.

Tax shelters: Forms of investment that temporarily protect income from being taxed; taxes commonly are deferred. For an investment to qualify as a tax shelter, money must be put at risk and there must be an expectation of profit. Tax shelters often will generate losses for their investors for some period of time, and these losses can be used to reduce the investors' taxable income. Such losses commonly result from depreciation of assets or interest paid on borrowed funds. Tax shelters can be used fraudulently; for example, a tax shelter may generate losses because it deliberately overvalues assets. The investors claim depreciation against these overstated values. Use of tax shelters was curtailed sharply by the Tax Reform Act of 1986.

Taxation and taxes: Taxation involves the means and mechanisms employed by governments to collect money or other valuable resources from people and organizations through the use of law. Taxes have come to constitute the chief source of revenue of the modern state.

Introduction and Background. In primitive societies, people voluntarily contribute their time or their resources to support projects and activities that benefit the public or collective good. Clearing a path through a forest or placing a log across a small creek are examples of cooperative activities that benefit the community in common. As societies become more complex, these voluntary contributions to the public good gradually are transformed into legally binding obligations on people to support certain activities that benefit the group or collective good. As trade and commerce expand, these legally binding obligations gradually evolve into increasingly complex systems of taxation.

In the ancient world, tribute was an early form of

taxation and an important source of revenue. Tribute was a payment made by one ruler to another ruler, by one nation to another nation, or by a vassal or subject to a lord. The payment of tribute acknowledged subjugation in return for protection from invasion and indicated bondage. Such payments might well be seen as a form of BRIBERY.

Under feudalism and absolute monarchies, rulers were under no obligation to submit their spending plans either to the people or to a legislature for a vote of approval or support. Taxes and other levies often were imposed on those people with little power or influence. Favoritism was common. Questions of equity or justice in levying taxes seldom were considered.

Taxation presupposes the existence of private property. If an absolute monarchy—a king or a queen, for example—owned every form of wealth in a society, there would be nothing to tax. No government, even a communist or socialist one, has ever concentrated all wealth in its own hands. Subject to certain limitations, people generally own certain household goods, possess some amount of money or other resources for exchange, and have some control over their own labor services. The private ownership of these and other goods and services makes taxation possible.

The more wealth a government owns, the less taxation is necessary. Certain governments own waterworks, electric power plants, and transportation systems, and they often receive substantial revenues from these operations. Many of these governments, therefore, are less dependent on taxation as a source of revenue. Such enterprises may operate at a loss if the government chooses to provide their services at low prices for the public benefit; in those cases, government ownership necessitates more rather than less taxation.

In addition to the existence of private property, the development of representative government also has contributed to the evolution of taxation. Certain types of taxation, to be successfully administered, require some level of cooperation on the part of taxpayers. If workers, for example, are to report tips and other gratuities voluntarily, they must have some confidence that the tax system is being administered properly and that the government is not spending their taxes in fraudulent or inappropriate ways. This requires that control of the government and the system of taxation it creates and administers ultimately must be in the hands of taxpayers.

Whatever system of taxation society implements, public understanding and support are vital. If taxpayers are expected to disclose and declare information about their income, their property, and themselves, they must have some level of confidence in their government and its system of taxation. When taxpayers begin to question the fairness or the honesty of the taxation system, they begin to resist disclosing and declaring information about themselves. Under these circumstances, noncompliance in the form of tax evasion or avoidance tends to increase.

Purpose and Functions of Taxation. Through the centuries, systems of taxation have changed dramatically. Taxing land in agrarian societies plays a very different role from doing so in urbanized, industrialized societies. The advent of the modern corporation and other changes in the form of business organization and ownership have contributed to new types of taxes and have presented new difficulties in administering and collecting taxes. Computerization and improved record keeping also have created new challenges as well as new opportunities to refine tax systems. Most important are shifts in the foundation upon which tax systems are based: people's beliefs and values and the degree to which the system of taxation reflects these.

The emergence of the notions of equity and justice as shared or collective ideals has affected modern thinking dramatically. In conjunction with the emergence of democratic institutions, particularly in the Western world, the notions of equity, justice, and other related ethical ideals set the stage for the ability-to-pay doctrine of taxation. This doctrine is related closely to egalitarian social philosophy. Rather than simply viewing tax systems as a means for raising revenue, these ideals suggest that taxes should be designed to reduce inequalities of WEALTH and income. Net worth and income typically are thought of as appropriate indices of a person's ability to pay. The concept of ability to pay implies the equal treatment of people with equal ability to pay. The principle states that public services should be funded by those who have the means to pay for those services.

With regard to taxing money income, tax systems can be proportional, progressive, or regressive. These terms describe how the tax system affects the distribution of income in a society. An INCOME TAX system is neutral if it does not change the distribution of money income in society. A tax system is distributionally neutral if it reduces each person's income in exactly the same proportion. Progressive taxation takes an increasing proportion of income as income rises; that is, higher percentage rates of taxation are applied to

A member of Americans Against Tax Hikes campaigns in Washington, D.C., in 1990. (AP/Wide World Photos)

higher levels of income. The assumption is that as an individual's income rises, ability to pay taxes also rises. Regressive tax structures do the opposite, increasing the tax burden on lower-income taxpayers. Sales taxes, although they appear to be proportional, have been assessed as regressive by some studies. The regressivity occurs because people with low incomes tend to spend a larger percentage of their income on taxable goods than do people with high incomes. People with high incomes save more and buy more non-taxed services.

Although using taxation as a means to redistribute income has become increasingly widespread in the modern world, debate continues over the purpose of taxation. If taxation is defined narrowly, its only purpose is to raise money to support the government. A

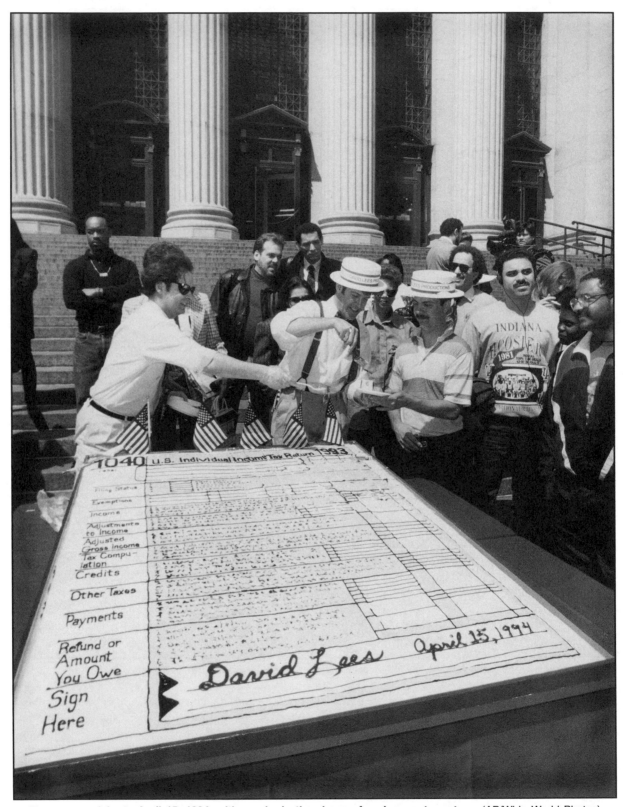

Taxpayers celebrate April 15, 1994, with a cake in the shape of an income-tax return. (AP/Wide World Photos)

broader definition also includes achieving certain goals such as changing the distribution of income and wealth

A problem associated with using tax policy to achieve socially desirable goals is deciding which goals are socially desirable. Even a specified goal, such as reducing a government's debt, might be accomplished through cutting government spending or through increasing taxes. If it is desirable to redistribute income, this could be accomplished by taxing some people at higher rates than others, allowing low-income individuals to pay no taxes, or granting subsidies—in effect, assessing negative taxes—to those with the lowest incomes, with the funds provided from the tax payments of higher-income taxpayers. In most democratic societies, a wide diversity of opinion regarding the proper objectives of taxation usually exists. Applying tax revenues to attain one socially desirable goal, such as reducing the BUDGET DEFICIT, may mean having to reduce spending for other worthwhile objectives, such as providing subsidies to low-income individuals.

A related problem rests on the premise that taxes are interdependent. Raising the rate of one tax often decreases the yield from other taxes. Increasing the tax on cigarettes, for example, means that the price of cigarettes will rise. Many smokers will not reduce their consumption of cigarettes in response to such a price change. They may have an addiction, or they may see the price increase as insignificant in their budgets. Thus, if consumption falls little as prices increase, more money will be spent on cigarettes. Demand for other products is lowered by that amount, and tax revenue generated by the sale of those products, such as from a sales tax, will decrease.

Taxes and government spending are interrelated in a number of other, often complex, ways. Continuing with the example of cigarettes, cigarette SMOKING is linked to a number of health problems, including lung CANCER and respiratory disease. To whatever extent tax policy can reduce cigarette smoking, the demand for health care ought to decrease in the long run. This should lower MEDICARE and Medicaid spending, which are funded through federal taxes, and perhaps decrease the need to build new hospitals.

Impact of Taxation. Different forms of taxation—an INCOME TAX versus a tax on commodities, for example—can better accomplish certain desired results. Reduction of inequalities of wealth and income through taxes is accomplished through means-tested or means-

based taxes, such as a progressive income tax, better than through other taxes. This tax cannot be shifted readily to others. Some taxes can be shifted to others, such as taxes that are placed on commodities imported from foreign countries. Although the company importing the product is legally responsible for paying the tax, it can shift part of the tax to consumers by increasing the price of the product it sells. The extent to which it can do so depends on how responsive consumers are to changes in price, that is, how much their use of the product will fall as its price increases.

In addition to redistributing income and producing revenue, taxes may influence the rates and patterns of private expenditures. Taxes can alter the "product mix" in the private sector. If higher tax rates are applied to tobacco, alcoholic beverages, or "gas guzzling" automobiles, for example, these products are made more expensive. If lower tax rates are applied to milk, meat, and vegetables, or if the production of these products is otherwise subsidized by the government, they are made less expensive. As a consequence, all other things being equal, people tend to purchase fewer of the former items and more of the latter. The government may desire to change the mix of products consumed, and the tax system is one means to achieve that goal.

Whether consumers as a group are better off or worse off as the result of such changes in the product mix is open to debate. Some people suggest that the product mix is best set by the market, through the laws of SUPPLY AND DEMAND. Others suggest that government, through various political processes and expressed in the system of taxes, ought to play a major role in defining the proper product mix. Their argument rests on the assumption that individuals may make choices that, although appropriate on an individual level, have harmful effects on society.

The impact of taxation on private expenditures can be seen in times of RECESSION or DEPRESSION, when governments typically reduce tax rates to stimulate the economy. Reduced taxes mean that businesses and individuals retain more of their income. This higher level of retained income encourages increased spending on goods and services, which in turn increases employment. The recession or depression is thus reversed.

In a similar fashion, during times of rapid economic growth, tax rates may be increased to slow the economy. Tax increases decrease the amount of money businesses and individuals have to spend on goods and services. This normally slows the growth in employment, and sellers find that they cannot increase prices as rapidly, so the rate of INFLATION falls.

Determining the role that a system of taxes should play is complicated by differing goals and value systems. There are several principles, however, that appear to be desirable. To whatever extent possible, taxes should not stifle the production of desirable goods and services, ought to be administered so as to avoid waste, and should neither call forth a widespread sense of social injustice or outrage nor arouse effective opposition. Governments must consider equity issues as well. A tax might be considered "fair" if it is assessed based on ability to pay; alternatively, fairness might mean, to some, basing taxes on the level of benefits received. Those two concepts of fairness often conflict. Political leaders must understand that certain types of taxes are more consistent with the prevailing opinions and sentiments of the community, state, or nation.

This discussion of the purposes and effects of taxation serves as an antecedent to the consideration of various types of taxes. As societies and economies have become increasingly complex, systems of taxation have done the same. This is reflected in the variety of taxes that have been devised and implemented to accomplish an increasingly wide range of objectives.

Classification and Types of Taxes. Given the variety of human societies and cultures, it is predictable that an enormous variety of taxes exists. Some countries are economically and technologically advanced, and others are underdeveloped; some are rich, and others are poor. Some societies have highly centralized governments, and others have decentralized or localized governments. Some have homogenous populations

Florida senator Connie Mack signs a 1996 pledge to reform the tax system. (AP/Wide World Photos)

with respect to ethnicity, race, language, and general style of life, whereas others are heterogeneous in terms of these factors. Such differences in cultural factors produce endless variations in types of taxes and systems of taxation.

The United States, for example, has a federal political system with a long-standing tradition of a complex combination of taxes at the federal, state, and local levels. Local functions traditionally have been financed locally through local taxes, state functions through state taxes, and federal functions through federal taxes. The federal government has tended to rely on a combination of personal INCOME TAXES, corporate taxes, SOCIAL SECURITY taxes, import and export taxes, and various excise taxes (on gasoline, alcohol, and tobacco, for example), as well as fees and taxes based on usage of a good or service, such as federal taxes on airline tickets. States generally have relied on state corporate and personal income taxes, sales taxes, and certain user fees and taxes. Local governments have tended to rely primarily on property taxes, but some impose sales and local earnings taxes.

In contrast to the United States, Canada has a national sales tax. In addition to its personal income taxes, corporate taxes, and excise taxes at the national level, Canada levies social security taxes, though the rate is lower than in the United States. This is because old age support in Canada is funded primarily from general revenue. The federal structure in Canada consists of ten provinces as well as numerous local or municipal governments.

Like the United States, Canada has a multilevel tax system. In addition to the aforementioned taxes at the national level, provincial governments levy personal and corporate income taxes in addition to sales taxes. Municipal government depends largely on property taxes. There is far more revenue sharing between Canadian federal and provincial governments than between federal and state governments in the United States.

Specific taxes can be classified and discussed in various ways. Taxes can be classified as business or personal. Individual income taxes, which are based on personal income, are an example of personal taxes; corporate income taxes are a form of business tax. Taxes can be categorized as to whether they are means-tested; that is, whether the amount of tax assessed varies depending on ability to pay. Estate taxes, which are based on an individual's net worth and payable at death, are linked to the ability to pay. General sales taxes and taxes on specific goods are not related to the ability to pay and therefore are not means-tested taxes.

Although there is not a perfect distinction, taxes commonly are classified as direct taxes or indirect taxes. A direct tax is one in which the legal taxpayer cannot shift or transfer the tax liability to others. Income taxes typically are classified as direct. Indirect taxes are those that are shifted, in part or in full, from the legal taxpayer to others. Taxes on the sales of commodities and import taxes commonly are shifted from businesses to consumers, in the form of higher prices. As such, they are indirect taxes. Such tax shifting may occur in various degrees.

Tax Reform. Criticism of the present tax system abounds, both of specific taxes and of the system in general. The U.S. federal income tax code has been subject to intense criticism. It is incredibly complex. As of the early 1990's, the INTERNAL REVENUE SERVICE (IRS) had more than four hundred forms on which to report income tax. Filing the required forms takes millions of hours for the United States as a whole and costs billions of dollars each year. Income taxes, because they typically tax interest earned, discourage saving. The United States has one of the lowest savings rates in the industrial world. This means that businesses that wish to borrow to finance investment in new factories or machinery often must acquire loans from other countries. A low rate of saving also means that many people will not save enough money during their working lives to finance their RETIREMENT.

Another problem is that the present tax system is easy to evade. Sophisticated computer technology that allows for the electronic transfer of money globally, massive money laundering operations by international drug dealers, and the increasing difficulty of monitoring tax returns all have contributed to this problem. The higher the rate of taxation, the more unjust it might seem to some taxpayers, and the more profitable it is to evade the tax.

There is a growing conviction that fundamental and comprehensive reform is needed. Simplifying the system is a major objective, and "flat-rate" taxation has been broadly proposed as a possible solution. All individuals would pay taxes on their income at one rate, and all business income would be taxed at another flat rate. Most or all TAX DEDUCTIONS, exemptions, and "TAX LOOPHOLES" that allow income to be sheltered from taxes would be eliminated. Two-bracket, or bilevel, tax structures also have been proposed.

Some reformers argue that taxation should be shifted from income to consumption, not only to simplify the code but also to encourage saving. Reformers have proposed a national sales tax on all retail sales as an alternative to income taxes. A similar option is a state or national value-added tax, which taxes the value added to the worth of a product at each stage of the manufacturing process. Such taxes have been used widely in Europe. Opponents charge that a value-added tax is a "hidden tax" that taxpayers do not realize they are paying.

There is no perfect tax or perfect tax system. Local property taxes are criticized as discouraging home ownership. Taxes on business hurt the economy and employment, critics charge. Reliance on property taxes on land, building, and sometimes personal belongings as the basic source of revenue for local governments means that wealthier communities have better schools, and, overall, better government services than do poor communities. As home prices increased through the 1970's, homeowners found themselves facing higher and higher property tax bills. People with fixed incomes, such as retirees, no longer could afford to keep their homes and pay the property taxes. In 1978, California passed Proposition 13, which reduced and capped property taxes. Taxes were based on a home's purchase price rather than an assessed value. As revenues fell, government services were cut. These cuts triggered widespread debate over taxation and tax reform, both in California and nationally.

—*Charles E. Marske*

Suggested Readings: *Canada-U.S. Tax Comparisons*, edited by John Shoven and John Whalley (Chicago: University of Chicago Press, 1992), provides a comprehensive overview of the similarities and differences of taxation and tax policy in the United States and Canada. Carolyn Webber's *A History of Taxation and Expenditure in the Western World* (New York: Simon & Schuster, 1986) offers a history of public expenditures and taxation as well as their relationship. *State Taxation of Business: Issues and Policy Options*, edited by Thomas F. Pogue with a foreword by Frederick D. Stocker (Westport, Conn.: Praeger, 1992), focuses on how state corporate income taxes affect economic conditions in the United States. For an interesting review of the relationship between corporate taxes and economic growth as well as of the interplay between the power of government and the influence of business, see Cathie Martin's *Shifting the Burden: The Struggle over Growth and Corporate*

Taxation (Chicago: University of Chicago Press, 1991). An insightful examination of the role of taxation throughout American history and an analysis of the discussion of taxation that occurred at the Constitutional Convention of 1787 is found in Roger H. Brown's *Redeeming the Republic: Federalists, Taxation, and the Origins of the Constitution* (Baltimore: The Johns Hopkins University Press, 1993).

For a thorough treatment of international taxation, the taxation of foreign corporations by the United States, and the taxation of aliens, *International Taxation in a Nutshell* by Richard L. Doernberg (St. Paul, Minn.: West Publishing, 1993) is useful. Problems with present-day tax systems and ideas for reform are discussed in a cross-cultural context, with reference to Australia, Canada, France, Germany, Italy, Japan, the United Kingdom, and the United States, in *Tax Reform and the Cost of Capital: An International Comparison*, edited by Dale W. Jorgenson and Ralph Landau (Washington, D.C.: Brookings Institution, 1993).

Taxes. *See* **Taxation and taxes**

Teach for America (TFA): Program in which recent college graduates, often from top universities, gain teaching positions in economically disadvantaged urban and rural schools. Wendy Kopp, a twenty-two-year-old senior at Princeton University, wrote a senior thesis on a plan to form a national corps of teachers; she subsequently raised more than twenty million dollars for her program and received considerable media attention for her accomplishments. She modeled the program on the Peace Corps. Generally lauded, her program has detractors, most notably writer Linda Darling-Hammond, who labeled the program a "fly-by-night operation." Proponents of the program point out that TFA does not circumvent traditional hiring practices; it places young graduates who are no less qualified than other teachers.

Teenage pregnancy: Adolescence is a time when youths mature physically and emotionally, begin to form closer relationships with other young people, and start taking practical steps to secure a positive future. When teenagers become pregnant, the normal process of smooth and gradual growth is seriously disrupted. Teen parents and their children are faced with difficult social and financial challenges. Unfortunately, teen pregnancy often is complicated by inadequate PRENA-TAL CARE, exposure to SEXUALLY TRANSMITTED DISEASES, and use of alcohol and street DRUGS. The increase in teen pregnancy indicates the failure of the society to encourage more responsible behavior among its young people and to provide appropriate socialization, education, and protection.

Increasing Incidence. Studies show that the behavior of American teenagers is at considerable odds with their stated VALUES. Most American teens say they believe SEX should be postponed until a person is twenty, and many say a person should not have sex before being married. Surveys of American teenagers indicate an increasing percentage of them are sexually active, and they start having sex at an earlier age. While they are more likely to use birth-control methods than before, the use remains inconsistent.

One of the unfortunate outcomes of increasing sexual activity among teenagers is the rising rate of adolescent pregnancy. American teenagers have the highest rate of pregnancy among the developed countries, and the gap is especially prominent with the youngest teens. Each year, one million American teens become pregnant, or one in ten youths between the ages of fifteen and nineteen. In contrast, the annual pregnancy numbers among Canadian teens has been declining steadily. For example, 39,600 Canadian teens became pregnant in 1984, as compared to 58,600 in 1975.

Causes. Many factors have been identified as contributing to the rising rate of teen pregnancy in the United States. Rearing of children in POVERTY and in families in which EDUCATION is not valued are strongly associated with pregnancy at an early age. Many other FAMILY aspects are seen as contributing to teen pregnancy, such as having a mother who had a child herself as a teen, poor communication within the family, family violence, poor discipline, and a permissive approach to early sexual activity.

The media is also seen as contributing to premature sexual activity. Many experts believe that American children see sex portrayed too much and too casually in the TELEVISION programs they watch. In various surveys of teen behavior, investigators find American teens spend more time watching television than attending school, regard television as a primary source of information, and say television follows only parents and peers as an influential force in their lives. American teens are further sexualized by explicit scenes in films and explicit lyrics in popular music.

Teens who have definite educational and other goals in life are less likely to become pregnant as a teen. Teens who abuse alcohol, drugs, and other chemical substances are more likely to become pregnant.

Many Americans prefer to believe teenagers are sexually innocent and ignore the evidence that shows this to be untrue. Operating in such an environment, some American public schools are reluctant to stir the controversies that often surround efforts to take a comprehensive approach to preventing unwanted pregnancies among teen students. Relying on an oft-repeated adult message to "Just Say No" to engaging in sex while a teen has been a popular approach to birth control among American educators, clergy, and politicians.

Parents are often unprepared to discuss normal sexual development and appropriate sexual behavior with their growing children. Parents who refuse to discuss the subject, who pass along incorrect information, and who take an unrealistic approach leave their child unprepared and unprotected.

The U.S. government spends several million dollars each year to provide services for pregnant adolescents and their babies, and the mothers face great odds of becoming and remaining dependent on government WELFARE. The social costs multiply as the cycle of poverty, poor PARENTING, increased health risks, and low educational attainment is perpetuated.

Effects. Teens who become pregnant face three immediate and difficult choices: keep the baby, have an ABORTION, or give up the baby for ADOPTION. About half of pregnant teens deliver a baby, with 40 percent electing to have an abortion. Some teens who want an abortion cannot obtain one, because of family and social pressures, inadequate financial resources, and distance from appropriate abortion services. Most of the teens who deliver keep the baby. Fewer than 10 percent give up the baby for adoption, although many more consider it and might select this option when given adequate information about and control over the process.

Pregnant adolescents have a greater chance to have complications while pregnant, to deliver prematurely, and to give birth to low birthweight babies, stillborn babies, and babies who suffer developmental problems later. Their babies are more likely to die suddenly, be hospitalized with serious illness, be injured, be poisoned, do poorly in school, and develop behavior problems. Those who have studied the problems occurring when teens give birth report the negative out-

A teenage mother with her child. (Jim Whitmer)

comes are more often caused by POVERTY, lack of EDUCATION, poor maternal nutrition, and inadequate medical supervision than by the mother's young age. Problems for the mother and child are increased when the mother has abused substances during pregnancy or has suffered from SEXUALLY TRANSMITTED DISEASES (one in six sexually active teens becomes infected). In addition, as many as one in five teens have been abused sexually or physically during pregnancy.

Those who become parents when they are teens have found it difficult to pursue further education and job-training opportunities. When they are able to find work, they usually are paid low wages. Many teens decide not to marry despite being pregnant; families headed by teenage single mothers often live in poverty. Teens who marry and become parents as teens often fail to stay married because of financial problems, inadequate emotional maturity, and poor social support.

Solutions. Analysts have suggested a number of ways to reduce the incidence of teen pregnancy. Prevention of unintended pregnancies among adolescents is the best solution. Common sense and study results indicate certain approaches are more likely to produce declining rates of unintended pregnancies. Adolescents need clear and accurate information about possible negative consequences of early sexual activity and inconsistent use of CONTRACEPTIVES. Teens need to be given the support and skills needed to resist cultural and PEER PRESSURE to engage in sex at an early age. Parents, extended families, schools, health-care professionals, and churches need to join together in a common effort to help teens avoid unintended pregnancies. Programs are needed to help teens achieve increased SELF-ESTEEM, through academic tutoring, vocational guidance, job placement, money management, and goalsetting. The media must reconsider its role in saturating teens in sexually explicit material and creating a false impression that having sex never has adverse outcomes. Teens need easy access to information they can understand on sexually transmitted diseases, use of alcohol and other dangerous substances, and effective contraception. They need to be able to obtain contraceptives at an early age, since the age when many teens first have sex is now from fourteen to fifteen years. Parents need help in learning how to be comfortable in discussing these controversial topics with their growing children, and how to be more effective in helping them avoid serious problems. Society must come to grips with the need to reduce poverty and to encourage children to attain higher educa-

tional goals, since these two factors are the most strongly associated with unintended adolescent pregnancy.

Once a teenager becomes pregnant, the primary aim must be to ensure the health of the mother and the unborn child. Pregnant teens need to be able to access affordable PRENATAL CARE delivered by trained and experienced professionals. Not only do teens need medical supervision of the pregnancy but also additional services to identify and help them deal with psychological problems, strengthen the teenagers' social support system, and enable teens to cope more effectively with the many challenges they will face in raising a child. Teens need professional counseling about their options early in the pregnancy, including information about abortion costs and services, adoption services, and prenatal services. Health-care professionals need to be able to detect early and intervene with teens who are dependent on dangerous substances, or who are victims of physical, emotional, or sexual abuse. Teens need clear information and effective help on how they can avoid another unintended pregnancy. Teenagers may also need information and help in eating a nutritious diet.　　*—Russell Williams*

SUGGESTED READINGS: Various opinions on sexual activity among adolescents are debated in Karin L. Swisher's *Teenage Sexuality: Opposing Viewpoints* (San Diego: Greenhaven, 1994). Judy Berlfein gives a comprehensive overview of issues and concerns related to adolescent pregnancy in *Teen Pregnancy* (San Diego: Lucent Books, 1992). Proper prenatal care is the topic explored in Fern G. Brown's *Teen Guide to Caring for Your Unborn Baby* (New York: Watts, 1989). Elizabeth Gleick and several other reporters offer dramatic examples of how teenagers and families are affected by adolescent pregnancy in "Teen Pregnancy: A Special Report, the Baby Trap" (*People Weekly*, October 24, 1994).

Telecommuting: Performing one's job at home through electronic means. Such technology as computers, modems, and fax machines has allowed offices and conference rooms to be replaced with remote meetings conducted by electronic mail (E-MAIL), conference calls, and faxes. Telecommuting began to occur on a wide scale in the 1980's as a result of two conditions: improvements in computer technology and the migration of large numbers of people out of metropolitan areas.

Telecommuting

Telecommuting allows this mother to work at home with her young son. (UPI/Corbis-Bettmann)

Until the 1980's, COMPUTERS were too expensive and bulky for many individuals and businesses to own. As new and cheaper means of building computers became available, computer prices dropped. Furthermore, use of even the simplified computers of the 1970's and early 1980's required advanced training. Even simple tasks, such as writing a letter, required knowledge of a computer language.

In 1984, Apple Computer launched its Macintosh line. The Macintosh computer was a landmark for the computer industry because of its ease of use, or "user friendliness." Apple introduced computers on which one could perform useful tasks, such as bookkeeping, without having to learn advanced computer languages.

Other computer manufacturers began to design easy-to-use computer systems, and SOFTWARE developers marketed such products as spreadsheets and databases.

Telecommuting became an option for many people as communication technologies improved. CELLULAR TELEPHONES, fax machines, pagers, and e-mail became affordable during the 1980's as the technologies changed. Cellular phones became cheaper to use as more cellular telephone companies entered the market. Fax machines evolved from slow and expensive early models to lightweight, portable, and affordable successors. E-mail became a widespread phenomenon as computer networks expanded across the United States and around the world.

As communication and computer technologies improved, social and economic changes also took place. During the late 1980's, economic conditions declined in large North American cities, for several reasons. On the global scale, two broad factors affected the United States' economic status. First, with the end of the COLD WAR, the United States' economy shifted away from defense-oriented spending. This resulted in massive LAYOFFS and UNEMPLOYMENT in defense industries, especially in Southern California. Second, the collapse of the Cold War coincided with increased globalization of economies. The global economy diversified as transportation of material goods became cheaper. The United States lost many high-paying manufacturing jobs to China, Singapore, Taiwan, and South Korea, where labor and natural resources were less expensive.

Social conditions in large American cities also changed during the 1980's. Illegal DRUGS, especially the introduction of cheap "crack" COCAINE, ravaged cities. GANGS, drugs, and increased inner-city VIOLENCE motivated many people to look outside the city for their livelihood. Pollution, traffic, and the higher cost of living in big cities also contributed to cities' decline.

As both economic and social conditions changed, many people and businesses found urban life to have more disadvantages than advantages and looked for viable alternatives. Telecommuting offered a way for people to live where they want and continue to work at occupations that once were limited to metropolitan areas.

The rise of telecommuting would not have been possible in the absence of these factors. In addition, attitudes of employers had to change. Businesses became increasingly willing to allow workers to perform their tasks outside the formal workplace. This trend occurred simultaneously with an increase in OUTSOURCING, or hiring outside contractors to perform various tasks. Employers focused on the task being performed more than on the number of hours employees spend in the office.

The rise of the service sector of the economy, particularly the information sector, also played an important role in the increase in telecommuting. Many manufacturing jobs cannot be performed at home because they require access to materials and machines available only at the workplace. Before the advent of computers and electronic data transmission, information-related jobs shared that feature. Information often was available only in the form of books, ledgers, or folders and ring binders full of paper. Employers were reluctant to allow these information sources out of the office, both because the information then would be unavailable for other employees' use and because of the fear that the INFORMATION would be lost. New information technology allowed information to be used simultaneously by many users and to be copied easily from the primary source to a worker's remote location.

The rise in telecommunication thus can be seen as the outgrowth of changes in technology, social and economic conditions, and workplace attitudes. Centralized workplaces never will be eliminated completely, because there always will be some materials and equipment that cannot be transferred economically to workers' homes. In addition, even though most communication can take place through electronic media, most workers and businesses realize the psychological importance of occasional face-to-face interaction. During the 1990's, business began to experiment with temporary offices and meeting rooms. Employees occupied these facilities only as needed, so that an office might be shared by numerous employees, saving the employer from paying rent on underutilized office space. This type of arrangement mixed the home office and the traditional office, offering cost savings to the employer and freedom of location to the employee as well as maintaining personal contacts among employers, employees, and clients.

Telemarketing: Business technique. Telemarketing is an aspect of "direct marketing" or "direct-response marketing," which includes mail-order catalog and similar marketing techniques designed to reach a relatively small target group of potential customers. Telemarketing is the systematic contact of customers by telephone (or, more recently, computer) in order to sell goods or services. Direct marketing by telephone has revolutionized the business world. Although it will never replace traditional sales techniques completely, telemarketing enhances a company's flexibility.

Generally, telemarketing is done in one of two basic ways: inbound and outbound. Inbound telemarketing is the use of 800, 888, and 900 TELEPHONE NUMBERS through which customers can place orders or use services. Typically, 800 and 888 numbers are used by customers to place calls to a retail order line, or business, to place an order for products or services. Numbers with an 888 prefix are relatively new additions to the long-used 800 number system, which ran out of num-

Telemarketing

bers. A call to an 800 or 888 number involves no direct cost for the customer; the charge is reversed to the company receiving the order. Such numbers have increased sales and profits for many companies because maintaining such lines is far less expensive than maintaining an outside sales staff.

Numbers with a 900 prefix charge a fee to callers. Charges accrue on a per-minute basis and are billed directly to the caller's phone company. Such numbers may result in fewer callers for the company than would 800 or 888 numbers, but the fact that a charge is made for the calls signals the potential that the callers are more serious customers and may yield greater sales in the long run. The company avoids the charges associ-

ated with 800 or 888 numbers. Some businesses are conducted entirely through 900 numbers, including various information services and "phone sex" lines.

The other major type of telemarketing is the outbound system. One lesser-used form is for office personnel to make arrangements for sales visits by outside salespeople, who are then given their schedules of visits. The major use of outbound telemarketing is the direct call to the potential retail customer. Using telephone lists that are compiled in a manner similar to direct mail lists (though sources such as purchased lists and responses to coupons and free offers), direct outbound telemarketers call the homes of customers and attempt to sell them goods or services. Such calls may

Telemarketers at work. (James L. Shaffer)

feature live marketers or may use computers that come on the line if and when a potential customer's telephone is answered. Computerized systems can play a recorded message and take orders.

Telemarketing can be seen as offering several advantages to business and customers. First, telemarketing can be vastly cheaper than conventional sales methods of the past. Inside salespersons using telephones and computers can make hundreds of contacts a day. Older methods such as door to door sales generated far fewer contacts and became ineffective as more women entered the workforce, leaving no one at home. Second, telemarketing creates sales in markets without retail outlets. Sales of products and services can be conducted directly in the homes of millions of persons, many of whom live far away from retail outlets or are shut in. Moreover, telemarketing creates demand for products where there ordinarily is little or none. Advertising that features telemarketing numbers attracts both inbound and outbound business.

Third, telemarketing can meet the needs of buyers who prefer not to shop in the retail environments ordinarily available. Music stores, for example, satisfy needs of younger buyers of music, but older buyers increasingly make their purchases through direct-market clubs or telemarketed numbers. Many companies depend entirely or to a large extent on catalogs and telephone solicitations for their sales.

Fourth, telemarketing takes advantage of "impulse buying," which, in a soft market, can be of immense value. Customers at home may be induced to purchase products they would not actively seek when in retail environments. Finally, telemarketing can be a tremendous source of data on clients and customers. Information gathered to make a sale by telephone can be sold to other marketers for further use.

Telemarketing is a useful tool for gathering information and redistributing it to other marketers. This very fact raises an important issue, that telemarketing creates problems for consumers, along with the benefits. First, telemarketing, especially the outbound type, is extremely invasive; that is, the call is made into homes, where, in many cases the calls are unwanted. Second, persistent telemarketers, under orders to make a sale at any cost, can be obnoxious. Although most telemarketers are careful to train personnel on proper courtesy, many are not, and these are the ones consumers remember and resent.

To provide some protection for consumers, the federal government, which regulates telephone lines through the FEDERAL COMMUNICATIONS COMMISSION, has regulated the use of telephone lines for business purposes. New regulations also enable phone companies to sell services to consumers to block calls to 800, 888, and 900 numbers. Furthermore, CALLER ID technology reports the number of the source of a call before a customer answers the phone. If the number is unfamiliar and the customer does not wish to answer the call, suspecting that the call may be originating from a telemarketing source, he or she simply does not answer. With a caller ID number in hand, a consumer may also telephone back and request to be removed from a list to stop further calls. Caller ID can be used in reverse. Callers to businesses may have their numbers recorded and put on telemarketing lists. For this reason and others, telephone companies began offering services to block the caller ID function.

The most difficult issue in telemarketing is the issue of PRIVACY regarding personal information. Most sales require customers to reveal credit card numbers and, in some cases, Social Security numbers. Such information can be used fraudulently, to the customer's detriment. Sharing and marketing of such information within the industry is vast, and some people fear the loss of privacy and the increased risk of theft associated with telemarketing.

Televangelism: Use of television broadcasts to disseminate religious teachings. Televangelism was pioneered by such preachers as Oral Roberts, a Tulsa, Oklahoma, Pentecostal minister who realized the potential of radio and TELEVISION as a method of carrying his message beyond a small community. From the early 1960's to the mid-1980's, Roberts' television ministry drew countless thousands of viewers into his fold and brought millions of dollars into his ministry's "war chest." With money pledged by viewers, Roberts built a large university with medical and legal professional schools, Oral Roberts University, and established himself as one of the leading purveyors of the Christian message. His upbeat television programs captured the attention of many viewers and set the stage for a church media revolution in the last quarter of the twentieth century. The television ministries of such well-known televangelists as Jerry FALWELL, Kenneth Hagin, Kenneth Copeland, Chuck Smith, and Pat ROBERTSON all patterned their programs after Roberts'.

Televangelists typically attempt to convert viewers to a particular understanding of the Christian faith, but

Televangelists Jim and Tammy Faye Bakker in 1987. (UPI/Corbis-Bettmann)

many also use the media to promote their own societal visions. Angered by a perceived erosion of "traditional" FAMILY VALUES in American culture, some televangelists have used their media constituencies to form political organizations to influence policy discussions in the broader community. Jerry Falwell, head of one of the more prominent "electronic" churches in America, the Virginia-based Thomas Road Baptist Church, formed a political organization called the MORAL MAJORITY to combat what he saw as social evils. Through his radio and television program *The Old Time Gospel Hour*, Falwell and his church reached millions of viewers each week with conservative religious, moral, and political messages. Pat Robertson, founder of the CHRISTIAN BROADCASTING NETWORK (CBN), parlayed his own influence among conservative protestant Christians into a run for the U.S. presidency in 1992.

Critics have assailed televangelists on a number of grounds. Liberal critics, in particular, have attacked televangelists for their dissemination of archconservative views, which are sometimes construed as examples of intolerance or fanaticism. Televangelists have also been criticized for their use of RELIGION to solicit donations from viewers; many televangelists have been suspected of operating their ministries primarily for their own enrichment, and some (notably Jim Bakker, who was prosecuted by federal authorities in the late 1980's for financial irregularities connected with the ministry he operated with his wife, Tammy Faye Bakker) have been accused of operating confidence schemes cloaked in a religious guise. Moreover, the personal integrity of some prominent televangelists has been questioned on other grounds; both Jimmy Swaggart and Jim Bakker, for example, drew headlines for their alleged involvements in extramarital sexual escapades.

Television: Dominant social influence of the twentieth century that ushered in a new age of home entertainment and information. Since virtually all topics of public interest appear in some form on television, public understanding of these matters is molded by the biases of television. Television orchestrates not only what we know of the world, but also how we acquire that knowledge.

Background. Television, begun as an experimental medium during the 1930's, was being utilized for limited commercial purposes by the end of the decade.

After a brief hiatus caused by World War II, commercial television grew rapidly. The FEDERAL COMMUNICATION COMMISSION (FCC) allocated the available airspace to three networks: The National Broadcasting Company (NBC), The American Broadcasting Company (ABC), and the Columbia Broadcasting System (CBS). From the early 1950's through the early 1970's, these networks controlled virtually all of television. Although some space had been reserved for educational TV, there was insufficient interest and inadequate funding for these stations to compete effectively.

Cable television grew slowly from inauspicious beginnings in the late 1940's. High costs, low demand, and regulatory constraints kept cable from becoming a threat to the networks. Then, in 1975, Home Box Office (HBO) made cable a more attractive option by using SATELLITE distribution and offering a wider range of programming. Soon, most cities were wired for cable. Complaints by the cable companies about hefty franchising fees and inadequate subscriber rates set by the FCC compelled Congress in 1987 to deregulate the industry. The companies used the revenues generated by higher rates to expand services and offer more channels. Consumer complaints of "price gouging" by a monopoly of cable companies caused Congress to resume regulating cable rates in 1992. This law also contained provisions that benefited the direct broadcast satellite (DBS) industry, a fledgling rival, and required the cable companies to carry local stations. Over the next several years, the cable companies attacked these provisions in court.

Meanwhile, a new potential rival—the telephone industry—began clamoring to provide home video services. Although presently banned by law, several important legal victories in the early 1990's began the process of relaxing regulations. In the future, the driving force behind many new expanded services, such as interactive television and video on demand, may well be the competition between telephone companies and cable systems for new subscribers.

Societal Effects. That television has dramatically and irreversibly altered American society no one debates. A pivotal point of contention between video advocates and those who feel the overall effects are nefarious, however, is whether programming is a reflection of the profound problems of society or a source of such problems.

The ascendancy of television, with the concomitant decline of the print-based culture, has helped shift principal thought patterns from an abstract realm to concrete images. Television watching is primarily visual; the rapidly changing images are processed in the nonverbal right brain without requiring the critical analysis characteristic of the left brain. An abundance of visually appealing but incongruous facts enter and leave the conscious mind at such speeds that reflection and evaluation are impossible. Knowing many isolated facts seems to be more relevant than understanding the implications and interconnections of these facts. Television is not only ubiquitous; as the epitome of impermanence, it has also elevated commingled visual images and instancy to a new type of knowledge, sensationalistic, impersonal, and fragmented.

Critics contend that society has been so transmogrified by television's distorted view that irrelevant trivia seems important and incoherence seems extraordinarily sane. Since all television is ultimately entertainment, even the phrase "serious television" becomes an oxymoron. Because of its inundating presence, American schools, churches, and political organizations have had to adapt to the forms and language of show business or be left behind.

The Future of Television. On the immediate horizon is a vast increase in entertainment and information services controlled through viewers' own television sets. The cable systems and the local telephone companies are vigorously competing to offer such services as video on demand, video games, interactive shopping, as well as many other types of informational services.

Since the rise of cable systems in the late 1970's, television has changed from being dominated by the three commercial networks to dozens of cable-carried channels, including those devoted exclusively to news, weather, sports, music, classic films, and shopping. Now local telephone companies are pursuing approval to construct new video networks with an even more dazzling array of options. The ultimate aim is to not only bring the theater and the retail store into the home, but also the workplace and the school. Fearing an unfair competitive advantage, the cable industry is seeking to block the "telcos'" access to this market. The telephone industry argues that the cable companies are attempting to thwart competition and stoutly denies that local telephone service costs would be inflated to help subsidize new video systems. This emerging rivalry comes at a time when both the cable and telephone industries confront complex challenges caused by governmental regulation.

While the telephone industry is contending with rivalry from competitive access providers, cable companies are trying to enter the telephone business. This competition for basic telephone service has augmented the local telephone companies' hope of eliminating constraints (imposed in 1984) against offering information services. The "INFORMATION SUPERHIGHWAY" bills considered, but not passed, by Congress in 1994, would have allowed telephone companies to provide video programming but, as a trade-off, mandated free competition for local telephone service. While legislative issues are pending, however, both telephone and cable companies are exploring new means of providing additional services. Interactive television devices are being field-tested by cable companies, and the telephone industry has installed one demonstration video dial-tone network. Advocates of easing restrictions on the telephone companies envision their equipment forming the infrastructure of the information superhighway, interconnecting homes, schools, libraries, and worksites. Opponents contend that the telephone and cable companies are more interested in maximizing revenues by offering more home shopping and recycled entertainment than in public service. Consequently, public INTEREST GROUPS endorse a provision requiring up to 20 percent of new video networks to be reserved for public access.

Regulation Issues. A revolution of the telecommunications industry is now in progress. As competing industries fashion a new world of interactive home video services, two important regulation issues are being debated.

The first issue is whether regulatory safeguards should be tightened before telephone companies are allowed to provide home video services.

The telephone companies are ready to move into the video service market as soon as Congress relaxes restrictions, but consumer groups want strong safeguards imposed to prevent new ventures from being subsidized by increased revenues from telephone customers. Also, cable companies would like authorization to vie for providing local telephone service. Telephone industry officials counter that regulatory authorities have found no grounds for concern about cross-subsidization; cable companies are merely attempting to postpone competition. Opponents to relaxed regulation fear that the greater resources and funds available to the telephone companies will crush their cable competitors and lead to a monopoly of the video market. Proponents argue that the telephone industry will have a competitive handicap against an entrenched monopoly, cable, as well as having to combat

A prospective buyer examines an array of televisions in a department store. (James L. Shaffer)

the emerging DBS industry. Excessive regulatory requirements on telephone companies will disable their free competitive access to the video market.

The second regulatory issue being debated is whether cable-television regulations should be relaxed because of increased competition for video services. The cable industry contends that the 1992 regulations, by reducing revenues, hamper its ability to provide new channels, to upgrade cable systems, and to invest in new technologies. Consumer advocate groups, allied with the cable companies on the telephone issues, part company on rate regulation. They claim that lower revenues are a natural result of limiting the excessive profits accrued by a monopoly. The cable industry would also like to rescind the provision of the 1992 law that secures access to cable programming by DBS

A woman displays a miniature television developed by a Japanese company. (Reuters/Corbis-Bettmann)

distributors. Supporters claim that this proviso has helped DBS become established as a cable competitor. On the other hand, the cable industry contends that this requirement is both unfair and unnecessary. DBS has authorized access to cable programs, while cable operators do not have a reciprocal access to exclusive DBS broadcasts. Satellite broadcasters reply that since they have less than one-half of one percent of the market share, it is too soon to think about modifying the law. —*George R. Plitnik*

SUGGESTED READINGS: Erik Barnouw in *Tube of Plenty: The Evolution of American Television*, 2d ed. (New York: Oxford University Press, 1990) traces the history of television from its inception through the development of cable systems and the evolution of fiber optics technology in the 1980's. The detrimental effects of television upon modern society are brilliantly exposed in *Amusing Ourselves to Death* (New York: Viking, 1985) by Neil Postman. T. Barton Carter, Marc A. Franklin, and Jay B. Wright in *The First Amendment and the Fifth Estate*, 3d ed. (Westbury, N.Y.: Foundation Press, 1992), comprehensively explore the history and development of regulations of the telecommunications industries.

Television, children and: Frequently debated issue of the effects of television viewing on children. Proponents state that TELEVISION offers unique opportunities for cultural enrichment and can stimulate learning. Those opposed claim that television induces a "drug-like" state detrimental to learning and undermines the educational values of society.

Background. Television is undoubtedly the most successful mass medium yet evolved. With 98 percent of American homes owning at least one set and 88.6 million viewers tuned in nightly, the effect on society is unparalleled. Although an affordable and reliable source of entertainment, ongoing debates among social scientists and educators stem from the question of whether television is ultimately beneficial or detrimental to society. The ensuing discussions usually focus on children, whose minds and emotions are still in critical stages of development. Opponents of television generally cast television as a brain-damaging "drug" that is undermining the educational system, while advocates assert that television offers unique opportunities for cultural enrichment and actually stimulates children's learning.

America's preschool children spend a greater proportion of their day (one-third of their waking hours) and more time weekly (an average of 27.9 hours) watching television than any other age group. Children six to eleven years old view an average of 24.5 hours a week. Many spend as much time watching television as they spend in the classroom. Considering that most children now spend substantial portions of every day captivated by television, it is imperative that the subsequent effect on cognitive development be accurately assessed.

Benefits of Educational Television. Some research indicates that programming devoted to enhancing specific learning abilities seems to fulfill its stated objective. Since proponents of television are not advocating programs devoid of educational value, the benefits of television will be examined solely in terms of educational programming for children.

Television has a vast, and as yet mostly untapped, potential to teach preschoolers to read. The dynamic nature of television's visual imagery, as well as its audio component, provide an exciting mechanism for illustrating the relationship between print and speech. Early studies assessing the role of television on reading readiness indicated that language skills acquisition was aided by viewing *Sesame Street*. Results of extensive field tests shape the design and language level of programming, focusing on a specific age group. This increases children's enjoyment and the subsequent value they place on the show.

An argument often voiced for incorporating television into the education curriculum lies in the fact that children seem to enjoy being taught when learning through this medium, as opposed to the more traditional methods of teaching. It is then assumed that this positive attitude toward learning will carry over to the entire educational experience. To counter the objection that watching television is primarily a passive activity while learning requires active participation, the possibilities of employing interactive educational television to elicit a more active role in learning are being diligently explored.

The level of active involvement in learning is a function of a show's format. The most important factors encouraging active participation by school-age viewers seem to be those of appeal, clear definitions, time allowed for contemplation, and encouragement of prediction. These factors, however, are not necessarily the norm for children's educational television.

Television as a Detriment to Learning. Opponents of children's television viewing center their arguments on three concerns. First, extensive television viewing

Preschool-aged American children on average spend about a third of their waking hours watching television. (Jim Whitmer)

is a completely passive activity that deleteriously affects cognitive development. Second, the family's values and beliefs are supplanted by the content of television shows because of children's natural tendency to copy frequently observed behaviors and the concomitant decrease in quality family time. Finally, a child's ability to problem-solve is stunted by television in two ways: The amount of time spent with television severely limits opportunities for practicing problem-solving skills, and children are led to assume that real-life problems mimic situations encountered on television. When children find that real problems often do not have definitive and quickly achieved resolutions, they may become frustrated.

Television perpetuates dependency, reduces the time available to work out basic family relationship skills, severely limits involvement in real-life activities, and stifles opportunities for learning clear and flexible self-expression. A child's need for fantasy is better gratified by devices of their choosing rather than the preprogrammed varieties offered on television. Their need for intellectual stimulation is best met by manipulating the environment.

Opponents also argue that television programming is designed to keep the viewer's attention focused on the screen. With more emphasis placed on formatting than on content, it presents material with constant intercutting, interruptions, and shifts in viewpoint that tend to induce a druglike entrancement. Some researchers have concluded that television viewing causes the mind to enter a nonthinking state. Excessive viewing by children results in less effective language skills, atrophied imagination, restlessness, and increased aggression.

Excessive television viewing is also counterproductive to the development of reading comprehension. Reading comprehension requires the reader to make a cognitive investment in the material by interpreting meaning from print and creating mental images based on the author's words. Television supplies an interpretation for the viewer and presents ready-made visual images: Viewers are denied the cognitive investment required of readers. Television may provide diversion, but reading allows and supports growth.

Educational Television for Children. The controversy surrounding children's television-viewing habits generally centers on content. Most opponents of television assert that television would be harmful to children even if all the programming were educational. Some researchers contend that if the content and format of children's television were shifted from entertainment to learning, a spectacular untapped educational resource would be unleashed. Others insist that the experience of television itself, regardless of content, seems to adversely affect a child's perception of reality and the development of left-brain skills. Instead of encouraging learning, children now expect to be entertained in school: If the lesson is not fun, then switch to a less boring channel.

Although most parents believe that *Sesame Street* is a positive educational experience (80 percent of two-to-five-year-olds watch the show), recent studies indicate otherwise. Disadvantaged children, regular watchers of *Sesame Street*, have not caught up to their more advantaged peers, and a new breed of well-prepared beginning students has not materialized. Although delightful entertainment for young children, *Sesame Street* apparently fails to effect a substantive educational benefit. Children may enter kindergarten recognizing numbers and letters, but there seem to be corresponding decreases in imaginative play, frustration tolerance, and perseverance and some confusion between reality and fantasy. The fast pace of such shows encourages frenetic behavior and leaves little time for the response and reflection that are important ingredients of a child's learning experience. *Sesame Street*, by over-stimulating a child, may also tend to create the psychological orientation leading to a shortened attention span, a lack of reflectiveness, and an expectation of rapid change in the broader environment.

Educational television advocates have proposed that by introducing presentations and class discussions about television in the school system, enhanced awareness and critical thinking skills could be fostered in children. Such active intervention methods would encourage students to identify and consider programming angles and techniques and to weigh advertising and entertainment messages. It is assumed that by altering a child's perception of television and influencing the manner in which television's content is processed, children would become less passive and increase their active cognition skills.

Neurological evidence suggests otherwise. The primarily visual nature of television during a child's formative years (up to about age twelve) mostly stimulates the brain's right hemisphere. Practicing language skills (reading, writing, and dialoguing) stimulates the left brain. Even educational television limits a child's opportunities to employ language, and language is the ultimate source of critical thinking. Childhood marks a transition from the completely nonverbal thought of infants to the primarily verbal thought patterns of rational adults. The greater the verbal opportunities, the greater the likelihood of a child's language growing in complexity and a concomitant sharpening of logical thinking skills. For children, the extended regression into nonverbal mental functioning during television viewing must be seen as a setback. Evidence suggests that the serious diminution of verbal abilities that first occurred among the "television generation" can be attributed directly to watching great quantities of television during those first twelve formative years.

—George R. Plitnik

SUGGESTED READINGS: Two works supporting the addictive nature of television and its adverse effects on cognitive development are *Television and the Quality of Life* (Hillsdale, N.J.: Lawrence Erlbaum, 1990), by Robert Kubey and Mihaly Csikszentmihalyi, and Marie Winn's *The Plug-in Drug*, rev. ed. (New York: Viking-Penguin, 1985). The effects of television on children are examined in editors Jennings Bryant and Daniel R. Anderson's *Children's Understanding of Television: Research on Attention and Comprehension* (New York: Academic Press, 1983) and John Condry's *The Psychology of Television* (Hillsdale, N.J.: Lawrence Erlbaum, 1989).

Information about the educational aspects of *Sesame Street* is presented in *"Sesame Street" Revisited*

Television addiction

(New York: Russell Sage Foundation, 1975), by Thomas Cook et al. Cogent reasons why children should not be exposed to any television are detailed in Gerry Mander's *Four Arguments for the Elimination of Television* (New York: William Morrow, 1978) and Marie Winn's *Unplugging the Plug-in Drug* (New York: Penguin, 1987).

Television addiction: Excessive attachment to television viewing. The majority of American adults believe that television viewing is addictive, but few believe that they are personally affected. Is TELEVISION truly an addictive medium, in the same sense that illegal DRUGS and alcohol can be physically addictive substances, or is it merely a seductive but harmless form of entertainment?

One means of determining whether television viewing can become addictive is to compare it with clinical criteria for addictions such as substance dependence. Five of the nine criteria for diagnosing substance abuse are particularly relevant to television ADDIC-

Critics contend that Americans spend too much time watching television. (Jim Whitmer)

TION; fulfilling four or more of these criteria ranks the addiction as "strong." The criteria are as follows: The substance is consumed in larger amounts or over a longer period than intended; the consumer recognizes that the use is excessive but is not able to reduce or control it; important social activities or responsibilities are interfered with or eliminated; excessive and prolonged use causes social, psychological, and physical problems that are exacerbated by continued usage; and withdrawal symptoms develop when substance use is eliminated or curtailed.

There is substantial evidence that these criteria can apply to many television viewers. For example, a 1990 Gallup Poll found that 42 percent of the respondents claimed that they spent too much time watching television. The problem seems to be worsening; the percentage of Americans who claim they watch too much television has increased from 31 percent in the late 1970's. Research also shows that viewers tend to withdraw from hobbies and family activities and often prefer to view in private; moreover, research indicates that passivity increases with television viewing and that, as passivity increases, the likelihood of becoming involved in more rewarding active experiences decreases. A potentially negative side effect of excessive television use is OBESITY caused by a lack of exercise. The addictive nature of television is also suggested by the fact that its elimination often produces intense psychological stress necessitating a period of severe adjustment.

Unlike the physical addiction of drugs, compulsive television viewing seems to fill an inner psychological need for passivity, self-annihilation, or regression into a state of dependence. Thus, strategies can be developed to regulate excessive or compulsive television viewing by taking responsibility for personal control, or by eliminating the source of temptation itself. The guidance and influence of family members can provide a positive influence to regulate excessive viewing. Finally, family role models and careful control of viewing time during childhood will most likely develop a proactive orientation toward television viewing that carries over to adulthood.

SUGGESTED READINGS: Evidence supporting the addictive nature of television is reviewed in *Television and the Quality of Life* (Hillsdale, N.J.: Lawrence Erlbaum, 1990), by Robert Kubey and Mihaly Csikszentmihalyi. In *The Plug-in Drug*, rev. ed. (New York: Viking-Penguin, 1985), Marie Winn affirms the insidious dangers of the druglike trance induced by television watching. In *Unplugging the Plug-in Drug* (New York: Penguin, 1987), Winn presents strategies for controlling television viewing.

Tenure: The principle that faculty members employed for longer than a probationary period should not lose their employment except for a number of well-defined causes. The protection afforded by tenure was first granted in college and university settings and later was extended to elementary and secondary faculty members. The principle of tenure is adhered to by practically all institutions of higher education and most state-operated elementary and secondary school systems. It also is found in many private elementary or secondary schools.

The idea is important in situations in which freedom of thought and inquiry is highly valued. Such freedom is a necessary part of the search for new knowledge and in the communication of such knowledge to others. Such a search and communication are the role of all education. With tenure, a faculty member is protected from loss of a teaching or research position because of a disagreement with the administration of the school. Lacking such protection, faculty members would be forced to adhere to popular opinions.

When a faculty member is first employed by an institution, there is a probationary period that can be as short as a year or as long as seven years. This period gives the institution the opportunity to evaluate the teacher's abilities and promise. During this trial period, the faculty member can be dismissed or not reemployed for a wide variety of reasons. The teacher does have to be given the chance for a hearing, as is required by DUE PROCESS of law. Once tenure has been granted, the faculty member holds the position on a permanent basis and cannot be released except for a few well-defined causes. These reasons vary from state to state and between types of schools. Generally, however, the following reasons are included: moral turpitude, incompetence, willful neglect of duty, repetitive negligence on the part of the faculty member, and financial crisis on the part of the institution.

The general public has a perception that the principle of tenure protects bad teachers and does not allow for their removal. As a response to public opinion, some states have stopped using the term "tenure" in describing a continuing contract while retaining the principle. There are two important points concerning this public perception. First, the probationary period affords the

Term limits

chance to decide on the ability of the teacher and, following that, the administration has a responsibility to help all members of its faculty to improve their performance continually. Second, if a teacher is not able to improve and meet expectations, the criteria of incompetence or negligence can be used to terminate the tenure faculty member. Establishing incompetence or negligence is not an easy task, and considerable administrative effort is necessary to prove such a case, but it is regularly done. Thus, the mechanism exists to dismiss the truly bad teacher while at the same time affording protection and job security to others.

Term limits: The proposal that the term of office for state and national legislators be limited to a specific length. Forms of term limitation have been adopted for state legislators in a number of states.

History. Although this issue became a major debate in the 1990's, Senator Dennis de Concini and several colleagues had unsuccessfully introduced a constitutional term-limits amendment in 1978 for members of Congress. The U.S. Constitution originally did not specify a maximum length of service either for members of Congress or for the president. This allowed individuals to occupy congressional seats for unlimited periods of time. The Twenty-second Amendment, adopted in 1951, however, provided term limitation for the president.

Debates. During the nineteenth century, there was a lively rotation of legislative seats. In the twentieth century, this has been replaced by longer terms for congressional members. In the second half of the twentieth century, on the average, 90 percent of all congressional members were being returned to office. This was due to the value of incumbency. In the 1970's, it was estimated that the value of incumbency

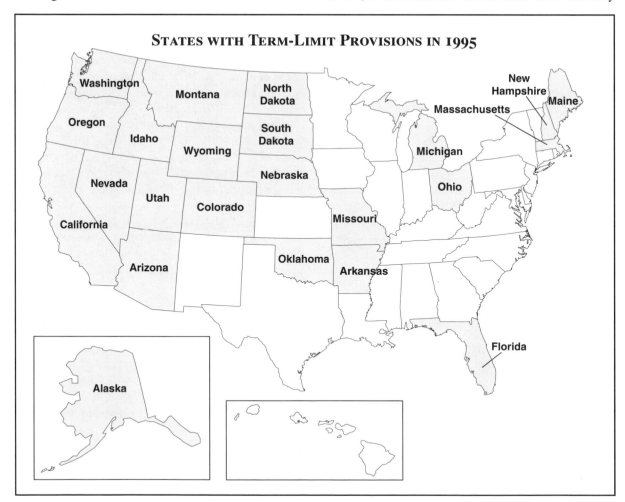

STATES WITH TERM-LIMIT PROVISIONS IN 1995

in a race for a House seat was worth $500,000, and for a Senate seat, $1,000,000. By the 1990's, those values had tripled.

The necessity to organize each house of Congress by the political parties encouraged development and dependency on the seniority system. This system tends to diminish the equal representation of individuals.

Being the chairperson of a standing committee confers immense benefits on the individual, advantages such as personal power and prestige; it also enables that person to ensure that the people represented will receive benefits out of proportion to a purely rational allocation of federal resources.

Arguments Against Term Limits. Opponents of term limits note that the people already have the power to limit terms. If the electorate so desired, it could replace the entire U.S. House of Representatives and one-third of the Senate every two years. This does not happen because many voters are pleased with the representation provided by their legislators. Term limits deny constituents their right to retain a good member of Congress in office if they so desire. Under term limitation, good and bad legislators are ousted equally and without distinction. The loss of senior, experienced legislators means the diminishing of an important check on other actors in the legislative process who would not be limited by term, such as lobbyists, legislative staff members, and executive department bureaucrats.

Arguments for Term Limits. Term limits would eliminate present disparities between senators and representatives based upon length of tenure. It would place each state, district, and citizen on a more nearly equal footing. New people, representing all walks of life and every age group, would be brought constantly and consciously into the system. Thus, U.S. citizens would be equally and fairly represented in Congress. Finally, term limits would eliminate entrenched incumbents and give the people a real choice at election time.

Terminal illness: Designation given when cure is judged no longer possible and a patient's probable life expectancy is six months or less. The problems related to terminal illnesses pose important and controversial social issues regarding ethics and finances. While these are of little concern to the patient who is told that the illness—cancer, AIDS, or some other fatal condition—is incurable and that only a few months of life

remain, society looks at the total costs and grapples with the ethical problems inherent in how to contain these costs. A growing proportion of the federal budget is devoted to MEDICARE, and one analysis showed that 7.5 percent of Medicare patients used more than a third of Medicare funds. As the population's average age increases, an ever greater share of these monies will be used to pay for the final stages of terminal illness.

For the patient facing a terminal diagnosis, three choices present themselves: to continue with intensive treatment, hoping for the elusive cure or extension of life; to accept the diagnosis and arrange for palliative care; or, in moments of depression, to consider SUICIDE. The patient's choice is personal and emotional and may be influenced by cultural background, length and severity of illness, and, more important, financial resources available.

Choosing to continue with expensive, aggressive treatment raises the question of who will pay the costs. It is during the few months or weeks preceding death that the greatest amount of financial resources is consumed. As complications become more frequent and severe, treatment requires specialized services and supplies. Increasingly sophisticated medical science can maintain precarious life but also adds to the costs. Procedures using organ or bone-marrow transplants, respirators, and artificial hearts, can easily approach one million dollars.

Many types of health insurance, including Medicare, may refuse payment for such care. Age may be a factor in determining whether money will be available for final curative efforts, with preference going to children and younger adults. Yet while society has an interest in limiting expenditures, it must also consider the ethics of restricting options for those without independent means.

The choice of palliative care, with goals of comfort and pain control, is now frequently handled in the patient's home by the family or other caregivers, often with the assistance of visiting nursing services. Some patients, lacking caregivers in their homes, are admitted to hospice units or nursing homes. Those patients who sign a living will specifying that no resuscitative efforts are to be used relieve their caregivers of this ethical dilemma. Recognizing the cost-effectiveness of this increasingly popular choice, many private health-insurance policies, Medicare, and other government insurance plans provide coverage for such care.

Those overwhelmed by a diagnosis of terminal illness, and perhaps by uncontrolled pain, may consider suicide as an escape. Though it avoids costly care, this is a passionately debated ethical issue. Attempts to legalize such acts have not been politically successful.

Terrorism: Use of terror as a means of coercion. Terrorists use threats or violence, such as beatings, bombings, and killings, in an attempt to intimidate a group or government into agreeing with their political demands.

Background. Terrorism has been used by groups throughout the world, including nationalistic groups such as the Provisional Irish Republican Army and the PALESTINE LIBERATION ORGANIZATION, religious fundamentalist groups such as the Islamic Jihad, Marxist groups such as the Italian Red Brigades, and racist groups such as the KU KLUX KLAN in the United States.

Individuals, countries, and small groups, whether state-sponsored or not, can attempt to coerce by a variety of means. For example, in 1970, a Canadian group, the Front for the Liberation of Québec, kidnapped the Minister of Labor in Québec's government and killed him after the Québec government refused to meet its demands. In many cases, the coercion involves violence not against state officials but against civilians. In 1972, Japanese Red Army terrorists, working on behalf of a faction of the Palestine Liberation Organization, machine-gunned civilians at Lod Airport in Tel Aviv, Israel. Twenty-six civilians were killed, and seventy-six were wounded; most of the casualties were Puerto Rican Christians on pilgrimage. In 1985, Sikh extremists, pressing for the creation of a Sikh state in the Punjab region of India, were apparently responsible for blowing up an Air India jet over the Atlantic Ocean. Because the flight originated in Toronto, many of the 329 people killed were Canadians. In 1993, anti-American Muslims detonated a bomb under the WORLD TRADE CENTER in New York, killing six and wounding more than one thousand. In April, 1995, domestic U.S. terrorists blew up the OKLAHOMA CITY Federal Building, killing and wounding dozens in the worst terrorist incident in recent American history.

Politics of Terrorism. How terrorism is defined can play an important role in promoting a political agenda. According to General Jorge Videla, president of Argentina from 1976 to 1981, terrorists include those who "spread ideas that are contrary to Western and Christian civilization." Guided by Videla's definition, elements of the Argentinean military conducted a "dirty war" against their own countrymen between 1976 and 1983. In this war, between six thousand and thirty thousand "subversive" Argentineans were abducted, tortured, and executed.

The term "terrorism" has considerable political force because of the common belief that terrorism is wrong and that terrorists are bad people. Successfully labeling one's opponents as terrorists makes them look bad, whether they are or not, and makes it less likely that their cause will receive sympathy.

Political differences between people sometimes result in disagreements about whether "terrorism" applies in a particular case. Those willing to support killing the innocent as a means for bringing about national liberation may not want this to be regarded as terrorism, since to classify it as such would give the impression that it is wrong, and thereby risk hurting the liberation movement. Those who believe in the movement may regard the killers as heroes or as freedom fighters,

U.S. DOMESTIC TERRORIST INCIDENTS, 1982-1992

Type and Target	Number
Type of incident	
Bombing attacks	130
Kidnapping; assaults; alleged assassinations; assassinations	11
Arson	8
Robbery; attempted robbery	5
Hostile takeover	4
Malicious destruction of property	4
Acts of sabotage	2
Hijacking	1
Type of target	
Commercial establishments	60
Military personnel/establishments	33
State and United States government buildings/property	31
Private residence/vehicle	18
Diplomatic establishments	17
Educational establishments	6
Total	**165**

Source: U.S. Department of Justice, Bureau of Justice Statistics, *Sourcebook of Criminal Justice Statistics—1993.* Washington, D.C.: U.S. Government Printing Office, 1994.

U.S. Citizens Killed or Wounded in International Terrorist Incidents, 1981-1993

	Total	Dead	Wounded
1981	47	7	40
1982	19	8	11
1983	386	271	115
1984	42	11	31
1985	195	38	157
1986	112	12	100
1987	54	7	47
1988	232	192	40
1989	34	15	19
1990	44	10	34
1991	21	7	14
1992	3	2	1
1993	1,008	6	1,002
Total	**2,197**	586	1,611

Source: U.S. Department of Justice, Bureau of Justice Statistics, *Sourcebook of Criminal Justice Statistics—1993.* Washington, D.C.: U.S. Government Printing Office, 1994.

whereas those who do not believe in the movement will be likely to regard the killers as terrorists.

Some reject the idea that whether or not someone is a terrorist is simply a matter of perspective, claiming that it is based on a misunderstanding of what terrorists and freedom fighters are really like and what their differences are. They claim that terrorists are not freedom fighters, since freedom fighters do not intentionally violate the rights of innocents, unlike terrorists. The 1972-1973 United Nations debates on terrorism show, however, that some are unwilling to apply the term "terrorist" to groups that have their approval, even if the groups deliberately kill the innocent.

In 1972, after a rash of terrorist incidents, including the killing of eleven Israeli Olympic athletes in Munich by a group of Palestinians, Kurt Waldheim, secretary general of the United Nations, proposed that the General Assembly consider "measures to prevent terrorism." Some states apparently regarded this as an attempt to undermine legitimate struggles for national liberation by branding them as terrorism. As a result of such concerns, the secretary general's proposal was amended to include the "study of the underlying causes of those forms of terrorism and acts of violence which lie in misery, frustration, grievance and despair." In the ensuing debates, a bloc of Arabic, African, and Eastern European nations would not classify "resisting oppression by all possible means" as terrorism. This bloc of nations was also reluctant to set limits on the methods of violence open to those whom they regarded as fighting legitimate wars of national liberation.

Terrorism: Pro and Con. Terrorists and their supporters offer a variety of reasons in support of intentional attacks on the innocent. Some claim that anything is permitted in the fight against world imperialism. This claim, however, is in direct conflict with modern developments in just-war theory, which sets restrictions on the kinds of behavior that are morally acceptable during war. One of these restrictions is that there should be no intentional attacks on innocent people.

Terrorists may reject such restrictions on the ground that no one is innocent. Many, however, regard this claim as implausible. Many victims of terrorism have no connection to the alleged injustices that terrorists aim to remedy. Many victims have no involvement in administering or enforcing the legal system that the terrorists want to change. Finally, before the victims were attacked, they posed little if any threat of harm to the terrorists.

Some terrorists say that when there is an extreme imbalance of power between belligerent parties, the party with the just cause has a right to self-defense, which includes using terrorism. It is not clear, however, that the right to self-defense includes the right to attack the innocent. Violence in self-defense may be justifiable against those who are a serious threat to one's safety, but innocent people do not constitute such a threat to terrorists or their people.

Terrorists also claim that justice cannot prevail unless they use terrorism. But even when terrorism seems to help win a war of national liberation, as it did in Algeria, it remains unclear whether terrorism directed at civilians was the only way that liberation could have been achieved: Would violence against military targets or nonviolent resistance have succeeded eventually?

Terrorists may say that because terrorism shortens the revolutionary struggle, terrorism brings about the greatest good for the greatest number and is, therefore, morally justifiable. This utilitarian rationale for terrorism faces at least three problems. First, instead of demoralizing the ruling class, terrorism may in fact strengthen their will to resist. Instead of turning the masses against the state by causing greater state repression, terrorism may in fact turn the masses against the terrorists by making the terrorists seem to be nothing more than especially dangerous criminals.

Second, even if terrorism does in fact shorten the revolutionary struggle, it does not necessarily bring about the greatest good for the greatest number. The new revolutionary regime may turn out to be worse than the old regime. And when a group uses terror to gain political power, it sets a dangerous precedent that its opponents may be all too willing to follow. Third, bringing about the greatest good for the greatest number is morally suspect if it involves disregarding people's rights.

Another rationale for terrorism, and one of this century's most popular, comes from Martinique-Algerian psychiatrist Frantz Fanon. In his *Wretched of the Earth* (1961), Fanon argued that using anti-colonial violence against persons is morally justifiable, since using such violence is the only way for the colonized person to be psychologically liberated and made whole.

There are several problems with Fanon's argument. It is not clear that violence against innocents would lead to psychological liberation instead of psychological degeneration. Also, a nonviolent approach to psychological liberation of the sort described by Martin Luther King, Jr., in such works as *Why We Can't Wait* (1963) seems morally preferable to Fanon's approach. Even if violence were the only way to achieve psychological liberation, such violence would not be automatically justifiable: Rape is not justifiable even if it is the only way a person can feel psychologically liberated.

Some terrorists seem to believe that their violence is justified as a way of taking revenge on another group that has treated their group unfairly. A reputed harm done to innocents in one group is put forward to justify harming innocents in another group. Many regard it as unfair to make the innocents in one group pay for what others have done to the innocents in another group. Some criticize this terrorist rationale on the ground that two wrongs do not make a right. Their thinking is that if it was wrong to hurt innocents in the first group, it would also be wrong to hurt innocents in the second group. —*Gregory P. Rich*

SUGGESTED READINGS: Bonnie Szumski's *Terrorism: Opposing Viewpoints* (St. Paul, Minn.: Greenhaven Press, 1986) juxtaposes pairs of newspaper articles on terrorism, the first taking one side of a question

and the next taking the opposing side. Benjamin Netanyahu's *Terrorism: How the West Can Win* (New York: Avon Books, 1986) is a series of antiterrorist papers by well-known statesmen, scholars, and journalists. Articles by terrorists and their opponents printed in the 1987 edition of Walter Laqueur's *The Terrorism Reader: A Historical Anthology* (New York: New American Library, 1978) provide an overview of terrorist theory and practice from the 1800's into the 1980's.

Terry, Randall (b. April 25, 1959, Rochester, N.Y.): Antiabortion activist. Terry, a former used-car salesman with a degree from Elim Bible Institute, is best known as the founder, director, and spiritual leader of OPERATION RESCUE. This nationally active antiabortion group, whose "rescues" usually take the form of clinic blockades, was established by Terry in 1988. The organization grew out of Project Life, created by Terry and his wife in Binghamton, N.Y., their hometown. Terry, who is noted for the outspoken character of his public statements, now acts independently of Operation Rescue, which has moved to Dallas, Texas, under the directorship of the Reverend Flip Benham.

Test-tube babies: Human infants produced through the extraction of eggs, the laboratory fertilization of those eggs, and their reimplantation into a mother. First utilized in the United States in 1981, the procedure differs from artificial insemination *in utero*, since the mother who donates the egg may not be the mother who carries the fetus through pregnancy. While the procedure provides hope for childless couples when the woman has damaged ovaries or Fallopian tubes, the procedure also established a business in "SURROGATE MOTHERS," leading some ethicists to question the separation of biological and genetic motherhood.

Texas v. Johnson (1989): U.S. Supreme Court case. In one of the Supreme Court's most controversial decisions, the Court ruled five to four that burning the flag as an act of protest is a protected political expression.

Gregory Johnson, one of many people protesting policies of the Ronald Reagan Administration, burned a U.S. flag in front of Dallas City Hall during the 1984 Republican National Convention. Several additional protesters chanted, "America, the red, white, and blue,

Operation Rescue founder Randall Terry is arrested and escorted from a 1988 protest at an Atlanta abortion clinic. (UPI/Corbis-Bettmann)

Gregory Johnson, who was acquitted of flag-desecration charges in *Texas v. Johnson*, poses with an American flag. (AP/Wide World Photos)

we spit on you." Johnson was arrested for violation of a Texas statute that made it a crime for anyone to knowingly or intentionally desecrate the national flag. In the statute, to "desecrate" was defined as to "deface, damage, or otherwise physically mistreat in a way that the actor knows will seriously offend one or more persons likely to observe or discover his action." No one was injured or threatened with injury. Several witnesses, however, testified that they were seriously offended by the flag desecration.

The Texas statute was ruled unconstitutional, along with versions in forty-seven other states, because it made it illegal to treat the flag in a disrespectful manner that offended bystanders. Treatment of the flag that was not offensive was not prohibited. Thus, an act designed to express criticism of the government, which the First Amendment protects as a right of freedom of expression, was prohibited when other people found it offensive.

Justice William Brennan wrote the majority opinion for the Supreme Court. He pointed out that the United States has a long history of protecting expression that is critical of the government. The form of that criticism is not always agreeable to the audience, but that is the nature of criticism. To not allow certain forms of criticism, including desecration of the national symbol of the government, would be to restrict the possibility of criticism. More than anything else, freedom of expression means freedom to criticize. Brennan argued that the best approach is to persuade the protesters that they are wrong, not to punish them. Chief Justice William Rehnquist disagreed with the majority opinion and argued that burning the flag is like an "inarticulate grunt" that deserves no constitutional protection.

Congress agreed and, urged on by President George Bush, attempted to pass a constitutional amendment. Amendments require a two-thirds majority vote of both the House of Representatives and the Senate and then ratification by thirty-eight of the states. Lacking the necessary votes for an amendment, Congress instead passed a federal law banning flag burning. The statute made it a crime to deface, physically defile, or burn the U.S. flag. In 1990, the Supreme Court struck down that law, too. Justice Brennan wrote, "If there is a bedrock principle underlying the First Amendment, it is that the government may not prohibit the expression of an idea simply because society finds the idea itself offensive or disagreeable."

In 1995, Congress again attempted to pass a constitutional amendment to prohibit flag burning. The resolution passed in the House, 312 to 120 votes in favor, but failed to pass the Senate. Since 1989, all the states but Vermont had petitioned Congress to pass the amendment.

Third World nations: The nations of Africa, Asia, and Latin America. The term had its origins in the post-World War II period, referring to a third alternative to the "First World" of developed, industrialized countries of the West and the "Second World" of the socialist bloc led by the former Soviet Union. The attempt to form alliances within the Third World is called the nonaligned movement.

Although many of the nations of Latin America and elsewhere had been independent long before World War II, the concept of a Third World emerged only after 1945 as a result of two important international developments. First, the European nations that had acquired colonies began to grant the nations of Asia and Africa independence. Second, the emergence of the Cold War rivalry between the West, led by the United States, and the socialist nations, led by the Soviet Union, created alliances that sought to win the support of both the older and the newer nations of the Third World. In 1955, several of the nations that make up this group convened the Afro-Asian Conference in Bandung, Indonesia, which led to the creation of a loosely structured nonaligned movement.

Third World nations generally have had a difficult time maintaining a coherent degree of effective cooperation. Their most common feature has been their relative impoverishment compared both to the industrialized West and to the former socialist countries. Most are dependent on exports of raw materials to the industrialized world in return for imported manufactured goods and capital. Other than that general common-ality, Third World nations vary from the huge states of India and China to the microstates in the Pacific. They range from states that have been independent since the early nineteenth century, such as those of Latin America—or even much longer, such as China or Thailand—to most of the states of sub-Saharan Africa, which emerged as independent states in their current form only since the late 1950's.

As a group, Third World nations have tried to press the industrialized nations to provide assistance for development with mixed success. Although they make up a large majority of the members of the United Nations, the veto held by the five permanent members in

Third World nations sometimes suffer from food shortages that prompt foreign aid. (Reuters/ Bettmann)

the Security Council and the domination of bilateral aid agencies such as the International Monetary Fund (IMF) and WORLD BANK by richer countries, has limited the ability of Third World nations to achieve a general equalization of wealth between rich North and poor South.

Some Third World nations have had more success than others in promoting economic development. China has pursued a socialist path that by the 1980's began to lead to rapid industrialization. Southeast Asian countries, such as Korea and Taiwan, and some Latin American nations have followed more market-oriented policies toward industrialization. India, using mixed policies, has seen a gradual but steady development since achieving its independence in 1947. Other Third World nations, especially many of those in Africa, have seen their economies stagnate. Many believe that the policies enforced by the IMF merely perpetuate the poverty of these nations.

Thomas, Clarence (b. June 23, 1948, Pinpoint, Ga.): U.S. SUPREME COURT justice. A former chairman of the EQUAL EMPLOYMENT OPPORTUNITY COMMISSION (EEOC) from 1982 to 1989, Thomas was nominated in 1991 by President George Bush to succeed Thurgood MARSHALL as only the second African American to serve on the Court. Critics contended that Thomas' qualifications for the job were slender and that his nomination was an instance of tokenism; leading CIVIL RIGHTS groups, including the NATIONAL ASSOCIATION FOR THE ADVANCEMENT OF COLORED PEOPLE (NAACP), refused to support his confirmation by the Senate. The confirmation hearings were further marred by charges of sexual harassment brought against Thomas by Anita HILL, a former subordinate at the EEOC. He vehemently denied the charges, labeling the pro-

ceedings a "high-tech lynching." Narrowly confirmed in October, 1991, Thomas quickly aligned himself with the Court's conservative bloc.

Three-Mile Island nuclear accident (March 28, 1979): Partial melting of the core in a nuclear reactor near Harrisburg, Pennsylvania. The accident was triggered when a plumbing crew accidentally shut off the water supply cooling the reactor core. An ensuing series of human and mechanical errors led to the rupture of many of the reactor's uranium fuel rods. Subsequently, bursts of radioactive gas escaped from the site, prompting evacuation of many local residents. The plant was closed, and cleanup operations continued for years. The Three-Mile Island incident focused

Supreme Court justice Clarence Thomas during his 1991 Senate confirmation hearings. (Reuters/Bettmann)

attention on the U.S. ANTINUCLEAR MOVEMENT, and in the accident's aftermath, nuclear plant cancellations far exceeded new orders.

Three-strikes laws: State and federal legislation requiring life sentences for three-time convicted offenders. In response to a perceived fear of crime on the part of the public, and following several high-profile incidents, politicians rushed to offer a variety of "get tough" proposals that would allegedly provide solutions to the crime problem.

When multiple offender and parolee Richard Allen Davis kidnapped and killed twelve-year-old Polly Klaas in California in 1993, public outcry swelled. The crime provided the impetus for California to pass a "three strikes and you're out" law in March, 1994. The previous November, the state of Washington had passed a law mandating life imprisonment without parole for "persistent offenders" convicted of a third "serious felony." By mid-1995, fourteen states and the federal government had three-strikes laws on the books.

The federal three-strikes provision is part of the VIOLENT CRIME CONTROL AND LAW ENFORCEMENT ACT signed by President Bill Clinton in September, 1994. The act requires life imprisonment for convicted offenders who have been convicted on two previous occasions of two serious violent felonies or one serious violent felony and a serious drug offense. The definition of "serious violent felony" is broad and includes such crimes as burglary and prostitution. Convictions before the law went into effect on January 1, 1995, are included in the "strikes."

The Washington law defines a "persistent offender" as one who is convicted of three crimes within the "most serious felony" category. The category includes crimes ranging from the promotion of prostitution to second-degree manslaughter to murder.

California requires a mandatory life sentence for a third felony, with a minimum of either twenty-five years or triple the normal sentence for the crime. For a second felony, the normal prison sentence is doubled. According to the California law, serious felonies include burglary, murder, felonies committed using a firearm, and the act of giving or selling drugs to a minor.

The Georgia legislature seemed to go even further, allowing only two "strikes" and providing for life imprisonment after a second "serious violent felony."

Unlike the others, however, the Georgia law includes a shorter list of eligible crimes, all of them clearly violent, such as murder, armed robbery, kidnapping, rape, and child molestation.

Both scholars and criminal-justice professionals expect that the three-strikes laws will have unintended results on the criminal-justice system. Prosecutors predict that, given the consequences of a third conviction, accused offenders will be much more likely to refuse a plea bargain and to insist on a trial. Jurisdictions will thus face both the cost of more criminal trials and—as serious cases must take precedence in the courts—the likelihood that nonfelony cases will become even more backlogged in the system.

The 1995 prison population in the United States stood at about 1.3 million, and that population is disproportionately made up of African American males. The incarceration rate of whites is 306 per 100,000; for blacks, the rate is 1,947 per 100,000, or more than six times as high. Many observers have predicted that under the three-strikes laws, the prison population could more than double within the next ten years; evidence suggests that the racial imbalance will persist.

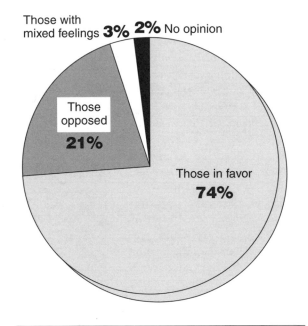

PUBLIC OPINION, 1994: THREE STRIKES LAWS

Those with mixed feelings **3%** **2%** No opinion

Those opposed **21%**

Those in favor **74%**

Source: George Gallup, Jr., ed., *The Gallup Poll: Public Opinion, 1994* (Wilmington, Del.: Scholarly Resources, 1995).

Like other mandatory sentencing schemes, the three-strikes laws seek to offer a simple solution to the complex problem of violent crime. In doing so, critics argue, such laws shift attention and resources from the causes and conditions that foster violent behavior and from other components of the criminal justice system such as juvenile justice, diversion, and early-intervention programs. Moreover, critics claim, although long mandatory sentences may prevent specific offenders from committing additional crimes, there is little evidence that such laws deter others.

Thurmond, Strom (b. Dec. 5, 1902, Edgefield, S.C.): Oldest member of Congress in U.S. history. Thurmond, who campaigned for president as a Democrat in 1948, was first elected to the Senate in 1954. A prominent opponent of racial integration, he became a Republican in the 1960's when mainstream Democrats embraced the CIVIL RIGHTS MOVEMENT. Political realities imposed by the large numbers of black voters in his state, however, have tempered his public pronouncements on race since the early 1970's. By the mid-1990's, Thurmond was said to be forgetful and almost completely dependent on his staff; critics charged that his advanced age made him unfit for his Senate duties, and some called for Thurmond to be stripped of his chairmanship of the powerful senate Armed Services Committee.

Timber Summit (1993): U.S. government-sponsored meeting on ENVIRONMENTAL ISSUES. The Timber Summit, held in Portland, Oregon, in April, 1993, at

South Carolina senator Strom Thurmond talks with Supreme Court nominee Ruth Bader Ginsburg in 1993. (AP/Wide World Photos)

The northern spotted owl, the focus of controversy at the 1993 Timber Summit. (AP/Wide World Photos)

the behest of the Bill Clinton Administration, brought together government officials, including Clinton and Vice President Al Gore, Jr., and representatives of groups on opposing sides of the debate over the logging of Pacific Northwest OLD-GROWTH FORESTS. Timber industry advocates argued that such logging was an economic necessity; environmentalists countered that continued logging would destroy irreplaceable natural areas and threaten native species such as the northern spotted owl. The resulting timber-management plan proposed by the Clinton Administration drew criticism from both sides in the debate.

Tinker v. Des Moines (1969): U.S. Supreme Court case. The Supreme Court ruled that the First Amendment protected free-expression rights of students as long as the expression was not disruptive, obscene, or a violation of the rights of other students.

Five members of the Tinker family wore black armbands to their elementary and high schools as a silent protest of U.S. involvement in the Vietnam War. School officials prohibited the wearing of the armbands, fearing that such a controversial act might disrupt the schools and the eighteen thousand students enrolled in the system. The Tinker children were expelled from school, and the family took the issue to court. Since there was no evidence of disruption in the schools, the Supreme Court found that their expulsion from school was an unconstitutional infringement of the Tinkers' freedom of expression. Justice Abe Fortas, in the majority opinion of the Court, wrote, "It can

Mary Beth and John Tinker, plaintiffs in *Tinker v. Des Moines*, display their controversial armbands. (UPI/Corbis-Bettmann)

hardly be argued that either students or teachers shed their constitutional rights to freedom of expression at the schoolhouse gate."

The Court found that student rights were not vastly different from those of adults. Political expression is protected, even when it is merged with conduct and takes largely symbolic form. Students may express their opinion on controversial issues so long as they do so "without materially and substantially interfering with the requirements of appropriate discipline in the operation of the school and without colliding with the rights of others." The Court noted that the Tinkers simply attended their classes and caused no interruption of school activities. They did cause discussion outside the classroom, but not disorder. Justice Hugo Black, a strong advocate of the First Amendment and freedom of expression, did dissent in this case. He argued that "it is a myth to say that a person has a constitutional right to say what he pleases, where he pleases, and when he pleases."

Later cases have placed more restrictions on high-school students. School administrators have on occasion been allowed to restrict the speech of students and to regulate content in a school newspaper. In the twenty-five years since *Tinker*, courts have generally supported the action of school administrators who have restricted the rights of expression of students when school activities seem threatened. There are increasing attempts to censor what students can write, read, or say at all levels of education. In 1989, the Student Press Law Center, an organization that monitors First Amendment controversies throughout the United States, received 615 requests for help from students who felt their constitutional rights of expression were being threatened. In 1990, the center received 929 requests for help. In the first six months of 1991, the center received more than eight hundred requests.

Tobacco farming: Controversial industry both attacked and defended by private, public, and government sources. The mid-1990's saw tobacco farmers faced by social and economic issues that threatened their livelihood. Decreasing government support for tobacco production, growing social restrictions on tobacco use, and greater reliance by tobacco companies on overseas tobacco supplies imperiled a valued source of small farm income.

For most of its history, the social and religious use of tobacco was accepted and largely unquestioned. In states like North Carolina, Kentucky, Tennessee, South Carolina, and Virginia, tobacco culture was an important feature of agricultural life for generations. Even though tobacco farming needed much labor, few crops brought in so much money from so little land. In 1993, for example, even though tobacco was less than 8 percent of the total cropland in Kentucky, it made up 43 percent of the total crop value. Farmers could earn more than twice as much from an acre of tobacco as they could from an acre of corn, wheat, or soybeans.

Tobacco farmers eventually found themselves and their crop attacked on several fronts. The 1965 U.S. Surgeon General's report linked tobacco use to higher cancer rates, and tobacco farmers found themselves condemned for producing a harmful crop. A steady decline in the social acceptance of tobacco use by the 1990's caused smoking to be banned on airline flights and influenced many states (including those in which tobacco was a major crop) to ban smoking in public buildings. The federal government almost completely eliminated support for research on tobacco production by 1995.

Tobacco farmers were slow to switch to other crops because of a long history of government support. Beginning in the mid-1930's, a federally sponsored program protected tobacco farmers from sudden changes in market demand by setting annual tobacco production levels and limiting surplus tobacco so that the crop value exceeded its production costs. This ended years of conflict between large tobacco companies (which tried to lower tobacco prices) and tobacco farmers (who sometimes used theft, arson, and other violent methods to restrict the tobacco supply and keep prices high). As part of the program, the federal government loaned tobacco farmers the difference between minimum support prices and sales prices. Thus, tobacco farmers could rely on a large and reliable income from the tobacco they grew.

As labor became more expensive in the United States, however, and as the quality and availability of tobacco in countries such as Argentina, Brazil, Kenya, and Zimbabwe improved, tobacco farmers in the United States found that even the federal program was at risk. As U.S. production costs rose, tobacco companies began to use cheaper sources of tobacco from overseas. This slow decline in the demand for U.S. tobacco meant the steady loss of income for tobacco farmers and the communities in which they lived.

SUGGESTED READINGS: Robert K. Heimann's *Tobacco and Americans* (New York: McGraw-Hill,

1960) is a good history of tobacco that is strongly biased against its link to increased disease. W. F. Axton gives a more balanced view of tobacco farming in *Tobacco and Kentucky* (Lexington: The University Press of Kentucky, 1975).

Tort reform: Use of legislation to change common-law tort decisions. Despite the general perception that private law is not political, there has been a long history of interest groups using the state legislatures to reverse or modify decisions of judges, especially in the areas of accident law and products liability. In the early part of the twentieth century tort reform was generally undertaken in reaction to conservative courts and tended to promote the interest of workers or consumers. In recent decades, however, tort reform at both the state and federal level has generally reflected the concerns of commercial interests that assert that many state judges have become too liberal.

Background. "Tort law" refers to the legal rights possessed by a citizen to be free of injury. Most tort law is COMMON LAW. Common law, unlike statutory law, has never been enacted by a sovereign; it has been developed, instead, through decisions of different courts over hundreds of years. Its authority derives from its long usage, the acceptance of its precedents by the courts, and ultimately the acceptance of its basic principles by society. Common law can always be changed by a state's sovereign. Thus, in seventeenth century England, the king could change common law (although he rarely did), just as today Parliament can change common law (which it does on occasion). Similarly, since in the United States every state has its own common law of torts, the sovereign of each state can change its common law of tort through legislation. In theory, although there is no federal common law in the United States, Congress has the power to change every states' common and statutory law of torts by virtue of the Constitution's supremacy clause.

Historical Cases of Tort Reform. The inspiration for reforming accident law for workers came when progressive lawyers and economists argued that the legal system was too difficult for the typical worker to navigate. These reformers argued that workers would be better off if industrial accidents were covered under an insurance policy paid for by the employer, whereby a worker would receive compensation for a work-related injury regardless of whether the worker could prove that the injury was the fault of the employer. The basic

TORT CASE RESOLUTIONS

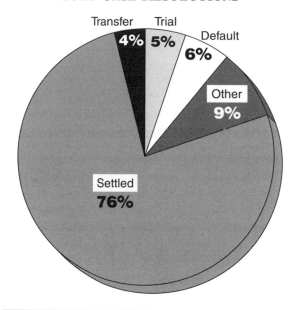

Source: Data are from *Newsweek*, March 20, 1995. Primary sources: Terence Dunworth and Joel Rogers, National Center for State Courts.

Note: Figures based on 1988 one-month caseload of thirty-three state courts.

idea was a tradeoff between the workers, who would receive a guarantee of compensation without filing a lawsuit, and the employers, who would as a result pay to each injured worker much less than they might have to pay to the occasional worker who actually won in court.

In 1910, New York became the first state to adopt a system of workers' compensation. By 1975, workers' compensation systems were compulsory in forty-six of fifty-one jurisdictions in the United States and in every province in Canada. The cost of the insurance scheme upon which workers' compensation relies has grown enormously: In 1960, employers spent $2 billion on administrative and insurance costs, while in 1992 they spent $62 billion. Workers' compensation, which was supposed to have taken a large number of accidents out of the courts, has gradually spawned its own set of complex legal questions, such as what counts as an injury "arising out of employment" and at what point workers' compensation ceases to be a worker's exclusive remedy. Furthermore, critics of workers' compensation have argued that its no-fault structure encourages fraud and discourages workers from assuming greater responsibility for their own safety.

Tort reform

The next widespread movement in tort reform concerned automobile accidents. Under a fault-based tort system, a car owner's insurer paid compensation only if a claimant could prove that the driver was at fault. In the 1960's, many scholars argued that in the case of automobiles, the tort system was expensive and inefficient: In New York in 1970, for example, fifty-six cents of every dollar put into the system was spent on administration and litigation. Just as with workers' compensation, progressive reformers urged various state legislatures to adopt a "no-fault" system in which victims of automobile accidents would be guaranteed to receive compensation upon proof of an injury caused by the insured automobile. Unlike with workers' compensation, however, the amount of compensation guaranteed by the no-fault legislation was not a small fraction but a somewhat sizable fraction of what the victim might have recovered through a successful suit under a fault system. For this reason, no-fault insurance schemes are generally perceived as more redistributive than workers' compensation. It is perhaps for this reason that no-fault automobile insurance has been a less successful reform movement—from 1970, when Massachusetts passed the first no-fault law, to 1995, only twenty-four jurisdictions passed no-fault reforms.

Contemporary Tort Reform. Tort reform since the 1980's has been driven by the perception that postwar common-law tort doctrine has generated a "tort crisis." Since the 1960's, judges have grown much more solicitous of plaintiffs and have rejected or reinterpreted precedents that made it difficult for plaintiffs to win. For example, family members, charities, and the government no longer enjoy immunity from tort claims, and changes in rules of evidence and proof of negligence have made it far easier to prove negligence in medical malpractice cases. The rejection of contributory negligence in favor of comparative fault, as well as the elimination of special privileges for landowners, mean that plaintiffs who are in some way "at fault" may still be compensated. The most important change came in the early 1960's, when the California Supreme Court repudiated a century of contract and tort precedents and declared that product manufacturers would be liable to consumers under a standard of strict liability instead of fault. By the late 1970's, almost every state supreme court had followed suit.

As tort law became more hospitable to plaintiffs, the number of lawsuits brought in the United States began to rise dramatically. A 1986 Department of Justice report noted significant increases in tort claims filed in federal courts in the areas of products liability, medical malpractice, and municipal government liability. The report also argued that jury awards for successful lawsuits were also increasing, giving as an example the fact that the average wrongful-death verdict for an adult male rose from roughly $250,000 to $1,000,000 between 1975 and 1985. Many insurance and manufacturing companies have used such reports to bolster their argument that state and federal legislation is needed to reverse some of the more extreme decisions of judges and juries.

Tort reform in the 1980's occurred mostly at the state level and was designed to make it more difficult for plaintiffs to bring tort claims and to limit damage awards if plaintiffs won. For the most part, tort reformers have not attempted to change the substantive legal doctrines developed during the 1960's and 1970's. The most important reforms included the following: The suspension or modification of the common law's "collateral source rule," which prevented plaintiffs' awards from being reduced if they had insurance or received compensation for their injuries from another source; capping the amount of damages a jury can award plaintiffs; allowing defendants to shift the cost of defense if plaintiffs filed "frivolous" lawsuits; restricting the right of plaintiffs to sue municipalities; restricting "joint and several liability," which forced relatively insignificant defendants who were found jointly liable with other, more significant defendants to pay large portions of a plaintiff's damages; and restricting or eliminating "punitive damages," which are damages imposed in addition to the amount designed to compensate plaintiffs.

The state tort reforms of the 1980's were made possible by the fact that Republicans began to make serious gains in state legislatures around the nation. The tort reformers were helped also by an increase in popular distrust of lawyers, which meant that arguments designed to protect the access gained by plaintiffs to the courts were met with skepticism. In 1994, Republicans took control of both houses of Congress, and the focus of tort reform moved from the state legislatures to the federal government. Despite a philosophical commitment to decentralization, the Republican Party's "Contract with America" promised to use Congress' national powers to reform state tort law. The proposed legislation would require state courts to adopt restrictive rules concerning products liability and punitive damages and would also make it more difficult to bring any sort of tort action into the federal courts.

—*Anthony J. Sebok*

SUGGESTED READINGS: The politics of contemporary tort reform are explained in Joseph Sanders and Craig Joyce's *"Off to the Races": The 1980's Tort Crisis and the Law Reform Process* (*Houston Law Review* 27, no. 2, p. 207). Michael Rustad and Thomas Koenig take a skeptical look at the "tort crisis" in *The Historical Continuity of Punitive Damage Awards: Reforming the Tort Reformers* (*American University Law Review* 42, no. 4, p. 1269).

Torture: Deliberate infliction of severe mental or physical pain or suffering upon a person. Torture is often used to acquire information or a confession from victims concerning themselves or a third party; torture may also be intended to punish victims for acts committed or suspected of having been committed either by the victims or a third party.

Throughout history, torture has been a common practice of governments, police authorities, and military agents. Torture is still widely practiced by governmental authorities throughout the world, despite the fact that it has been regarded since the early twentieth century as a violation of the international law of war. Moreover, with the gradual growth following World War II of modern human rights treaties, freedom from torture has been recognized as a basic human right. Article 5 of the Universal Declaration of Human Rights adopted by the United Nations General Assembly in 1948, asserts that "no one shall be subjected to torture or to cruel, inhuman or degrading treatment or punishment." In 1966, the General Assembly adopted the International Covenant on Civil and Political Rights, which similarly prohibited torture. This legal instrument did not enter into force until 1976.

However, in the meantime, the United Nations began to draft legal instruments concerned solely with prohibition of torture and related acts. In December, 1975, the U.N. General Assembly adopted a nonbinding declaration on the subject of torture, calling upon countries to eliminate torture and other inhuman or degrading punishment by legislative action, to treat torture as a criminal act, to investigate incidences of torture, and to train police forces in such a way as to ensure compliance with the nonuse of torture. A decade later, in 1984, the General Assembly adopted a binding Convention Against Torture and Other Cruel, Inhuman, or Degrading Treatment or Punishment, which obliges ratifying parties to take domestic legislative and executive action to outlaw and punish acts of torture. The convention also created a

A suspected Viet Cong guerrilla is tortured in 1966 during the Vietnam War. (UPI/Corbis-Bettmann)

Committee Against Torture to receive reports from governments regarding their compliance with the convention's provisions.

Several regional attempts to eradicate torture as a legitimate action of governments have also been undertaken. In 1985, the Organization of American States, in its Inter-American Convention to Prevent and Punish Torture, defined governmentally sponsored torture to be a crime. Similarly, the European Human Rights Convention contained provisions combating the use of torture. The Council of Europe also sponsored a European Convention for the Prevention of Torture and Inhuman or Degrading Treatment or Punishment, which forbids torture and provides for a Special Committee of experts to visit prisons and detention facilities of member governments in order to protect inmates from practices proscribed by the Convention. The European Regional Regime relies heavily on publicizing treaty violations and is considered one of the most effective systems for preventing the use of torture.

Despite the many global and regional efforts to prevent and punish torture, there are still pervasive violations of international norms in this area, especially in situations involving civil war, rebellion, and political instability. The eradication of this practice, then, has yet to be fully realized, despite the determined efforts of human rights advocacy groups such as Amnesty International and Human Rights Watch.

Total quality management (TQM): Formal system commonly used in the manufacturing, service, and health-care sectors of the North American economy. TQM encompasses employees and processes as well as final product quality. The manufacture or provision of products or services is viewed as being part of a continuum that exists to achieve a stated goal or mission. Each component has established standards of quality (design, construction, timeliness, customer satisfaction, and the like). According to TQM doctrine, all components in the process are important, all contribute to the final product, and all persons or organizational entities become accountable when assessing success or failure.

Trade deficit: When the value of the goods a country imports in a year is greater than the value of its exports, the difference is called the country's trade defi-

cit. Before 1982, U.S. trade deficits were small and temporary. Deficits in some years typically were offset by surpluses in other years. Since 1982, the United States has experienced large and chronic trade deficits. Many analysts believe that low rates of saving by individuals and huge federal government budget deficits are largely responsible for increases in the U.S. trade deficit.

Throughout most of the 1980's, the United States was plagued with the problem of the "twin deficits." The first deficit, the budget deficit, was the significant gap between what the federal government spent and what it collected in taxes. The budget deficit had to be financed by borrowing funds, thus adding to the national debt. The second deficit was the trade deficit. Some economists contend that high trade deficits reflected an underlying loss of U.S. international competitiveness. Others argued that trade deficits were primarily the consequence of the federal government's budget deficits and mounting national debt. In simple terms, the national debt is linked to the trade deficit because the borrowing country receives money from the lender, money that may be used to buy imported goods.

Chronic budget and trade deficits have become major concerns for domestic and foreign investors. In the absence of reform or policy changes, the twin deficits posed the threat of stifling current and future standards of living, leading to drastic cuts in social programs and tax increases for future generations.

Because domestic uses of funds exceed the domestic sources of fund for a country with a trade deficit, the excess must be borrowed from abroad. Further, because federal budget deficits lead to government borrowing and increase the national debt, many analysts contend that these deficits raise interest rates and depress private borrowing and investment. Lower current investment means lower capital formation in the future. Therefore, higher deficits can lead to lower current and future levels of output in the economy. Although economists disagree concerning the severity of the social and economic effects of mounting budget and trade deficits, most agree that the problems are real and the consequences loom large.

Finally, the growing dependence of the United States on a steady flow of foreign capital to finance its budget and trade deficits has caused a shift in market confidence and negative perceptions by foreign investors. These attitudes may pose substantial risk to the U.S. economy, because foreign lenders may become less willing to lend to the United States. Reducing the trade deficit requires economic policy that encourages domestic savings and reduces the budget deficit, thus reducing the need to borrow from and buy from other countries.

Transcendental meditation (TM): Controversial "technology of consciousness" alleged to produce benefits for mind, body, behavior, and environment. Introduced to the West in 1957 by Maharishi Mahesh Yogi, TM became well known in the 1960's when the Beatles learned the technique. TM is sometimes begun for stress management, but its primary purpose is to allow individuals to develop higher states of consciousness. Proponents claim that TM also has wider implications as a way to develop harmony and coherence in collective consciousness. Skeptics have disputed the technique's efficacy.

Transsexuals: People who believe that they are trapped in the body of the wrong sex. Some transsexuals undergo surgery to alter their bodies and legally change their assigned sex.

"Transsexuality" is the term used to describe the rare condition when an individual feels that their gender identity, or psychological sense of gender, does not

Students at Iowa's Maharishi International University practice transcendental meditation as part of their classwork. (UPI/Corbis-Bettmann)

Transsexuals

match their body. While the reason is unknown, it is more common for someone with a male body to have a female gender identity than vice versa. In some cases it is discovered that the person has internal body structures that are partially male and partially female, but in most cases, there is no explanation for the conflict.

Throughout history, transsexuals have had few options: cross-dressing (transvestism); finding a homosexual partner and taking the role of the opposite sex; or remaining in psychological distress. In the last half of the twentieth century, however, physicians devel-

oped medical and surgical procedures that allowed a person to change their sex-related physical features. Such operations allowed these individuals to change both their social role and their legal sex in order to match their psychological sex.

Transsexual surgery is accomplished in many steps over a period of years. Male-to-female surgery involves removing the testes, penis, and internal genitalia, and creating an artificial vagina from the remaining tissue; facial hair is removed and hormones are taken to enlarge the breasts and soften the skin.

Transsexual Korean War veteran Bridgette Poi Brusseau at a 1986 news conference after her failure to win election as a Connecticut veterans' post commander. (UPI/Corbis-Bettmann)

Female-to-male surgery involves removal of the internal genitalia and the addition of an artificial scrotum and penis; hormones are taken to increase growth of facial hair; and breasts may be surgically removed.

Psychosocial adjustment, too, must be slow and gradual. Physicians generally require that surgical candidates undergo preoperative psychiatric evaluation and practice living as the opposite sex for months or years before any irreversible steps are taken. Long-term individual and group counseling is also recommended, both pre- and postoperatively. Some individuals manage the transition well, finding a long-awaited psychological wholeness and freedom; others find it difficult to cope with the stresses of repeated surgery, the financial drain, and the anger, confusion, or prejudices of their friends, family, and co-workers.

Sex reassignment, like *in vitro* fertilization or surrogate motherhood, is a controversial procedure. Some people consider it unethical for philosophical or religious reasons; others consider it to be a waste of medi-

cal funds and skill. Some view it as one of many elective medical procedures that help people in their pursuit of happiness. The American Psychiatric Association considers transsexuality to be a mental disorder (called gender dysphoria); yet if the psychological conflict is resolved through successful sex-change surgery, the mental disorder is considered to be gone, even though there has been no change in the transsexual's psychology. Despite its controversial social and medical status, the legal status of sex reassignment is clear: It is an individual's private medical decision and has full legal standing.

Treason: Crime of attempting to overthrow a government, criminally aiding a foreign power, or giving aid or comfort to an enemy of a state. English law traditionally divides the offense into at least two categories: high treason, involving offenses against the crown, and petit treason, involving offenses against another subject. U.S. law states that treason is either of two

Convicted traitors have traditionally been sentenced to death. (James L. Shaffer)

kinds of acts: secret attachment of allegiance to a foreign power or the lending of aid or comfort to an enemy power or its representatives. Treason is usually punishable by long jail terms or execution.

Treaties: Agreements between sovereign states. A treaty does not become binding until it is ratified by the parties; under the U.S. Constitution, for example, ratification requires the consent of the Senate. A treaty may take many different forms (as a detailed contract, joint declaration, or simply an exchange of notes); it may be of unlimited duration or for a fixed period of time; and it may cover a wide variety of subjects. Treaties between several states, known as multilateral conventions, are usually negotiated at diplomatic conferences. Multilateral conventions typically prescribe a number of ratifications to bring a treaty into force.

Triage: Emergency aid system. Originally a French word meaning to sort into three groups, triage was first used during World War I to categorize wounded soldiers. Those in group 1 had received major injuries and would surely die; those in group 2 had slight wounds and would recover; and those in group 3 could survive only with medical help. Doctors who had to set priorities thus gave their attention to those in group 3. Triage methods have also been suggested for allocating the world's food supply. For example, advocates say, in regions with permanent food shortages, starvation may be inevitable. Countries with minor shortages can manage unaided. International help could thus focus on countries with temporary food emergencies where the likelihood of eventual recovery is good.

Tribalism: Native American value system that considers the tribe to be the primary political, social, and cultural mode of organization. Tribalism extends beyond mere ethnic or regional identification. The Native American emphasis on community often places the needs of the tribe above those of the individual, thus requiring both loyalty and sacrifice. In return, the tribe furnishes the individual with a meaningful place in the world.

Given the diversity of Native American life, sociologists are unwilling to provide an exact definition of the term "tribe." Various definitions that include common language, religion, or cultural forms always meet exceptions. Anthropologists note that the typical unit of social organization before European contact was the band or the village. Some historians maintain that the concept of the tribe took root when white colonists and traders needed to identify political bodies with which to conduct parleys and sign treaties. Native Americans responded to the pressures of European settlement by developing formal political systems similar to those of Europeans. Political organization provided boundaries that helped to identify socially and culturally related individuals. The modern tribe can thus be understood as a political unit, but the underlying sense of identification that Native Americans have with the tribe is far greater, extending into cultural and spiritual grounds.

The subsistence nature of early native life required strong commitment to the survival of the community as a whole. The concerns of the individual were often subordinated to the needs of the group. This necessary commitment influenced native culture. Social norms that contributed to the healthy functioning of the community developed. In many native cultures, for example, individual acquisition of material goods was seen as disruptive to the group and was therefore frowned upon. Religious beliefs also reinforced the primacy of the community. Many native religions regarded the death of the individual as an affair of little concern, since the community would continue to live on. These cultural and religious values persisted after the tribe became the dominant mode of social and political organization.

Both Christian reformers and land-hungry settlers in the nineteenth century recognized tribalism as the force that ensured the survival of Native American culture. Hostile to the survival of that culture, the U.S. government determined to destroy the tribes and force the Native Americans to assimilate into white society. Native languages and culture were suppressed, tribal lands were parcelled as individual lots, and the power of tribal leaders was eroded as government officials undertook most decision making. Despite the concerted attack on tribalism, many Native Americans continued to identify with their tribes and to maintain their customs and rituals. The INDIAN REORGANIZATION ACT of 1934 reversed government policy, recognizing the tribe as the primary political unit and the value of native culture.

Tribalism remains a core value and source of strength for many Native Americans. Continued efforts to integrate Native Americans into American society have met with mixed success because the traditional commitment to the community continues to be a central cultural and spiritual value for Native Americans.

Truancy: Unexcused absence from school. The modern English word "truant" comes from a Middle English word roughly translatable as "vagrant." Prior to the mandatory school-attendance laws enacted in the decades preceding World War I, the word had a much more general meaning, and it still occasionally refers to people avoiding duties other than school. Its primary modern referent, however, is to children of certain ages who stay away from school.

Although education is not specifically mentioned in the Constitution, federal courts have consistently upheld taxation for public schools and mandatory school-attendance policies, provided that states do not specifically mandate public schooling rather than private schooling or home-schooling. The latter are increasingly popular alternatives for families opting out of the public-school system.

In most states, school attendance or its equivalent is legally mandated from age six or seven (occasionally earlier) through age sixteen or seventeen (occasionally later). Children with unexcused absences from public or private school are officially designated as truants, or the state's legal equivalent of that term, unless they fall into another legal category such as home-schoolers, expelled students, or children in custody. Institutionalized juveniles may still attend some sort of school, and school attendance may be a condition of juvenile probation for those old enough to consider dropping out. Penalties for truancy may include school suspension or expulsion, juvenile probation, or various penalties to the parents such as fines or loss of custody. Truancy is not a delinquent offense, but it is one of the most common juvenile status offenses. It is by far the most frequent status offense causing children under sixteen to be petitioned to juvenile court and, according to some studies, its frequency as a status offense is exceeded only by alcohol-related offenses for juveniles sixteen to eighteen.

Since the early 1970's, there has been a prevailing tendency to handle status offenders separately from delinquent offenders in the juvenile justice system. There is a strong statistical correlation between truancy or other status offenses, such as running away, and more serious delinquent offenses, which would be felonies or misdemeanors if committed by adults.

There is also a strong statistical correlation between status offenses and the victimization of juveniles by abusive or negligent adults such as parents or guardians, as well as a strong correlation between school attendance and completion and later successes in life or work.

This poses a troublesome dilemma for the school system and the juvenile justice system in dealing with truancy and related status offenses. On the one hand, chronic truants are among the most likely children to have special needs that might be met by remedial, rehabilitative, or social programs. On the other hand, they are among the most likely children to cause trouble for school officials, police, and society in general. For instance, truancy is one of the typical warning signs for possible gang affiliation.

Merely mandating school attendance will not solve the many interrelated problems that plague children and society. However, it may be a necessary first step. Some schools take further steps, such as calling all parents of absentees every day or rewarding previous truants and dropouts for attendance. While the days of the full-time truant officer are mostly over, some police departments do periodic roundups of offenders at known truant hangouts.

Official juvenile offense data, especially for status offenses like truancy, are somewhat inaccurate and incomplete because of local variations in the ways such cases and data are handled. Criminal justice databases often lump truancy together with "all other juvenile offenses except traffic," while school records often lump excused and unexcused absences together. A total absenteeism rate above 5 percent is considered indicative of a truancy problem within a school system. Self-report data and longitudinal studies suggest that truancy is frequent among juveniles who commit other more serious offenses and may be a major factor in the development of delinquent or criminal careers.

SUGGESTED READINGS: Robert Drowns and Karen Hess discuss social and legal aspects of truancy in *Juvenile Justice*, 2d ed. (Minneapolis: West Publishing, 1995). For the political and educational aspects of truancy, see Pat Carlen, Denis Gleeson, and Julia Wardhaugh's *Truancy: The Politics of Compulsory Schooling* (Philadelphia: Open University Press, 1992).

Trudeau, Pierre (b. Oct. 18, 1919, Montreal, Québec, Canada): Prime minister of Canada from 1968 to 1979 and from 1980 to 1984. Educated at the Univer-

Canadian prime minister Pierre Trudeau endorses the addition of the Charter of Rights and Freedoms to the Canadian Constitution. (UPI/Corbis-Bettmann)

sity of Montreal, Harvard University, and the London School of Economics, Trudeau was an influential journalist and law professor prior to entering politics in 1965 as a member of Parliament for the Liberal Party. Trudeau became minister of justice in 1967, where he gained notoriety for liberalizing laws regarding divorce, homosexuality, and abortion. In 1968, he was elected prime minister, a position he held (save for nine months in 1979 and 1980) until 1984. A charismatic figure, Trudeau oversaw the establishment of official bilingualism, adoption of the CHARTER OF RIGHTS AND

FREEDOMS, and the patriation of the Canadian constitution in 1982 from Great Britain to Canada.

Trump, Donald (b. June 14, 1946, New York, N.Y.): Entrepreneur and real estate tycoon. Trump became famous for his brash business deals and his flamboyant lifestyle in the 1980's, as he amassed a huge real-estate empire that included the opulent Trump Tower in New York City and several casinos and hotels in Atlantic City, New Jersey. In 1989, he took over Eastern Air-

Donald Trump at a 1990 news conference promoting his ill-fated airline shuttle. (UPI/Corbis-Bettmann)

lines' bankrupt shuttle business, financing the deal with junk bonds purchased through the notorious firm Drexel Burnham Lambert; in the 1990's his empire verged on collapse. Trump's relationships with his first wife, Ivana, and his second wife, Marla Maples, have been frequent tabloid fodder.

Tuberculosis (TB): Infectious disease caused by the bacterium *Mycobacterium tuberculosis*. This disease has plagued humans since ancient times and remains a major cause of sickness and death worldwide. Tuberculosis has unexpectedly increased in the U.S. since 1984, particularly in urban centers.

Tuberculosis is spread by droplets produced when an infected person coughs, sneezes, talks, or sings. Tuberculosis infections most commonly affect the lungs, but all parts of the body can be involved. Usually, close and prolonged contact with an infected individual are necessary in order to transmit the disease. The traditional risk factors for developing tuberculosis include poor sanitation, poverty, malnutrition, and overcrowding. Tuberculosis is easily spread in prisons, nursing homes, and homeless shelters because large numbers of individuals are housed in close proximity to one another.

In 1960, public-health officials predicted the eventual disappearance of TB in the U.S. The disease had been declining for several decades, but, in 1984, a reversal of this trend was observed. By 1995, 10 million Americans were infected with tuberculosis. Two thousand Americans die annually from this disease. Formerly a disease of the elderly, TB has been most commonly seen in twenty-five to forty-four-year-olds since the mid-1980's. TB has become a disease of minorities: From 1985 to 1992, 70 percent of all reported U.S. TB cases occurred among Hispanics, non-Hispanic blacks, and Asians and Pacific Islanders.

The resurgence of tuberculosis has been correlated with increases in the numbers of poor and homeless individuals, intravenous drug use, and increased immigration from countries that have a high prevalence of TB. However, the most important factor in explaining the increase in TB is the AIDS epidemic, which began in the early 1980's. Individuals infected with the HUMAN IMMUNODEFICIENCY VIRUS (HIV), the causative agent of AIDS, have a tuberculosis risk that is one hundred to five hundred times greater than the general population. The HIV virus inhibits the immune system, which normally protects against the tuberculosis bacterium, thus leaving its victims prone to infection. Individuals with AIDS may develop many secondary infections in addition to TB; however, TB is the only bacterial disease that an HIV-infected person can transmit to healthy individuals.

Exposure to tuberculosis can be assessed by a skin test. Antibiotics and other drugs are available for treatment of active cases of TB. The most effective are isoniazid (INH), rifampicin, streptomycin, and ethambutol. These prescribed medications must be taken for long periods of time, usually six to nine months. Compliance with this prolonged treatment has been a serious problem. When treatment is not complete, there is a serious risk that the bacteria will not be completely eliminated and the disease will recur, often with a new population of bacteria that have developed resistance to the medication. The emergence of tuberculosis bacteria that are not killed by the conventional treatments is an increasing public-health problem; there is no effective treatment for infected individuals, resulting in the spread of these resistant bacteria in the general population.

Turner, Ted (Robert Edward Turner III; b. Nov. 19, 1938, Cincinnati, Ohio): Media tycoon. Turner is the founder and owner of Cable News Network (CNN), which transmits news throughout the world by satellite. In 1976, he became one of the first broadcasters to use a communications satellite to relay programs to local cable television companies. Turner's company, Turner Broadcasting System, Inc. (TBS), owns the CNN Headline News network, Turner Network Television (TNT), and the Atlanta Braves baseball and Atlanta Hawks basketball teams. Both Turner and his wife, actress Jane Fonda, have been active supporters of peace movements and environmental causes; he has also generated controversy with his purchase and "colorization" of black-and-white films and his networks' broadcast of programs supporting abortion rights.

Tutu, Desmond (b. Oct. 7, 1931, Klerksdorp, Transvaal, South Africa): South African religious leader and human rights activist. The first African to be appointed archbishop of Cape Town, Tutu is head of the Anglican church throughout southern Africa. For many years one of the most prominent critics of South Africa's apartheid system, Tutu in the 1980's helped to organize the antiapartheid United Democratic Front; in

Ted Turner and wife Jane Fonda at a 1991 awards ceremony. (AP/Wide World Photos)

1984 Nobel Peace Prize winner Archbishop Desmond Tutu. (UPI/Corbis-Bettmann)

1984, he received the Nobel Peace Prize for his work. Following the South African government's transition to majority rule, Tutu has remained an active spokesman for human rights and has often been critical of his country's majority-black government.

Twelve-step programs: Addiction-recovery programs modeled on the techniques of the ALCOHOLICS ANONYMOUS association. Founded in 1935, Alcoholics Anonymous adopted both Christian and Eastern philosophical principles. The group espouses an often successful method of dealing with alcoholism (the twelve steps) that has come to be applied to all manner of compulsive behavior, including gambling addiction (Gamblers Anonymous), eating disorders (Overeaters Anonymous), and drug addiction (Narcotics Anonymous). Twelve-step groups attribute these disorders to physical, emotional, and spiritual problems that they consider to be diseases; the medical community, however, is divided over this characterization. The twelve steps are a series of behavior-modification principles that guide the participant into surrendering to a higher power, taking action through personal inventories, making amends to others, and spreading the message.

Two-career families: Families in which both the husband and wife pursue careers and family life simultaneously. In a two-career family, the careers of both

Twelve-step programs are employed at many addiction treatment centers. (James L. Shaffer)

Typecasting

the husband and the wife are typically considered equally important.

A career, as distinguished from a job, includes occupations that provide greater opportunity for advancement, involve upward progress in earnings and prestige, and demand high levels of personal commitment. Furthermore, careers require substantial education or training. Higher levels of education for women, less rigid role expectations for men and women, and changing economic conditions have contributed to the increase in two-career families since the 1960's. An accurate estimate of the number of two-career families in the United States today is not possible because of the difficulty in classifying occupations as careers.

This family structure differs from the traditional pattern of male breadwinner and female homemaker. Husbands and wives have more interchangeable roles in a two-career family. Household management and child care become complex when both spouses have careers, since neither spouse can devote all of his or her time to these activities. Some research suggests that dual-career couples, in an effort to maximize both careers, share tasks more than the single-earner household. Other studies have found that women tend to perform more housework and child care than their husbands, regardless of a career. Two-career families do not have as many financial concerns as single-earner families, but dual incomes alter the marital relationship. Since women in two-career families provide financial resources, dual-career families tend to have a more equal distribution of power.

Typical challenges of the two-career family focus on balancing family life and occupations. Each spouse's commitment to the job is limited in a two-career couple. Employee absenteeism and turnover may be greater with dual-career employees because of an employee's involvement with both work and family. Corporations, however, can actually increase their profits by working creatively with dual-career couples on such issues as child care, parental leave, flex time, job sharing, and other alternative work patterns. Because of potential conflicts of interest regarding both careers, job relocation and promotions may become problematic.

Social scientists have identified several interpersonal problems resulting from the stresses of two-career families. Role overload occurs from the demands of the many roles played, such as spouse, parent, employee, and friend. Interference takes place when work demands one commitment and family another. Two-career families must also deal with negative social attitudes, since some segments of society still do not completely approve of this family form.

In spite of the difficulties faced by two-career families, the lifestyle offers many advantages. Careers allow both the husband and the wife opportunities for achievement and personal satisfaction. Career couples tend to be intellectual companions and to experience a sense of collegiality. Marital satisfaction is high in families where the wife pursues a career by choice. Children of two-career families have higher educational and achievement goals and develop greater independence and resourcefulness. Two incomes also provide a higher standard of living and can offer greater social prestige.

Typecasting: Concept used by dramatists to describe the pairing of an appropriate actor's personality or image with the requirements of a dramatic role. Many actors owe their success to their ability to render faithfully the part of a certain "type" of person, for example a criminal or a housewife. The term, however, often carries negative connotations; a typecast actor may become the victim of a stereotyped image, and the range of roles available may be effectively limited. Members of minority groups often complain that they are typecast as a result of their ethnicity and are thus denied the chance to play a variety of roles.

Tyson, Mike (b. July 1, 1966, New York, N.Y.): Professional boxer. Tyson became the youngest world heavyweight champion in history in November, 1986, when he knocked out Trevor Berbick for the World Boxing Council title at the age of twenty. In 1987, he unified the title by capturing the championships of the World Boxing Association and the International Boxing Federation, and he reigned as undisputed heavyweight champion until his shocking February, 1990, loss to James "Buster" Douglas. His stormy eight-month marriage to actress Robin Givens was marked by allegations of domestic abuse, and in October, 1991, while waiting for a championship match, he was indicted on rape charges. He was convicted of having raped beauty pageant contestant Desiree Washington in an Indianapolis hotel, and he was sentenced to six years in prison. After serving three years of his sentence, he was released in May, 1995, and resumed his professional career; his public appearances continued to draw protests from women's rights groups.

Mike Tyson (right) during a 1991 fight with Razor Ruddock. (AP/Wide World Photos)

U

Unabomber case: Campaign of terror conducted over a seventeen-year period by an individual apparently obsessed with eliminating the evils of technology from modern society.

The Unabomber case began in 1978 with a series of bombings. The first targets of the bomber were associated with universities or airlines; thus, the FEDERAL BUREAU OF INVESTIGATION (FBI) codenamed the case "unabom" (for "university and airline bomber"), and the individual responsible came to be known as the Unabomber. In sixteen attacks between 1978 and 1995, three people were killed, and twenty-three others were injured.

The Unabomber's explosive devices, handcrafted of wooden and metal parts, were mailed or delivered to victims. Bombs were specifically designed to blow up a single human target; the victims were all college professors, business executives, or people associated with computers. The FBI believed that the bomber had a grudge against modern technology.

As time went on, investigators gathered a few meager clues. The bomber appeared to be based in Northern California, so a task force of thirty investigators from the FBI, the Bureau of Alcohol, Tobacco, and Firearms (ATF), and the U.S. Postal Service was set up in San Francisco. In 1987, a witness saw a man leaving a bomb package outside a computer store in Salt Lake City, Utah, and a composite sketch of the suspect was created. In 1989, the bomber sent a brief note to *The New York Times* in which he described himself as an anarchist. Subsequently, he seemed to have adopted a radical environmentalist philosophy seeking to defend "wild nature." After the April, 1995, bombing, which killed a lobbyist for the California timber industry, one hundred new investigators were added to the Unabomber task force.

In July, 1995, the Unabomber sent a letter to the *San Francisco Chronicle* in which he warned of a planned attack on an airplane flying out of Los Angeles; emergency measures were quickly instituted at all California airports. A few days after making his initial threat, the bomber sent copies of a 35,000-word manuscript to *The New York Times*, *The Washington Post*, and *Penthouse* magazine. He said that if his manifesto were published by September 24, he would call off his campaign of terror. After much discussion and soul-searching, and with the approval of the FBI and the U.S. Attorney General, the newspapers collaborated in publishing the document on September 19, 1995.

In April, 1996, law-enforcement officials received their first major break in the case. Acting on a tip from a New York social worker who believed he recognized passages in the published manifesto, federal agents arrested the informant's estranged brother, Theodore Kaczynski, at his isolated Montana cabin. Bomb-making equipment and a typewriter that appeared to match that used to produce the manifesto were found in the cabin, and most observers believed that the elusive Unabomber had at last been caught.

Underemployment: Employment of people at less than full-time hours or in occupations that do not fully utilize their education or skills. In the 1990's, as the United States shifted toward what scholars such as Daniel Bell labeled the postindustrial society, service industries began to dominate the economy. Restaurants, retail outlets, health-care providers, and similar service industries started to shape the labor market as the number of traditional production jobs in factories declined. With this growth in the service-oriented economy came an increase in the problem of underemployment. Employers found that using part-time or temporary workers could reduce labor costs. By definition, underemployment results in a sacrifice of productive potential, even though it may be efficient from the perspective of a particular employer.

Many workers who lost full-time jobs in manufacturing found that the only employment available was part-time, that is, less than forty hours per week. Similarly, young workers entering the labor market for the first time encountered difficulty in obtaining full-time employment. Rather than finding permanent positions with full-time hours, new workers often discovered they were scheduled to work half-time (twenty hours per week) or less. These part-time positions generally paid less per hour and provided fewer fringe benefits, such as HEALTH INSURANCE, than full-time production jobs.

A second type of underemployment occurs when a

worker is employed at a job that does not require the level of education or skills the worker possesses. A person with a college degree working at a job that does not require more than a high-school diploma could be considered underemployed even if the job were in the same general field as the worker's education. A registered nurse working as a nurses' aide or an accounting major working as a supermarket cashier are examples of underemployed people.

Although underemployment may not be as serious an issue as UNEMPLOYMENT (when a person has no job), widespread underemployment contributes to a variety of social problems. First, underemployed workers suffer from numerous personal hardships created by trying to earn a living while working less than full-time hours. For example, if they are unable to pay for decent housing, the underemployed may end up homeless or living in squalid conditions. In addition, a lack of money to pay for routine preventive medical care may cause underemployed people to neglect their health or that of their children. Problems of this type are similar to those of unemployed people, differing only in degree.

Second, underemployment may be a factor in workplace CRIME. Employees who feel underpaid or exploited may not hesitate to steal from their employers or may ignore crimes committed by coworkers. By the 1990's, loss of inventory to employee theft had become a major financial burden for many companies. Some criminologists believe that the increasing number of underemployed workers is directly related to a rise in employee theft.

Underemployment may also play a role in the rising rates of VIOLENCE by workers toward one another and toward supervisors. In 1994, it was reported that violence by coworkers was a leading cause of on-the-job injury and death in many U.S. industries. In industrialized societies, people are trained from early childhood to see work as a source of satisfaction and identity. When circumstances force people into underemployment, frustration, unhappiness, and an increase in irrational behavior may result.

SUGGESTED READINGS: Joel A. Devine and James D. Wright's *The Greatest of Evils: Urban Poverty and the American Underclass* (New York: Aldine de Gruyter, 1993) paints a vivid picture of the cycle of poverty to which chronic underemployment contributes.

Underground economies: Market sectors that operate outside the law. Participants in an underground economy do not want their behavior known to the government, for various reasons. They may be engaging in practices that are illegal, such as PROSTITUTION or the sale of drugs. Some activities in underground economies are not in themselves illegal but involve lawbreaking, commonly the illegal avoidance of INCOME TAXES. Much of the underground economy operates on a cash basis, and sellers of goods and services may fail to report their cash income to the government. Participants in an underground economy also may wish to avoid government regulations of various types.

Undocumented person: Term used by those who object to the negative implications of "ILLEGAL ALIEN." People who enter the United States without permission for the most part do not intend to commit additional crimes or otherwise to violate the law. The term is used mostly in reference to Mexican nationals who cross into the United States seeking work but is also applied to students and tourists who overstay their visas. In the eyes of the law, both groups are in the United States illegally and are subject to DEPORTATION if discovered.

Unemployment: In the United States, people age sixteen and older are classified as unemployed if they do not have a job, have been searching actively for employment in the prior four weeks, and are currently available to work. Other countries have similar official definitions. When people are unemployed, not only do they lose their income and financial resources, but they also may lose their self-confidence and eventually develop low self-esteem. People with no financial resources and low self-esteem are a major potential source of family abuse, CRIME, and social disruption.

The Unemployment Rate. The unemployment rate is the number of unemployed people divided by the number of people in the labor force (the number of employed people plus the number of unemployed), multiplied by one hundred. Several factors, including new technology, overall economic conditions, and work reorganization affect the unemployment rate. The highest unemployment rates in U.S. history were recorded during the GREAT DEPRESSION. In 1933, 24.9 percent of the labor force was unemployed. During World War II, in 1944, the U.S. unemployment rate hit its lowest recorded level, 1.2 percent.

The unemployment rate is a controversial indicator

Unemployed workers stand in a bread line during the Great Depression. (UPI/Corbis-Bettmann)

of actual unemployment in a society because it excludes many people who are qualified to work. For example, the official unemployment rate in 1983 was 9.6 percent, or 10,717,000 people. *Working: Sociological Perspective* (1987), by Robert Rothman, reports that the actual number of unemployed people was more than twice that number. There were more than 1.6 million discouraged workers, people who would have worked if offered jobs but who were not actively searching for jobs because they believed there were no jobs or that they were not qualified for those that might exist. Further, about 4 million people were excluded from employment because they were attending school or had home or child care responsibilities. These people are not counted as part of the labor force. Finally, there were 6 million people working in part-time jobs who sought or would have preferred full-time jobs. They were included as employed people in the government statistics even though they sought additional work.

Unemployment has plagued all industrialized nations. In Japan and the Scandinavian countries, the unemployment rates typically are lower than in the United States, whereas in Canada and in the Western European nations, they tend to be higher than in the United States.

Types of Unemployment. Labor analysts discuss three forms of unemployment. Each one has different causes and consequences, and each affects unemployed people differently. Frictional unemployment exists when people are temporarily out of work while changing jobs or seeking new jobs. Some frictional unemployment results from LAYOFFS—decisions to dismiss employees because of bankruptcies, closing plants, or technological displacement. Most frictional unemployment, however, is the result of the normal circulation of people between jobs and between schools and jobs.

Seasonal unemployment is caused by periodic variations in the demand for certain skills and tasks. For example, farm work and the construction trades are affected by the weather, and retail sales work peaks during holiday periods. Countless blue-collar workers face this form of unemployment in response to shifting sales or periods of retooling for new seasonal products. U.S. unemployment figures adjust for seasonal variations.

A laid-off worker with the forms needed to collect federal unemployment insurance. (Reuters/Corbis-Bettmann)

Unemployment

Finally, structural unemployment refers to a chronic gap between the number of jobs that the economy produces and the number of people available for work. This gap can be caused by a combination of social, technological, economic, and demographic forces that render certain groups of workers unemployable even during economic prosperity. For example, automation is displacing large numbers of unskilled and semi-skilled workers. Geographic movement of industries across international boundaries may create jobs in one country at the cost of jobs in another one. Structural unemployment occurs when workers do not have the skills needed to perform jobs that are available to be filled.

The Costs of Unemployment. Financial loss is the most immediate and direct consequence of unemployment. The loss of income and of benefits such as HEALTH INSURANCE results in a rapid deterioration of lifestyle, including the potential loss of housing, delays in educational plans, reduced medical care, and reductions in recreation and food budgets. In the case of prolonged unemployment, families are forced to use savings and even to sell their personal property, such as cars and homes. Furthermore, the combination of the loss of a job and of income disrupts family relationships. In extreme cases, the STRESS of these disruptions and changes in plans can lead to DIVORCE, spouse abuse, CHILD ABUSE, and other family problems.

At the community and social levels, unemployed people may be excluded from social and community plans that require the expenditure of money. This can lead to social isolation. Work life provides a significant amount of the social life of many people. Their friends are their coworkers. Thus, then work ties are cut, participation in community life declines.

The costs of unemployment go beyond financial and social problems. Loss of a job commonly is interpreted as a judgment of incompetence of the worker. Unemployed people therefore are traumatized, and their SELF-ESTEEM may fall. STRESS and DEPRESSION are common responses to unemployment. Many of those who find new jobs do not fully recover their self-esteem. Harvey Brenner testified before the Joint Economic Committee of the Ninety-eighth Congress (testimony reported in *Technology and Structural Unemployment: Reemploying Displaced Adults*, 1986) that when the unemployment rate rises by 1 percent, 4.3 percent more men and 2.3 percent more women are admitted to state mental hospitals for the first time. Further, 4.1 percent more people commit SUICIDE, and 5.7 percent more are

An unemployed woman holds her young son as she fills out a job application.
(Jim West)

murdered. This evidence links economic hardships to other social problems. It is tempting to infer that unemployment causes these other problems, but the various factors involved make proof of causation all but impossible.

Governmental Unemployment Policies. The U.S. federal government, along with state governments, offers a wide range of programs for unemployed workers. Programs offer temporary income assistance until an unemployed worker finds another job and help in preparing for and finding that new job.

Unemployment insurance has been the main program providing income assistance to unemployed workers for more than sixty years. The program provides weekly benefits to workers who lost their jobs, whether or not the job loss is permanent. Benefits are paid for a limited period of time. In 1991, the percentage of unemployed who claimed unemployment insurance benefits varied greatly across states, ranging from 20.7 percent in Virginia to 60.0 percent in Alaska. When the unemployment rate in a state is very high, the Federal/State Extended Benefit Program provides additional weeks of benefits. The Emergency Unemployment Compensation program, enacted in 1991 and amended in 1992, enables unemployed workers who have exhausted their unemployment benefits to receive further payment.

Title III of the Job Training Partnership Act (JTPA) of 1982 was the first comprehensive federal program for more than two decades to offer training assistance to displaced workers. Under this program, states receive federal funds to help displaced workers obtain employment through training and related employment services. The funds for the program are used primarily to provide classroom training, on-the-job training, and job search assistance to participants. Reports on the first two years of operation show that JTPA programs helped displaced workers find new jobs. The Office of Technology Assessment pointed out that the programs served 96,100 workers in the initial nine months, and another 132,200 workers were newly enrolled in the full program for the fiscal year of July, 1984 to June, 1985. This was, however, less than 5 percent of the eligible workers.

Trade Adjustment Assistance (TAA). This program provides income replacement benefits, training, and related services to workers who become unemployed because of competition from imports in their industry. It was established in 1962, but served very few workers until eligibility requirements were revised in 1974.

The number of workers served by TAA peaked in 1980, at 585,243. The program was cut substantially during the 1980's. Qualified workers are eligible for both training and cash benefits. Benefits can last for up to one year if the recipients take part in an approved JOB-TRAINING PROGRAM.

Despite unemployment insurance, JTPA Title III, TAA, and several other federal and state programs, there is no law that directly helps reduce unemployment. In a free-market economy, unemployment is a norm. Even when the economy is strong, many people are unemployed.

Some sociologists explain that unemployment is essential to the operation of a capitalist economy. Unemployment has been used as leverage at the bargaining table and has provided a reserve labor force that can be drawn back into employment when profit and investment conditions require it. Although unemployment is essential for employers, it has a devastating effect on unemployed people and their families. Among minority groups and youth, the consequences are more widespread because these groups tend to have unemployment rates higher than those of other groups. For example, in 1990, when the overall unemployment rate was 5.5 percent, the unemployment rate for whites was 4.7 percent, for Hispanics 8.0 percent, and for African Americans 11.3 percent. The unemployment rate among persons under twenty years of age typically is two to three times as high as the overall rate.

—Max Kashefi

SUGGESTED READINGS: Unemployment in Canada and in the United States is contrasted and explained in Vivek Moorthy's research, *Unemployment in Canada and the U.S.: Lessons from the 1980's* (New York: Federal Reserve Bank of New York, 1989). Jennifer Gardner explores the similarities and differences among displaced workers in the 1980's and 1990's in "Worker Displacement: A Decade of Change," *Monthly Labor Review* (April, 1995). For a discussion of the export of jobs from the United States to lower-wage areas overseas, see Barry Bluestone and Bennett Harrison, *The Deindustrialization of America* (New York: Basic Books, 1982).

Unification Church: Religious sect formed in 1954. The Unification Church was founded by the Reverend Sun Myung Moon, who was born in Korea in 1920. Moon's theology, which calls for the unification of all humanity under the leadership of the Messiah, Moon

Uninsured motorists

A mass wedding sponsored by the Unification Church in 1995. (Archive Photos, Paul Barker, Reuters)

himself, is at variance with both Christian doctrine and American conservative thought. Nevertheless, after he established U.S. residency in 1971, Moon's staunch anticommunist, procapitalist positions and his fierce espousal of "family values" enabled the Unification Church to work in partnership with the American RE-LIGIOUS RIGHT. In 1984 and 1985, Moon served a U.S. prison term for conspiracy to commit tax fraud and other charges. This crisis seems to have only strengthened the church, which has extensive U.S. business holdings that include such media outlets as the influential conservative newspaper *The Washington Times*. Church members are frequently derided as "Moonies," and the church has been the target of much criticism for alleged brainwashing and coercion of prospective members. While the church provides variable membership figures, it appears to have fewer than ten thousand U.S. members and fewer than two million worldwide.

themselves, their passengers, and anyone they might injure in an accident, along with covering the costs of any damage incurred in an accident for which they are at fault. Some drivers, however, do not carry insurance. Even when they are at fault in an accident, it can be difficult for the other party to collect damages from them because most uninsured motorists are poor. Without insurance—which they do not purchase because they cannot afford it—they have no means of paying for damages they cause.

Several U.S. states have passed laws requiring drivers to be insured, but those laws are not enforced severely. Some drivers purchase additional coverage on their automobile insurance policies that covers them for any damage caused by an uninsured motorist; in effect, they are forced to pay to protect themselves instead of uninsured motorists taking responsibility for their own actions.

Uninsured motorists: Legal issue. Most drivers carry insurance policies that cover medical costs for

Union of Concerned Scientists (UCS): Advocacy group founded 1969. Formed by faculty and students of the Massachusetts Institute of Technology (MIT) in response to concerns over NUCLEAR WEAPONS proliferation and the conduct of the VIETNAM WAR, the UCS grew into an organization of more than 100,000 members interested in a host of environmental, scientific, and military issues. UCS members have long monitored the condition of aging nuclear power plants and the related performance of the Nuclear Regulatory Commission; UCS investigations exposed safety violations at the Yankee Rowe plant in Massachusetts and the Trojan plant in Oregon that led to the closing of the plants in the 1990's. In the 1980's, the UCS effectively opposed the Ronald Reagan Administration's STRATEGIC DEFENSE INITIATIVE, or "Star Wars" proposal, deriding the proposed antimissile system as ill-conceived and unrealistic. The UCS publishes the quarterly journal *Nucleus* and numerous briefing papers, fact sheets, and action guides on nuclear power, arms control, environmental issues, and related topics.

United Auto Workers (UAW): U.S. labor union. Officially the International Union, United Automobile, Aerospace, and Agricultural Implement Workers of America, the UAW was founded in Detroit in 1935. The UAW has more than 1,200 local unions throughout the United States; its membership was important in the 1955 merger of the Congress of Industrial Organizations (CIO) and the American Federation of Labor (AFL). In 1968, the UAW withdrew from the AFL-CIO but rejoined it in 1981. Union officials meet with employers to work out agreements about working con-

Striking United Auto Workers members in 1993. (Jim West)

ditions and wages. Membership in the UAW includes automobile, aircraft, agricultural, bank, insurance, hospital, university, and local government workers.

United Farm Workers (UFW): Labor union representing predominantly Hispanic farmworkers founded in 1966 by César CHÁVEZ in California.

Chávez was born in 1927 in Yuma, Arizona, into a family that had migrated from Mexico to pick agricultural crops in the Southwest. As a young man, Chávez became involved in efforts by the National Farm Labor Union and the Community Service Organization to better the lives of farmworkers. In 1959, Chávez founded the National Farm Workers Association (NFWA) in Delano, California, to organize workers to struggle for better pay and conditions. The association held its first convention in the fall of 1962.

In 1965, the farmers' union of the AMERICAN FEDERATION OF LABOR-CONGRESS OF INDUSTRIAL ORGANIZATIONS (AFL-CIO) struck Delano grape growers. The workers in the Delano fields earned less than

United Farm Workers president César Chávez addresses a 1970 meeting. (UPI/Bettmann)

$1 per hour and faced harsh conditions: no toilets in the fields, unregulated exposure to agricultural chemicals, and, when drinking water was available, a fee was often charged. The NFWA joined the strike, employing nonviolent tactics such as picketing and marching. They persisted with nonviolence despite threats and beatings by growers.

The NFWA began a boycott of grapes to pressure growers into signing, initiating a tactic that later became their trademark. Robert Kennedy, then a member of the Senate Subcommittee on Migratory Labor, lent his support to Chávez and the NFWA's effort, winning it much favorable publicity. After strikers marched the 250 miles from Delano to Sacramento, the state capitol, the first grape grower signed a contract with the NFWA.

In 1966, other growers invited the United Brotherhood of Teamsters to organize in their fields, preferring it to Chávez's association. Faced with such opposition, the NFWA merged with the AFL-CIO's farmworkers union to form the United Farm Workers. A bitter struggle against growers ensued, during which the newly formed UFW organized a largely successful national boycott of table grapes. In July, 1970, in a major victory, twenty-three growers representing 42 percent of all California grapes signed contracts with the UFW.

Next, the UFW organized workers in the lettuce fields around Salinas, where the Teamsters Union again competed for the same workers. The UFW stuck to its nonviolent stance despite Teamster violence. When a court ruling ordered the end of the boycott, Chávez refused to comply and was jailed. Twenty days later, the boycott was ruled constitutional, and Chávez was released. Still, only a few growers signed contracts, and the strike ended unsuccessfully in 1971.

During the 1980's, rulings unsympathetic to the union made field organizing difficult and costly. The union concentrated its efforts instead on extending its grape boycott and serving its members by constructing housing and establishing a radio station for farmworkers.

In April, 1993, César Chávez died, and Arturo Rodriguez, the UFW's first vice president, took over his office. Rodriguez revived the union's field organizing, bringing in four thousand new members by 1995.

United Nations (U.N.): International organization. Formed in 1945 in the aftermath of World War II, the United Nations was created primarily to prevent war. The organization also works to promote international cooperation in economic, social, cultural, and humanitarian affairs and to foster respect for human rights.

Structure. The United Nations is composed of six main organs: the General Assembly, the Security Council, the Economic and Social Council (ECOSOC), the Trusteeship Council, the Secretariat, and the International Court of Justice. The General Assembly, the only organ in which every member nation is represented, originally had 51 members; by 1995, the number had grown to 185. Each state has one vote, and issues are decided by a two-thirds vote on "important" questions and by a majority on others. The General Assembly's resolutions are not binding on its membership.

The Security Council, originally an eleven-member body, was enlarged in 1963 to fifteen members, of which five (the United States, China, Great Britain, France, and the Soviet Union—its place later taken by Russia, with the support of the Commonwealth of Independent States) are permanent; the remaining ten are elected by the General Assembly for two-year terms. Decisions on "substantive" matters require concurring votes from nine members, including the concurring votes of the five permanent members.

This voting structure gives effective veto power to each permanent member on most matters of importance. Decisions on procedural issues also require concurrence of nine members but may not be vetoed. Created primarily to maintain international peace and security, the Security Council may take a variety of actions in the case of armed conflict, including calling for a cease-fire, imposing economic sanctions, and taking military action.

The ECOSOC, a fifty-four-member body of representatives elected by the General Assembly, engages in studies and makes recommendations regarding economic and social problems. The Trusteeship Council was created to administer the League of Nations mandate territories as well as colonies put under its jurisdiction as U.N. trusts. The granting of independence to the world's remaining colonies during the latter half of the twentieth century resulted in the Trusteeship Council being declared defunct.

The Secretariat is the United Nations' civil service, with responsibilities for carrying out the decisions of the General Assembly and Security Council and of maintaining day-to-day operations of the organization. The head of the Secretariat is the secretary-general,

Former First Lady Eleanor Roosevelt examines an early mission statement of the United Nations. (UPI/Corbis-Bettmann)

who is elected for a five-year term by the Security Council and General Assembly. The secretaries-general through 1995 have been Trygve Lie, Dag Hammarskjöld, U Thant, Kurt Waldheim, Javier Perez de Cuellar, and Boutros Boutros-Ghali.

The International Court of Justice is a fifteen-member court located in The Hague, The Netherlands. It renders decisions on cases voluntarily brought to it by national litigants. It also may issue advisory opinions when requested to do so by an international organization.

In addition to the six principal organs, the U.N. system embraces more than a dozen autonomous agencies and organizations known as "specialized agencies." These agencies, the work of which is coordinated by the ECOSOC, carry out a variety of nonpolitical functions of importance to the international community. As of 1995, these agencies were the International Atomic Energy Agency, International Labor Organization, Food and Agricultural Organization, WORLD BANK (International Bank for Reconstruction and Development), WORLD HEALTH ORGANIZATION, International Development Association, International Finance Corporation, International Monetary Fund, International Civil Aviation Organization, Universal Postal Union, International Telecommunications Union, World Meteorological Organization, International Maritime Organization, World Intellectual Property Organization, International Fund for Agriculture Development, United Nations Industrial Development Organization, and World Trade Organization.

Accomplishments. The United Nations' accomplishments can be grouped into two general categories: economic and social activities and political and security operations. The former activities, primarily the work of the specialized agencies, have brought substantial benefits to humankind. Certain diseases (smallpox and yaws, for example) have been eliminated in various regions of the world. Millions of illiterates have been taught to read and write. About 30 million refugees have been housed and fed. Starvation has been averted for countless numbers of people, and economic development has been supported in the less developed states of the world. Transportation has been made safer and communication made easier between states as a result of multilateral cooperation.

The role of the United Nations in the political sphere has been mixed and more controversial. There is general agreement that the United Nations has failed to maintain international peace and security as mandated in the U.N. Charter. The Security Council, in some cases, has been unable to mobilize military force to stop aggression or counter threats to the peace. Although the United Nations played a role in the defense of South Korea when North Korea invaded it in 1950, the action of the Security Council in creating a U.N. Command was possible only because of the absence of the Soviet Union from the Security Council. The real defense of South Korea was the work of the combined forces of South Korea and the United States. Throughout the Cold War, the ineffectiveness of the Security Council was attributed to veto power within the Security Council, but the problems of peacemaking and enforcement measures have proven to be more formidable. The great powers consistently have refused to put their military forces under international command, as specified in the U.N. Charter.

Peacekeeping. As an alternative to the use of enforcement measures to keep the peace, the United Nations has developed a technique, known as peacekeeping, for limiting conflict. The first peacekeeping force was the United Nations Emergency Force (UNEF), created in 1956 to facilitate the withdrawal of British, French, and Israeli forces from Egyptian territory.

The UNEF and most subsequent peacekeeping forces had missions that were different from peacemaking (the original intent of the U.N. Charter) in several important ways. The most important of these is that peacekeeping forces are not intended to fight. They are neutral to all the parties to the conflict and operate only with the consent of the host country. Most peacekeeping forces have been small in number and not armed for combat. Their primary mission has been to monitor cease-fire agreements. Peacekeeping operations have been deployed in the Sinai Peninsula, Cyprus, Lebanon, the Golan Heights, Afghanistan, Rwanda, Kashmir, Cambodia, Iraq, El Salvador, Nicaragua, the Congo, Namibia, Croatia, and Bosnia. As of 1995, thirty-three missions had been launched, most of them successfully contributing to ending or diffusing conflict.

Beginning in the 1980's, the goals of PEACEKEEPING MISSIONS were expanded beyond monitoring cease-fire agreements to include providing humanitarian assistance, supervising elections, and helping to build administrative structures. At the beginning of 1995, the United Nations had seventeen peacekeeping missions in operation, totaling seventy-three thousand troops and police officers at an annual cost of $3.6 billion, more than three times the regular U.N. budget of about $1 billion.

On balance, peacekeeping has proven to be one of the most dynamic and successful missions of U.N. practice, but it has not been without controversy. In several operations—notably in the Congo in the early 1960's, Somalia in 1993, and Bosnia during the mid-1990's—U.N. forces intervened in situations in which the parties had not agreed to stop fighting and therefore became involved in the countries' internal struggles. These crises led to bitter criticism of the United Nations by states dissatisfied with U.N. actions.

One of the greatest impediments to a more effective use of peacekeeping has been the inability of the United Nations to secure adequate funding. In the 1960's, the Congo operation put the United Nations in debt because of the refusal of some states to pay for peacekeeping. The United Nations has been saddled with an ongoing indebtedness since then.

The United Nations and World Politics. The politics of the United Nations has reflected the changing trends of world politics. Throughout the Cold War, powers of both the East and the West sought to use the United Nations for their respective ends. During the first decade of the United Nations, the Western powers dominated it, and the Soviet Union found itself on the defensive. By the mid-1950's, the political complexion of the organization began to change as former colonies became independent and joined the United Nations. These new nations began to dominate the General Assembly and tilted its politics against the West. During the 1950's and 1960's, the General Assembly vigorously and successfully pushed the cause of decolonization.

Having completed that process by the 1970's, the General Assembly focused on promoting economic development in the Third World. A confrontational posture toward the West resulted in a decline of Western support for the organization. Financial pressure, caused in part by reduced United States support, forced a reconsideration of Third World strategy. By the 1980's, the General Assembly began to consider some of the reforms demanded by the West. Among these reforms were a stronger voice in the budget for the main contributors and a reduction in bureaucratic waste and inefficiency.

The end of the Cold War in the early 1990's raised hopes that greater harmony among the great powers might permit more cooperation within the United Nations. The overwhelming support given to the U.S. effort to liberate Kuwait in 1990-1991 was one indication of that possibility. As the United Nations completed its first half century, however, its limitations were all too evident. It was faced with a seeming inability to curb aggression, a lack of financial support, bureaucratic waste and mismanagement, and a voting arrangement that conflicted with political realities. Nevertheless, there was widespread agreement that the United Nations contributed to making the world a safer place and that with further reform it might do even more.   —*Joseph L. Nogee*

SUGGESTED READINGS: The definitive history of the origins of the United Nations is by Ruth B. Russell, assisted by Jeannette E. Muther, and titled *A History of the United Nations Charter* (Washington, D.C.: Brookings Institution, 1958). A classic theoretical study is Inis L. Claude, Jr.'s *Swords into Plowshares: The Problems and Progress of International Organization* (New York: Random House, 1971). An authoritative analysis of peacekeeping is *The Blue Helmets: A Review of United Nations Peace-Keeping* (New York: United Nations, 1990), produced by the United Nations' Department of Public Information. A useful overview is Peter R. Baehr and Leon Gordenker's *The United Nations in the 1990's* (New York: St. Martin's Press, 1992).

United Nations International Children's Emergency Fund (UNICEF): Organization founded by the United Nations General Assembly in 1946. UNICEF is devoted to the eradication of malnutrition, disease, and illiteracy among the world's children. In 1965, UNICEF won the Nobel Peace Prize; in 1979, the organization was designated as the main agency to help children worldwide. Its services include advocacy for children's rights, education in health care and nutrition, and immunization against childhood diseases. At the 1990 World Summit for Children UNICEF was credited with helping to save the lives of three million children annually.

United States v. Lopez (1995): U.S. SUPREME COURT case. The *Lopez* decision established, for the first time in nearly sixty years, limits to the federal government's power under the commerce clause of the Constitution. The Court struck down a federal law that prohibited anyone from possessing a firearm within one thousand feet of a school. The defendant had been convicted under the statute, but his conviction was reversed by the Court, which concluded that the carrying of a gun near a school has no reasonable relation to interstate commerce and thus did not fall within the regulatory power of the federal government.

United Steelworkers v. Weber (1979): U.S. SU-PREME COURT decision stating that voluntary AFFIRM-ATIVE ACTION plans were legal and not in violation of the CIVIL RIGHTS ACT OF 1964. The Court ruled that voluntary plans were legal if narrowly tailored, meaning that they had to be designed to remedy manifest imbalances in the workforce, be temporary in nature,

and leave some avenues of advancement open to those employees who did not fall into a preferred group. The case applied to private employers, but in subsequent cases, the Court applied similar arguments to the public sector as well.

Universal Declaration of Human Rights (UDHR, 1948): United Nations General Assembly statement on human rights as a common standard for all peoples and nations. The declaration was prepared by the United Nations Commission on Human Rights as a general

Brian Weber celebrates the Supreme Court's 1978 agreement to hear his case, which was decided against him in *United Steelworkers v. Weber.* (UPI/Corbis- Bettmann)

guideline for member nations to follow in passing internal human rights legislation. The UDHR was followed by two subsequent international conventions adopted in 1966 and entered into force by 1976: the International Covenant on Civil and Political Rights (ICCPR) and the International Covenant on Economic, Social, and Cultural Rights (ICESCR). These two covenants form an important part of international human rights law and, with the UDHR, constitute what is popularly referred to as the International Bill of Human Rights.

The importance of human rights in the United Nations was underscored by the announcement that 1968, the twentieth anniversary of the adoption of the UDHR, would be the International Year for Human Rights. On December 10 of each year (the anniversary of the adoption of UDHR), the United Nations celebrates Human Rights Day. Several international conferences have focused on aspects of human rights; for example, environment- and development-related rights issues were discussed at the EARTH SUMMIT held in Rio de Janeiro, Brazil, in June, 1992. A global Conference on Human Rights was held in Vienna, Austria, in June, 1993.

The UDHR recognizes the inherent dignity and equal and inalienable rights of all human beings; reaffirms faith in fundamental human rights; explains that all human beings are born free and equal in dignity and rights; insists that there be no distinctions of any kind based on race, color, sex, language, religion, political or other opinion, national or social origin, property, birth, or other status. Some of the numerous rights propounded by the declaration are those of life, liberty, and security of person; recognition and equality before the law; the right to a fair, impartial hearing; the right to be presumed innocent until proven guilty; the right to privacy; the right to freedom of movement; the right to seek asylum from persecution; the right to a nationality; the right to own property; the right to freedom of thought, conscience, and religion; the right to freedom of opinion and expression; the right to freedom of peaceful assembly and association; the right to work; the right to equal pay for equal work; and the right to form and join trade unions. Citizens of all nations are also protected from slavery, torture and inhuman treatment, arbitrary arrest, detention, or exile.

According to the UDHR, all children are entitled to social protection and are declared to have the right to free education at the elementary level, which is compulsory. The declaration makes an adequate standard of living, including appropriate food, clothing, housing, and medical care, a human right and also propounds the right to security in the event of unemployment, sickness, disability, old age, or widowhood.

The primary significance of the UDHR lay in its formulation of a universally applicable ideal for all nations to emulate despite cultural differences. Although the declaration's principles have been often breached by member nations, the UDHR nevertheless offers a useful public standard for gauging national achievements in the field of human rights.

Upward Bound program: Government program established in 1965 to help youth from low-income families achieve a college education. Part of President Lyndon B. Johnson's GREAT SOCIETY program and first directed by Sargent Shriver, head of the Office of Economic Opportunity, the Upward Bound program provided funding for additional schooling for low-income students. The typical project supplements regular school with full-time summer school and part-time school, including weekends, during the school year. This additional schooling is provided largely within existing institutions, paying for extra time for teachers to prepare students for university-level studies. This preparation can include time away from home: for example, summers spent in college dormitories, while attending school.

The program has been almost universally hailed as a success and has grown considerably since its first implementation. It targets low-income students from urban and rural areas.

Urban renewal: Cooperative program between developers, municipal authorities, and the federal government targeting blighted areas and residential slums for commercial redevelopment. Though initiated by the Housing Act of 1949, urban renewal addressed housing needs as only one element of a strategy to stimulate urban economic growth.

Like most redevelopment programs, urban renewal owes its existence to private interests. Business leaders opposed to the federal presence in urban affairs first suggested urban redevelopment as an alternative to public housing in the late 1930's. Local developers preferred subsidies and programs that would benefit their operations directly to projects that threatened to monopolize valuable land downtown for housing programs they considered virtually nonprofit. As the battle over housing continued, some private firms delved into redevelopment without government assistance.

The earliest example of private redevelopment was the Stuyvesant Town project of 1943. Designed by Robert Moses for the Metropolitan Life Insurance Company, Stuyvesant Town replaced several blocks of housing and businesses in an East Side New York neighborhood with a series of high-rise apartment towers and open spaces. Metropolitan Life had chosen the Stuyvesant Town neighborhood not because of any need to rehabilitate local housing but rather to capitalize on the area's desirable location with a series of luxury apartments. Most residents evicted before the project began were denied the possibility of moving back to the completed Stuyvesant Town by exorbitant increases in rent, while persons of color were automatically disqualified by restrictive covenants quietly imposed by Metropolitan Life officials.

Several cities took New York's lead and organized redevelopment boards that were only strengthened by the passage of housing legislation in 1949. Stuyvesant Town was not perfect, but it gave officials around the country a model for redevelopment that Moses personally guaranteed. In fact, cities that lacked renewal authorities hired Moses to reinvigorate their downtown areas with more office towers and sleek apartment buildings. Affordable housing remained a secondary concern, with many developers neglecting their responsibilities as outlined by federal urban policy. In the first fifteen years of urban renewal, less than 1 percent of all federal funds were spent relocating families. The startling realization that two-thirds of those evicted were African Americans prompted many activists to brand the program "Negro removal."

In light of these shortcomings, critics of urban renewal suggest that its few accomplishments came at the expense of minorities and the poor. They point to cynical developers who scuttled public-housing initiatives for the benefit of free enterprise only to turn around and receive government subsidies for commercial redevelopment. Others choose to interpret urban renewal as a fluid concept that eventually did serve public interests. Libraries and schools constructed with renewal funds, along with property allocated to colleges, universities, and even hospitals, satisfied needs found wanting before the advent of urban renewal. Social programs directed at preserving neighborhoods and promoting cohesion in lower-income areas supplanted the "federal bulldozer" projects that

had so aptly characterized earlier renewal efforts. The urban renewal program came to an official end in 1974, yet it left a legacy of unanswered questions concerning the compatibility of sincere housing efforts and commercial redevelopment of the aged urban core.

Urbanization: Process of people moving from rural to urban areas in great numbers. Urbanization does not simply refer to a specific number of people concentrated in a certain geographic area; rather, the proportion of the population living and working in a city and its suburbs serves to classify an area as urban or rural.

According to the 1990 U.S. Census, 77 percent of the U.S. population lives in urban areas. Roughly three-quarters of the people are concentrated on 16 percent of the land, with more than 50 percent of these urban dwellers located along the coastlines.

The U.S. Bureau of the Census designates a locale as urban in terms of the actual number of people living in a given area. If there are 2,500 inhabitants or more, the city, village, or town is designated as "urban." Given this definition, the United States has approximately seven thousand urban locales.

There are a number of characteristics that are unique to the urban lifestyle. First, in contrast to rural life, urbanization involves a tremendous mixing of people from a wide range of backgrounds, cultures, and histories. Second, along with this human heterogeneity, there is also great variety in work skills, occupations, and statuses, all of which serve to categorize people into classes and arrange them into neighborhoods.

Third, cities are ever-changing entities. The look and feel of a city or neighborhood for one generation will likely be quite different for the next. Fluctuations in the economy, changing industry demands for labor, variation in immigrant flows from different parts of the world—these and many other factors contribute to changes in a city over time. Some find opportunity and vibrancy in this ongoing process, while others view the lack of consistency as problematic and destabilizing, with those most affected being the poor and the working classes.

Fourth, the nature of social relationships in cities differs from that in the country. In a rural setting, it is common for people to know their neighbors and their life histories. In contrast, in a city, a person can live quite anonymously, virtually as a stranger in a sea of people. Relationships with others become much more a matter of choice. From the societal perspective, the drawback of such anonymity and selective choice of social groups is that social order is more difficult to maintain. It must necessarily be kept by more formal means, such as through laws and by enforcers of the law (typically a police force). These impersonal means of control are usually not as effective as such traditional, social sanctions as shame, ostracism, or fear of embarrassment to the family, sanctions that can often be more easily applied in a rural setting.

Nevertheless, most countries are swiftly urbanizing. As they do, the earth's inhabitants are coming into increasingly close contact with one another. The challenge of the reality of globalization is the utilization of effective communication and interaction skills among the diversity of world cultures.

V

V-chips: Computer chips added to television sets to enable users to block the reception of unwanted transmissions. V-chips became the centerpiece of the federal government's mid-1990's effort to regulate broadcasts of violent, sexual, or otherwise potentially offensive material. Proponents, including President Bill CLINTON, lauded v-chips as technological developments that would allow parents to control their children's viewing habits without the need for governmental interference that would infringe on the rights of broadcasters. Skeptics saw the programming of v-chips as likely to prove too difficult for most users; others argued that associated ratings systems would serve to attract young viewers to violent or sexual shows.

Vaccination and immunization: "Immunization" refers to the process by which an individual is rendered immune to a specific disease or toxin, often with the aid of a specially prepared vaccine; "vaccination" is the act of administering a vaccine. Immunizations are available for many diseases, including diphtheria, pertussis, tetanus, polio, mumps, German measles (rubella), red measles, and hepatitis; it is often recom-

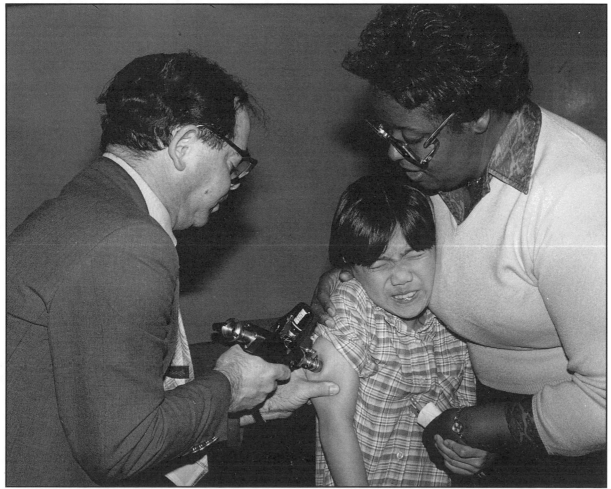

A child receives a shot as part of a vaccination program. (Impact Visuals/Harvey Finkle)

mended that everyone be immunized against these diseases. Vaccines are also available for other diseases such as influenza, plague, cholera, and yellow, typhoid, and Dengue fevers; these vaccines are administered to persons with specific needs. Rabies vaccine is given to domestic pets; smallpox has been completely eradicated through the application of an immunization program.

Vaillancourt v. The Queen (1987): Supreme Court of Canada case. In the *Vaillancourt* decision, the court ruled that a defendant who had taken part in an armed robbery could not be prosecuted for murder committed by an accomplice during the course of the robbery. The court concluded that the defendant could not "objectively foresee" that murder would result from his actions; in effect, the ruling meant that Canadians could not be charged with "constructive" murder.

Valdez Principles (1989): Name given to the September, 1989, "code" generated by a coalition of environmentalists, religious groups, and investors, the Coalition for Environmentally Responsible Economies (CERES). CERES proposed a "conduct code" for judging businesses to be environmentally responsible and thus deserving of investment or career consideration. The fifteen-point code calls on corporations to address the effects of their products and processes on the environment, communities, and their employees, with special emphasis on pollution prevention, energy efficiency, biotic conservation, and corporate accountability and responsibility. The Valdez Principles are modeled after the 1977 Sullivan Principles, which governed American business conduct in then-segregated South Africa.

Values: Beliefs that people hold—individually and collectively—about what is right and wrong, good and evil, precious and worthless, beautiful and ugly, or sacred and profane. Value judgments affect everything we do: from the ways that individuals spend their money to the interests that nations defend. Social issues emerge from questions or conflicts about values. Solutions to those issues depend on the values that govern human life.

Philosophical Background. How important is money? When should ABORTION be permitted? Should Québec separate from Canada? What kinds of education about sex or drugs should schools provide? How should "FAMILY VALUES" be defined? Should affirmative action programs be discontinued? Is the death penalty right or wrong? How high should taxes be in the United States or Canada? Is religious faith desirable? All those questions are about values. Answers to the social issues that they raise depend upon the value commitments that people make.

People can and do take different positions on social issues, which shows that they have different values or that they interpret the same values differently. Such differences may exist because people come from different cultures or communities, neighborhoods or nations, races or religions. Those social factors produce different perspectives that affect what values people hold and influence the particular evaluations that people make.

People make value judgments when they say, for example, that "abortion is wrong" or that "the death penalty is right." Does the variety of values, and especially the arguments that conflicting value judgments can produce, mean that value judgments are culturally relative and even personally subjective? Or are at least some value judgments objectively grounded and true for everyone? For centuries, philosophers have debated such questions, which are themselves at the core of many social issues. Agreement about how to answer those questions is not universal, but philosophers emphasize the importance of inquiry about the values that people hold. For example, much can be learned by asking, "Is this value judgment true, and, if so, why?" Much can also be learned by asking, "What makes some values positive (courage, for example, or honesty and trust), and what makes others negative (hatred, for example, or selfishness and infidelity)?"

Nothing is good or right simply because someone values it. In fact, to say that something is valuable simply because someone values it would contradict a fundamental point that values make: The differences between what is valuable and what is not depend on more than an individual's feelings or a culture's preferences. We know this because our value judgments can be mistaken. We often criticize, change, or even reject them because we learn that they are wrong. Thus, while people may not agree about values, the questions that values raise—which ones do we hold, how should we evaluate those values, which values matter most—are themselves social issues. Those issues require careful attention because so much depends on

A civil rights advocate calls for the recognition of fundamental values. (Photo Agora/D. Michael Hostetler)

A protester makes a value judgement about capital punishment. (Impact Visuals/Alain McLaughlin)

how people answer them. In particular, the pursuit of such inquiries can cause people to find more common ground about values than their disagreements suggest at first glance.

Population Factors. People are defined by the values they hold. Likewise, who they are influences what matters most to them. Census data and public-opinion polls shed light on all these areas.

According to the U.S. Census Bureau, Americans numbered about 250 million in 1990, an increase of 10 percent from 1980. Canada's population in the 1990's has exceeded 28 million. Updates by the U.S. Census Bureau showed that the population of the United States in 1995 was about 262 million, which included an increase of 2.47 million persons in 1994 alone. Of that number, 816,000 were immigrants. The American people are the most diverse of any nation on earth. When Canada's population is added, the diversity of the North American region increases still further.

Focusing specifically on the United States, population projections made by the Census Bureau indicate that the U.S. population will rise to about 394 million by the year 2050. Of that number, 53 percent will be non-Hispanic whites, a decline from 74 percent in the mid-1990's. The estimates indicate that the African American population will remain stable, rising from 12 percent to 13.6 percent. Asians will provide 8.2 percent of the U.S. population in 2050, up from 3.3 percent in 1995. Hispanics will make up 24.5 percent of the population, a large increase from 10.2 percent in 1995. Another significant change will be that by 2030, the non-Hispanic white population of the United States will constitute less than half of the people under the age of eighteen, but three-fourths of the population over the age of sixty-five.

What Matters Most? The size and diversity of the U.S. population raise important questions about values. One of them concentrates on how Americans decide what is valuable. James Patterson and Peter Kim, authors of an extensive public-opinion survey called *The Day America Told the Truth* (1991), found that 70 percent of the American people believed that the nation has no living heroes. A similar number thought that American children have no meaningful role models. More than 90 percent reported that they—and they alone—determine by themselves what is morally right or wrong.

In a followup study, *The Second American Revolution* (1994), Patterson and Kim found that, despite an apparently individualistic approach to value judgments, Americans displayed considerable consensus on several major issues. Americans were eager for new leadership that could rejuvenate the economy, improve American schools, provide better health-care access, make their cities safer, and curb drug abuse.

As illustrated by examples from Patterson and Kim's findings, solutions to those social issues will require Americans to keep evaluating their values. For example, when Americans were asked what they would most like to change about themselves, neither increased intelligence nor improved employment topped the list. The idea of becoming a "better person" did not make the rankings at all. Instead, a substantial majority thought outward appearance more important than the inner self. They wanted most to be rich and thin—the American Dream of the 1990's, as Patterson and Kim called that hope.

The Day America Told the Truth also testified that violence has been running far and wide in American society. According to Patterson and Kim, one out of seven Americans reported that they were sexually abused as children. Of that number, 75 percent were women. Twenty times more rapes are reported in the United States than in Japan, England, or Spain. Patterson and Kim also discovered that one-third of the people they surveyed owned handguns, and almost as many had rifles or shotguns. They judged that one in seven Americans carries a weapon on their person or in their car.

Among the world's industrialized nations, the United States is by far the most violent. The U.S. homicide rate has been twenty times higher than in Western Europe, forty times higher than in Japan. Guns were used in 75 percent of U.S. killings, as compared to 25 percent of those in other industrialized nations. As for violence in American entertainment, *The Day America Told the Truth* reported that children's television programming has averaged twenty-five violent acts every hour, a rate up 50 percent from the early 1980's.

Next, when considering the executive and legislative branches of the federal government, organized religion and the nation's educational system, the military and the media, or business, banking, and organized labor, Patterson and Kim found that the percentage of Americans who expressed a great deal of confidence in major social institutions has been in decline. When Patterson and Kim asked their survey participants to evaluate some seventy American occupations, the results echoed the decline of confidence in American

PUBLIC OPINION, 1994: SHOULD THE GOVERNMENT PROMOTE TRADITIONAL VALUES?

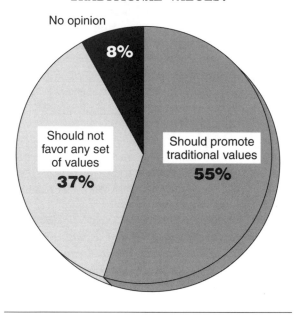

No opinion
8%

Should not favor any set of values
37%

Should promote traditional values
55%

Source: George Gallup, Jr., ed., *The Gallup Poll: Public Opinion, 1994* (Wilmington, Del.: Scholarly Resources, 1995).

institutions. Member of Congress, Wall Street executives, labor-union leaders, lawyers, and evangelists joined organized-crime bosses and drug dealers in the twenty occupations that Americans rated lowest for honesty and integrity. Of the twenty occupations that ranked highest in that regard, many were neither prestigious nor high-paying. The U.S. presidency, for example, did not make that list, tying for only twenty-eighth in the Patterson-Kim reckoning, slightly ahead of the nation's often-maligned press. Roles such as firefighter and paramedic came out on top, with educators, doctors, scientists, airline pilots, and flight attendants joining Catholic priests, Jewish rabbis, and Protestant ministers to round out most of the preferred list.

Turning to community involvement, *The Day America Told the Truth* showed that two-thirds of Americans never gave time to community activities or to solving community problems. One-third of Americans had never given money to a charitable cause: among those who did give, the average American donated less than 1 percent of his or her annual income. Slightly more than half of the American population felt a moral responsibility to help the poor, with some 42 percent

convinced that people are poor because they are lazy or because of other faults of their own.

Patterson and Kim detected relatively few hardcore racists, but they did find a "new racism" directed toward African Americans in particular. They defined the "new racism" as the view that blacks now have the same chances for success as anybody else in America and that those who have failed economically or socially have simply not taken advantage of the opportunities that the nation offers.

According to Patterson and Kim, these findings did not mean that Americans lacked love for their country. More than 90 percent of the American people think of themselves as patriotic; more than four out of five (81 percent) affirm that the United States plays a special part in the world; and 75 percent think more patriotism is needed. Most Americans—95 percent—have a deeply favorable opinion of their country.

Still, public-opinion polls in the mid-1990's have also consistently shown that less than 20 percent of the American people believe that American character has changed for the better since the 1970's. In fact, *The Day America Told the Truth* showed that Americans have been deeply concerned about moral decay in the United States. Americans may rationalize their problematic behavior by saying "everyone else is doing it," but that justification sparks no celebration. To the contrary, Americans have deep worries about public safety and national health. They do not want to be cheated, lied to, stolen from, raped, mugged, or murdered. Nor do Americans want untrustworthy leaders, dysfunctional institutions, and unsatisfying jobs.

The Day America Told the Truth indicated that nearly six in ten Americans would gladly give three weeks annually to do volunteer work that would help to solve the nation's basic social problems—or so they said. A similar percentage would accept, even if not so gladly, a heavier tax burden to improve American education and to safeguard the environment, two aims that Patterson and Kim identified as causes that could help to unify American life. The authors' optimism on those points may be excessive, however, for Americans remain divided about how to improve education as well as about what it means to safeguard the environment when economic values conflict with environmental ideals. Nevertheless, education and the environment are two areas where Americans are substantially united in the belief that special attention must be paid.

In summary, the Patterson-Kim polls suggested that there are millions of Americans who would respond to

Conservative leaders such as the Reverend Jerry Falwell called for an emphasis on "family values" in the 1980's and 1990's. (AP/Wide World Photos)

the right kind of call for help. Waiting for wise leadership, efficient organization, and moral vision to tap them, there are tremendous reservoirs of American energy that can serve the common good. That recognition may help to explain why Patterson and Kim found that an overwhelming majority of Americans (81 percent) want schools to teach morals to American children. Whose "morals" and what content those values should contain are, of course, questions far more easily asked than answered. Yet the consensus reported about the importance of such teaching remains significant.

Turning to Religion. Value judgments and social issues are often linked to religion. On this point, the surveys done by Patterson and Kim revealed another mixture of views. Perhaps because Americans think of God in so many different ways, the researchers found that 90 percent of the American people believed in God. Belief in life after death was also affirmed by 82 percent. The latter affirmation entertained the reality of hell as well as heaven, but only a few (4 percent) seriously thought they might be destined to spend eternity with Satan. That belief, however, did not mean that Americans take evil lightly. To the contrary, Patterson and Kim found that 55 percent of Americans testified not that the devil is merely a figurative of symbolic power but instead that Satan is a particular—even personal—power, and one that is all too real. In fact, the numbers of Americans who hold this belief may be growing. A 1995 *Newsweek* poll indicated that 66 percent of all adult Americans—and 85 percent of evangelical Protestants—believe in the devil's existence.

Despite those high percentages, analysis reveals neither a definite consensus about religious meanings nor a clear indication that such beliefs make much difference on people's attitudes and actions about a variety of important social issues. Six out of seven Americans, for example, thought that it was all right not to believe in God. Interest in God's will was lukewarm at best, at least if allegiance to the Ten Commandments or to the teachings of organized religion measure such concern. Most Americans did not know, to say nothing of consciously obeying, the public-policy positions held by the country's major religious institutions. Americans even pick and choose among the Ten Commandments, and apparently they do so without much

A Quaker school in Brooklyn, New York, emphasizes the teaching of values. (Hazel Hankin)

fear of divine judgment. While Americans did still tend to have a sense of sin, they also tended to define "sin" for themselves, an outcome that fits the facts that half of the American population has not attended a religious service in the last three months, and one in three has not done so in the past year.

What Patterson and Kim discovered about American religious experience did not end there, however. They also found a marked difference between those who are superficially religious and those who are truly serious about religious commitment. Most Americans belong in the former category, but Patterson and Kim noted that 14 percent of the American people described themselves as "very religious." The Patterson-Kim profile of "very religious" Americans looked like this: The vast majority (99 percent) were under the age of sixty-five. Their educational level was quite high—one in four had been graduated from college, and two out of three had done some college work. Women outnumbered men. Patterson and Kim found the latter point consistent with other important results of their survey, which repeatedly revealed that women have higher moral standards than men and that deeply religious Americans act more ethically than most other Americans.

Compared to those who defined themselves as "not religious at all," very religious Americans ranked higher than other people on value commitments that most persons would accept as defining citizenship in a civilized society. The "very religious" were not perfect, but *The Day America Told the Truth* showed them to be significantly more truthful and committed to their families than were the nonreligious. Less prone to drug use or criminal activity, they were also less likely to carry weapons or to rationalize behavior because "everybody's doing it." The poll also showed that deeply religious Americans are significantly more dedicated workers, more satisfied with their lives, and more prepared to die for their beliefs than their nonreligious counterparts. In addition, the deeply religious are less likely to be racially prejudiced and are more likely to be kind, optimistic, giving, and forgiving than the majority of Americans. Far from being Karl Marx's "opiate of the people," religion in deeply religious Americans apparently does not hinder compassion and caring but instead can be a vital force for constructive social change.

The figures about deeply religious Americans are much smaller than other poll findings from the 1990's, which include reports such as the following: 88 percent of Americans sometimes pray to God, 43 percent have attended a religious observance in a typical week, 33 percent have had a powerful religious experience, and 22 percent have indicated that religion is the "most important" influence in their lives. Clearly, however, there is tremendous religious interest and personal piety in the United States, much more than the conventional wisdom about the secularization of American society may admit. That sign could be a hopeful one for American life, although the depth and quality of religious commitment and the difference such commitment makes remain fundamental value questions.

Looking Ahead. In his famous 1863 Gettysburg Address President Abraham Lincoln expressed the hope that the United States could have "a new birth of freedom." Closely linked with American value commitments to justice, equality, and respect for individual human rights, freedom is one of the values that Americans emphasize the most.

Lincoln also once observed that although Americans want freedom, they do not all mean the same thing when they use the word. His observation remains as accurate as his Gettysburg hope was profound. Americans do not agree completely about what "freedom" means; probably they never will. Yet, at the close of the twentieth century and the beginning of the twenty-first, Americans may well agree that the United States still needs a new birth of freedom—especially if "freedom" is understood to include higher ethical standards, less violence, more compassion, and better racial relations than the society has experienced in the past. As they struggle with modern social issues, which include defining those values and enacting public policies to put them into practice, Americans will discover whether they have changed for the better.

—*John K. Roth*

SUGGESTED READINGS: Drawing on data from the 1990 U.S. census, Sam Roberts provides a detailed description of the American people in *Who We Are: A Portrait of America Based on the Latest U.S. Census* (New York: Times Books, 1993). James Patterson and Peter Kim's *The Day America Told the Truth: What People Really Believe About Everything That Matters* (New York: Prentice-Hall, 1991) is a fascinating resource for anyone interested in American beliefs and values. William J. Bennett offers additional statistical information about beliefs and values in *The Index of Leading Cultural Indicators: Facts and Figures on the State of American Society* (New York: Simon & Schuster, 1994).

In *The Second American Revolution* (New York: William Morrow, 1994), Patterson and Kim turn their appraisals to forecasts about the future of American Life. Ben J. Wattenberg's *Values Matter Most: How Republicans or Democrats or a Third Party Can Win and Renew the American Way of Life* (New York: The Free Press, 1995) examines how American politics can and should respond to the fact that the solutions to social issues depend on the values that people hold. Robert J. Samuelson's *The Good Life and Its Discontents: The American Dream in the Age of Entitlement, 1945-1995* (New York: Times Books, 1995) argues that Americans should avoid either excessive optimism or unwarranted pessimism as they seek a realistic and balanced appraisal of the nation's strengths and weaknesses.

In *Trust: The Social Virtues and the Creation of Prosperity* (New York: The Free Press, 1995), Francis Fukuyama explores a wide range of national cultures and shows how their success and failure depends on the presence or absence of social trust. George H. Gallup, Jr., and Timothy Jones provide important information about religious beliefs and values in the United States in *The Saints Among Us* (Harrisburg, Penn.: Morehouse, 1992). Finally, for discussion of the philosophical background concerning value questions, see John K. Roth and Frederick Sontag's *The Questions of Philosophy* (Belmont, Calif.: Wadsworth, 1988) and Norman Melchert's *Who's to Say? A Dialogue on Relativism* (Indianapolis, Ind.: Hackett, 1994).

Vanier, Jean (b. Sept. 10, 1928, Geneva, Switzerland): French-Canadian spiritual writer and founder of l'Arche (The Ark), a community for the handicapped. Vanier, a Roman Catholic layman, began the first l'Arche community in Trosly-Breuil, France, in 1964, convinced that the voice of God speaks through the suffering of the poor and the outcast. L'Arche communities, which can now be found throughout the world, are examples of communal living that attempt to live out the simplicity of love and hope witnessed in the Bible. Vanier's vision is informed by the conviction that truth is learned through suffering and that God's power is revealed in human powerlessness.

Vanier Institute of the Family: Private Canadian nonprofit organization founded 1965 by Governor-General Georges Vanier and his wife Pauline Vanier to promote the well-being of Canadian families. The institute sponsors research and analysis on demographic, economic, social, and other influences on Canadian family life, serves as an information resource for students of family issues, and provides advice on family issues to interested parties. Membership includes representatives from the fields of business, education, health, and community services as well as the general public.

Vasectomy: Surgery used to permanently end a man's fertility. The term refers to the cutting of the vas deferens, the tubule that carries sperm from the testes to the urethra. When the tube is cut, sperm cannot mix with the fluids that form semen; in this way, vasectomy makes men infertile without altering any other sexual functions. Despite its ease, since vasectomy is rarely reversible, it is generally used as a means of birth control only by men who are sure that they do not want to father children.

Vatican II (1962-1965): Council of the Catholic Church that sought to modernize worship, open interreligious dialogue, and involve the Church in the concerns of the world.

Pope John XXIII said that his inspiration for the council was "a flash of heavenly light," and he announced it as a "council to promote the unity of all Christian communities." The council met two months each year for four years and produced sixteen documents aimed at changing Church attitudes and practices.

The council reversed the Church's long-standing opposition to interfaith dialogue by affirming other Christian groups as possessing some elements of the one, true church. It regarded Protestants as "separated brethren" rather than heretics and schismatics. It also affirmed the right of people to choose their religion, and it encouraged religious liberty. It acknowledged whatever truth and goodness might be in other religions while still enjoining Catholics to proclaim Jesus Christ as the Lord and Savior of all humanity.

One of the council's primary goals was to update the Church in order to meet the needs of modern times. Some regarded the attempt as a reversal of the principle that had guided the Church since the Fourth Lateran Council in the sixteenth century, which said that "men must be changed by religion, not religion by

1636

men." In the spirit of modernization, the language of liturgy was changed from Latin to the vernacular. The change affirmed the diversity of cultures in the world and the importance of meeting local needs. This replaced the traditional mentality that the Church is monolithic, and addressed criticism that for all its expansion across the globe, the Church was still strongly Western and European.

The council recognized the spiritual priesthood of the laity, allowing them to participate in the Mass and encouraging them to read the Bible. The Church was seen not as a hierarchy but as a community of people working in their appropriate roles. Collegiality, or sharing of power, between the bishops and the pope was proclaimed, though the acts of the bishops were not regarded as effective without the endorsement of the pope.

Declaring that spirituality cannot be separated from social concerns, the Church sought to engage social problems—a trend it began in the late nineteenth century when it addressed such things as the role of government in society and economics and the right of labor to organize. Since World War II, the Church has globalized its social vision to include such things as providing the moral foundation for political, economic, and strategic issues. Vatican II supported this expanding vision by affirming the dignity of humans as creatures in the image of God, the excellence of freedom, equality as the basis for social justice, and the interdependence of people and their societies.

Critics of Vatican II see in the documents inconsistencies resulting from the clash between the conservatives, who wanted only to clarify traditional teaching, and progressives, who wanted to restructure the Church. Some call on the Church to follow through on the reforms it began. Supporters of the Council hail it as the beginning of a globally minded Church.

Vegetarianism: Philosophy and set of dietary practices that are against meat-eating. Vegetarians do not eat meat, poultry, or seafood; vegans extend these prohibitions to include eggs, dairy products, and, often, honey.

Surveys yield widely different results regarding the number of vegetarians. In the United States, estimates range from about five hundred thousand to eight million. Researchers have a difficult time counting practicing vegetarians because many people who occasionally eat meat and seafood call themselves vegetarians even though they do not meet the definition.

Several different arguments contribute to the vegetarian philosophy, and most practicing vegetarians tend to emphasize some of these arguments over others. In a 1991 survey conducted by the Vegetarian Resource Group, members of this organization cited the following reasons as important: health (81 percent), animal rights (81 percent), ethics (76 percent), and environment (75 percent).

Many people become vegetarians for health reasons, arguing that avoiding meat increases their vitality. In the 1960's and 1970's, the American Dietetic Association (ADA) expressed concern about the quality of vegetarian and vegan diets, which were often characterized as "food faddism" or "quackery." Over time, the ADA's position has become increasingly accepting of vegetarianism, although it still expresses concern for vegan diets, which exclude dairy products. In 1993, the ADA expressed its official position as "vegetarian diets are healthful and nutritionally adequate when appropriately planned."

People also become vegetarians for animal rights reasons. They oppose the ways in which animals are slaughtered, and they feel that animals have rights similar to those of humans. Many vegetarians find the practices associated with factory farming (large-scale animal agriculture) to be particularly disturbing. Vegetarians often hold animal rights views in conjunction with a concern about ethics.

People who become vegetarians for environmental reasons are motivated primarily by concerns for soil and water CONSERVATION; they hold that intensified cattle ranching depletes environmental resources. They also argue that more people could be fed if people were to consume grains directly rather than using them to feed cattle. Jeremy Rifkin outlines these concerns in *Beyond Beef: The Rise and Fall of Cattle Culture* (1992), which the American Council on Science and Health (ACSH) criticizes as providing an overly simplistic view of how eating less meat can solve environmental and hunger problems.

Still other vegetarians are motivated by reasons such as economics, taste, and religion. Seventh-day Adventists, Jains, and Hindus are especially likely to follow a vegetarian diet.

Many organizations provide information and support for people interested in vegetarianism. For example, in the United States, the Vegetarian Resource Group, the American Vegan Society, and the North American Vegetarian Society actively promote the vegetarian lifestyle; Canadian groups include the Toronto Vegetarian Association and the Vegetarians of Alberta.

SUGGESTED READING: In *A Vegetarian Sourcebook: The Nutrition, Ecology, and Ethics of a Natural Foods Diet* (Arlington, Va.: Vegetarian Press, 1983), Keith Akers provides a thorough overview of vegetarian nutrition and ethics.

Veterans: Strictly, soldiers and former soldiers who have served in combat. In modern America, the term has become more ambiguous; it has come to connote any member of the military who served in active duty during a conflict, whether in combat or not. In addition, former members of the military who have served at least four years on active duty, regardless of the type of duty, have legal status as veterans.

American society recognized during the colonial era an obligation toward those wounded or maimed while in the military. In 1789, the new government of the United States assumed the burden of caring for former members of the Continental Army who were unable to support themselves. This tradition continued throughout the nineteenth century, as the federal government established and maintained homes for former servicemen who had been incapacitated or who were otherwise unable to support themselves.

Since the beginning of civilization, former military members have formed organizations based on their status as veterans. In the United States, that tendency had its first great flowering after the Civil War. The Grand Army of the Republic, an organization of former members of the Union Army, remained a conservative force in American politics well into the twentieth century. The twentieth century veterans' movement has been shaped by mass participation in the century's world wars. Whereas previously veterans' groups tended to be formed around veterans of specific wars, the twentieth century saw the creation of more broadly based groups. Organizations such as the American Legion, the American Veterans of World War II, Korea, and Vietnam, and the Veterans of Foreign Wars are composed of veterans from several periods. Other groups such as the Disabled American Veterans focus on veterans with similar needs. Still other groups exist for women veterans and for veterans of certain units or duties.

In 1924, the government initiated a system of bonuses, payable in twenty years, for veterans of World War I. In 1932, during the Great Depression, unemployed veterans marched on Washington demanding an early payment. In late July, U.S. Army troops under the command of General Douglas MacArthur forcibly dispersed the marchers. In 1936, President Franklin Roosevelt signed a law providing for immediate payment. During World War II, in an attempt to avoid the problems stemming from the World War I bonus as well as to ease the return of millions of veterans into the workforce, Congress passed legislation known as the G.I. Bill, which provided educational opportunities for veterans after discharge. Approximately half of the nation's 16 million veterans took advantage of the G.I. Bill, which helped millions to enter the middle class.

The VETERANS ADMINISTRATION (VA) was created in 1930 as an independent agency under the president. The Department of Veterans' Affairs replaced the Veterans Administration in 1989 as a cabinet-level agency. The department has responsibility for administering retirements, survivor benefits, hospitals, cemeteries, educational assistance, home loans, and most other federal programs for former service members. In the mid-1990's, veterans made up roughly 10 percent of the U.S. population.

Veterans Administration (VA): Agency coordinating benefits and services for U.S. military veterans. The Veterans Administration was established by Congress as an independent agency of the United States government in July, 1930. The enactment combined several agencies that had previously offered various services to veterans, and centralized the system. In October of 1988, Congress approved elevation of the agency to cabinet level. The VA was renamed the Department of Veterans Affairs and became the fourteenth cabinet position on March 15, 1989.

The secretary of the department is nominated by the president, with the advice and the consent of the Senate. The department's headquarters are in Washington, D.C., and regional offices are maintained throughout the country. Other facilities include hospitals, outpatient clinics, domiciliaries, and various other field stations.

The Department of Veterans Affairs is authorized to administer federal laws and programs that relate to benefits established by Congress for veterans, their dependents, or surviving spouses. These programs include: vocational rehabilitation and disability compensation for disabled veterans; guaranteed loans for

A World War I veteran salutes a 1987 Veterans Day parade in Denver. (UPI/Corbis-Bettmann)

homes, farms, and business property; life insurance and burial benefits; and educational training.

The department administers the Soldier's and Sailor's Civil Relief Act, the Veterans Pension and Re-adjustment Assistance Act of 1967 (benefits for surviving widows and children), the Montgomery G.I. Bill (educational benefits for all veterans serving 180 or more days), Public Law 894 (vocational rehabilitation for war veterans), and other pertinent legislation.

One of the VA's primary activities is the operation of veteran's hospitals and the provision of medical care. The largest centralized U.S. health-care system, VA facilities and hospitals are located throughout the country, providing medical care to ill, injured, or disabled veterans, whether or not the medical condition is connected with service in the military. In addition, the VA, along with other health-care providers, makes available a limited number of beds for veterans in non-VA facilities. Outpatient medical and dental care, long-term care, and other medical services are also pro-

vided. The goal of VA medical care is to return veterans to their communities as rehabilitated, independent, and self-supporting members of those communities. In addition to providing direct patient care to former services members, the VA also conducts extensive medical research in the areas of cancer, mental health, cardiac disease, age-related health problems, and medical conditions specifically related to military service.

The department also provides services to assist military personnel with re-adjustment to civilian life, aid to families of service members serving abroad, and numerous other programs. The VA can also assist persons who wish to appeal denials of particular benefits or payments and discharge classifications.

Veto power, presidential: U.S. executive-branch privilege of nullifying legislation. Under the U.S. Constitution, presidents are given a qualified veto over

President Ronald Reagan vetoes a 1985 bill to provide aid to farmers. (UPI/Corbis-Bettmann)

bills passed by Congress; however, Congress can override vetoes via a two-thirds vote of both houses. A "pocket veto" occurs when a president declines to sign a bill shortly before Congress adjourns. Presidential veto is part of the Constitution's CHECKS AND BALANCES system; the power ensures that legislative authority is not solely in the hands of the legislature. The power of the presidential veto is considerable. From George Washington to Jimmy Carter, of 1,380 formal vetoes, only ninety-four were overridden; during the same period, presidents also exercised 1,011 pocket vetoes.

Vietnam and the United States: Following the end of the VIETNAM WAR, normalization of relations between the United States and Vietnam was widely debated. At issue were economic and political advantages for both countries, human rights considerations, and the possible continued detention of American prisoners of war by Vietnam.

Background. The United States and Vietnam fought a long war during the 1960's and 1970's that poisoned relations between them. The Vietnamese believed they were fighting for their political independence. Americans typically believed that they were fighting communist aggression.

The war ended with the evacuation of the United States military. The communist government in Hanoi was able to defeat the remnants of anticommunist opposition and exert its dominance over all of Vietnam by mid-1975.

In the years immediately following the war, the United States kept in place an embargo against Vietnam instituted during the war. When Vietnam invaded Cambodia in December, 1978, American and Vietnamese animosity deepened, and the chances of rapprochement grew dim.

As the world economic system began to tighten in the late 1970's, the United States and Vietnam began to reassess the absence of a political and economic understanding. By the mid 1980's, the United States realized that Vietnam would be a useful ally in a growing dispute with the People's Republic of China. Also, Vietnam would be useful in maintaining stability in Southeast Asia. Political stability in the region, plus an alliance with Vietnam, would quite probably mean new economic opportunity for America.

During the same period, Vietnam realized that the United States would be a useful ally, especially after

the fall of the Soviet Union. American help in maintaining stability in Southeast Asia would most certainly mean American investment capital, which could only impact Vietnam's economy in a positive manner.

By the mid-1990's, Vietnam had taken steps to reapproach the United States. These steps included moderating communist rhetoric vis-à-vis the United States, agreeing to withdraw troops occupying Cambodia since 1978, and liberalizing foreign-investment laws. Also, American delegations were allowed into Vietnam to investigate reports of prisoners of war (POWs), while the remains of POWs discovered buried in Vietnam were returned to the United States.

For its part, the United States announced in 1990 that it would no longer insist that Cambodia's United Nations' seat be occupied by a coalition that included the Khmer Rouge, Vietnam's enemy. In December, 1990, the United States announced that it would be willing to begin formal talks concerning the normalization of relations as soon as Vietnam made steps toward resolving the POW issue.

Vietnam and the United States

In November, 1991, the United States and Vietnam began talks in New York City on restoring relations. In 1994, President Bill CLINTON ended the trade embargo against Vietnam, which had been in effect since the war. In July, 1995, Clinton proclaimed the normalization of relations between the two countries.

Threats from senators and congressional representatives to block Clinton's action by withholding funds from a projected Vietnam embassy seemed to be only bluster. The quiet private and public response from the United States indicated general agreement that the time had come for normal diplomatic relations with the former enemy.

Economic and Political Advantages. For the United States, the economic advantages of normalized relations were manifold. Access to Vietnam's labor pool would mean cheaper wages for American producers, resulting in higher profits. Access to Vietnam's market would also mean more customers for American manufactured and agricultural goods. Vietnamese raw materials, such as oil, rubber, and mineral deposits, would translate into lower costs for American producers, also increasing profits.

Politically, the United States would gain an ally in an explosive area of the globe. The historically fluctuating relationship between the United States and the People's Republic of China could leave America vulnerable in East Asia. Normal relations with Vietnam would act as a political lever in the region, protecting American interests in the event of problems with China. Because Vietnam has the strongest military force in Southeast Asia, the country could, as an American ally, be depended upon to protect American interests.

For the Vietnamese, the economic advantages included a market for Vietnam's underutilized workforce. An economic understanding with the United

Billboards in Hanoi advertise U.S. products following the 1994 lifting of the U.S. economic embargo on Vietnam.
(Reuters/Corbis-Bettmann)

U.S. assistant secretary of state Richard Solomon and Vietnamese prime minister Vo Van Kiet at a 1992 meeting in Hanoi. (UPI/Corbis-Bettmann)

Villagers watch as a U.S. team searches in 1991 for the remains of an American pilot downed during the Vietnam War. (UPI/Corbis-Bettmann)

States would mean a lower unemployment rate and higher wages for Vietnam's workers. Another advantage for Vietnam was that the United States could provide a huge market for their industrial and agricultural surplus. Finally, American investment capital would result in a higher output of Vietnam's underdeveloped natural resources, resulting in a higher standard of living for the average Vietnamese citizen.

Politically, the United States would represent a counterforce to the giant People's Republic of China on Vietnam's northern border. The Vietnamese would be able to rely on American military and economic strength to guarantee their autonomy, especially since the fall of their primary protector, the Soviet Union, in the early 1990's. An economic and political understanding with the United States would translate into a greater degree of freedom of action in Vietnamese foreign policy, especially in Southeast Asia.

Human Rights. One of the major stumbling blocks to the normalization of relations between Vietnam and the United States was Vietnam's poor record on human rights. Those opposing a rapprochement claimed that Vietnam needed to improve its treatment of political dissidents and to end its program of "re-education" before diplomatic ties were established.

Complicating the issue was the fact that Vietnam had shown no willingness to tolerate open political dissent. In November, 1991, for example, Dr. Nguyen Dan Que was sentenced to twenty years in prison for, among other things, his activities as a member of Amnesty International.

In certain respects, Vietnam had attempted to improve its record in human rights. The system of "re-education" camps had been largely dismantled, and the International Red Cross was allowed to visit the last of these camps. Also, several political prisoners convicted of anticommunist activity were released.

Many argued that making Vietnam improve its record on human rights a prerequisite to diplomatic relations was putting the cart before the horse. Only by instituting relations, they argued, would liberal political and economic ideas, such as democracy and capitalism, be allowed to filter into Vietnam. Certainly, the twenty-year American policy of nonrecognition had not exposed Vietnam to American institutions.

Another argument for establishing relations with Vietnam prior to a full Vietnamese commitment to human rights had to do with the People's Republic of China. One of the primary functions of normal relations would be to confront China indirectly about its human rights abuses. Using subtle diplomatic pressure indirectly on China's southern border might effect some moderation of Chinese treatment of political prisoners and dissidents.

MIA and POW Issue. Another major barrier to formal relations was American insistence of a satisfactory Vietnamese accounting of MIAs (soldiers missing in action); in 1990, fully 82 percent of the American public believed that living American POWs were being held in Vietnam. This was quite probably the result of several popular motion pictures produced between 1978 and 1989, the common theme of which was the rescue of American POWs from the jungles of Vietnam.

The belief in living POWs was reinforced in 1988 when President Ronald Reagan announced that the United States would operate on the "assumption" that at least some of the MIAs were still alive. Supporting the assumption, a top Soviet intelligence officer testified before members of the U.S. Senate that Soviet agents had interviewed American POWs in 1978.

Vietnam claimed that there were no live American POWs and extended offers to aid American officials in accounting for MIAs. On one of these occasions, between 1985 and 1987, the remains of eighty-eight POWs were returned to the United States. Also, the U.S. Defense Department continually discounted reports of MIA or POW sightings in Vietnam and finally assumed that all but one were dead. The one surviving MIA was kept officially "alive" as a symbol to Vietnam of continuing interest in the issue.

Some Americans claimed that the POW/MIA issue was being kept alive for political reasons. That argument posited that certain American politicians kept the pressure on Vietnam in order to garner votes from veteran's groups so as to further their careers. One of the key points of the political argument was the MIA statistics from World War II and from the Korean War. In World War II, eighty thousand MIAs were never accounted for. In Korea, eight thousand MIAs were never recovered. In Vietnam, 1,618 MIAs remained

unaccounted for by 1990. Those who claimed that the MIA/POW issue was merely a domestic political issue asked why the MIA issue was critical to American-Vietnamese relations when it was not critical to Axis-American relations, or as critical to North Korean-American relations. The final, deciding argument on the issue was, apparently, that the United States could get an accurate accounting of MIAs only by having diplomatic relations with Vietnam.   *—Tim Palmer*

SUGGESTED READINGS: Several issues on postwar relations are discussed in editor Robert E. Long's *Vietnam Ten Years After* (New York: The H.W. Wilson Company, 1986). Gary R. Hess provides an excellent description of the problems of rapprochement in *Vietnam and the United States* (Boston: Twayne, 1990). A comprehensive treatment of the entire Vietnam War, plus an exploration of postwar developments, can be found in George C. Herring's *America's Longest War: The United States and Vietnam, 1950-1975*, 2d ed. (New York: Alfred A. Knopf, 1986). Postwar events in Vietnam are described by Melanie Beresford in *Vietnam: Politics, Economics, and Society* (London: Pinter, 1988).

Vietnam War: Conflict between the United States and North Vietnam that took more than fifty-eight thousand American lives and created deep divisions within American society between supporters and opponents of the war.

Background. The Vietnam War followed a long tradition of Vietnamese struggles against invading nations, including France, which colonized Vietnam in the nineteenth century. The Vietnamese finally scored a decisive victory at Dien Bien Phu in 1954, effectively ending French rule.

The subsequent Geneva Agreement of 1954 divided Indochina into four parts: Laos, Cambodia, North Vietnam (ruled by Ho Chi Minh's communist government), and South Vietnam (with a pro-Western government led by Ngo Dinh Diem). National elections were to occur in 1956 to determine reunification of Vietnam, but the governments of the United States and South Vietnam (The Republic of Vietnam), fearing Ho Chi Minh's popularity, refused to hold the election.

From 1956 to 1964, the United States supported South Vietnam's resistance to the North's efforts to unite all of Vietnam under Ho Chi Minh. As the North escalated its attacks, the number of United States military advisers rose, reaching sixteen thousand by the time of President John F. Kennedy's assassination in November, 1963.

Buddhist opposition to the political corruption and anti-Buddhist actions of the Diem government, including the Buddhist monk Quang Duc's suicide by fire, precipitated a coup in early November, 1963, which led to the arrest and execution of Diem and his brother, Ngo Dinh Nhu, head of the Saigon secret police. A period of political instability followed until the accession to power in June, 1965, of General Nguyen Van Thieu and Air Marshal Nguyen Cao Ky.

A confrontation between two United States destroyers and North Vietnamese warships in the Gulf of Tonkin in August, 1964, led President Lyndon B. Johnson to ask Congress for authorization to use increased force. The resulting Gulf of Tonkin Resolution permitted the president to use "all necessary measures to repel any armed attack against the forces of the United States and to prevent further aggression." The American role quickly changed from adviser to principal combatant.

American Involvement. Beginning in 1965, the United States increasingly led the war effort, rapidly building up its forces in Vietnam. United States soldiers and their South Vietnamese counterparts faced dual enemies: the Viet Cong (communist guerrillas in the South) and the North Vietnamese Army.

The United States began its official air war against North Vietnam in early 1965. In the same year, General William Westmoreland, American commander in Vietnam, ordered American ground forces into direct combat. In November, they confronted the North Vietnamese Army for the first time, in a monthlong series of battles in the Ia Drang Valley that produced an American victory but cost 247 American lives.

As the war progressed into the 1970's, the United States continued to bomb North Vietnam, enemy positions in the South, and the Ho Chi Minh Trail (a network of supply trails and roads stretching from North Vietnam southward through Laos and Cambodia into South Vietnam). The massive bombing, however, failed to cut off supply lines or to break the resolve of the North Vietnamese. On the ground, United States forces took a heavy toll on the enemy but ultimately proved no more successful than the air war at forcing an end to communist efforts in the South.

The Tet Offensive. In January, 1968, during the Vietnamese holiday known as Tet, the Viet Cong launched a sudden attack in Saigon, and much of the city became a battleground. Viet Cong entered the U.S. Embassy compound and nearly overran the main embassy building.

Similar attacks hit scores of other sites throughout South Vietnam, including the ancient city of Hue. The communist forces caused great devastation and executed large numbers of Vietnamese. Although the captured areas were retaken, with huge loss of life to the North Vietnamese and Viet Cong, what remained in the minds of Americans back home was the realization that no place in South Vietnam was safe from the enemy. The Tet Offensive raised serious doubts about the ability of the United States to win the war.

Hundreds of antiwar demonstrations occurred in the weeks following Tet, and on March 31, President Johnson announced that he was limiting further bombing of the North to an area just north of the border to try to draw the Ho Chi Minh government into peace negotiations. He added that he would not be a candidate for reelection. On April 3, North Vietnam agreed to begin peace talks.

Withdrawal. In 1969, President Richard M. Nixon ordered the "Vietnamization" of the war, the gradual turning over of the war effort to the South Vietnamese while simultaneously reducing the number of American service personnel in Vietnam (which had reached 550,000 in 1968).

As Americans withdrew, the war became increasingly unpopular both in Vietnam and at home. Many servicemen felt that the war could not be won by South Vietnam and that American deaths had been in vain. Drug use grew among servicemen, as did acts of violence against officers. The invasion of Cambodia by American and South Vietnamese forces in 1970 led to demonstrations on college campuses throughout the country. At an antiwar protest at Kent State University in Ohio, four students were killed by National Guardsmen; at Jackson State College in Mississippi, police killed two students.

To move peace negotiations forward, President Nixon ordered renewed bombing of the North in April, 1972, and the mining of North Vietnamese harbors. On December 18, he ordered the bombing of Hanoi and Haiphong. Finally, a peace agreement was signed on January 27, 1973, providing for the cessation of hostilities, withdrawal of all foreign forces (but not the North Vietnamese) from South Vietnam, and the freeing of prisoners of war. The final United States troops left for home within the next sixty days, and close to six hundred American prisoners of war were released and flown home. Yet the war did not end.

A U.S. Marine waist deep in a muddy Vietnam river in 1966. (UPI/Corbis-Bettmann)

A U.S. soldier moves across a devastated Vietnamese hillside in 1971. (UPI/Corbis-Bettmann)

The End. The final North Vietnamese push began on March 11, 1975. Large numbers of South Vietnamese troops deserted, and hundreds of thousands of Vietnamese refugees fled the advancing armies. The United States began to evacuate remaining Americans and pro-American Vietnamese. As April passed, President Thieu withdrew his forces to the Saigon area for a last stand. He later resigned in a final attempt to achieve a cease-fire and flew to Taiwan.

The end came on April 30. Final evacuations were carried out from the roof of the U.S. Embassy, concluding shortly before 8:00 A.M. Two hours later, General Duong Van Minh, Thieu's successor, surrendered. Cambodia already had fallen to the communists; Laos would follow before the end of the year.

The Cost. More than fifty-eight thousand U.S. servicemen and women died in the war. More than 300,000 were wounded, about one-half of them seriously; approximately ten thousand lost at least one limb. In all, nearly 2.5 million people died, mainly Vietnamese, Cambodians, and Laotians.

In the United States, increasing numbers of Vietnam veterans suffered POST-TRAUMATIC STRESS DISORDER. Suicides, broken marriages, lost jobs, drug addiction, and alcoholism afflicted many. Veterans exposed to AGENT ORANGE, a defoliant used in Vietnam, reported such ailments as cancer, chloracne, and personality changes, as well as birth defects in their children.

Social and political divisions proved difficult to overcome. Supporters and opponents of the war differed as to whether the war was justified, whether it could have been won, and if not who was to blame—political and military leaders, antiwar activists, the media—or if other forces made the result inevitable, such as ignorance of Vietnamese history and culture, initial overconfidence, or limited objectives that delayed the final outcome so long that the United States lost the will to support the war. Many attempts have been made to heal the personal suffering and the divisions within society, ranging from construction of the VIETNAM WAR MEMORIAL in Washington, D.C., to journeys by veterans back to a more peaceful Vietnam.

—*Edward J. Rielly*

SUGGESTED READINGS: George Esper's *The Eyewitness History of the Vietnam War, 1961-1975* (New York: Ballantine Books, 1983) offers a chronological overview of the war, with eyewitness accounts and some of the war's most famous photographs. *Vietnam at War: The History, 1946-1975* (Novato, Calif.: Presidio Press, 1988), by Lieutenant General Phillip B. Davidson, is a comprehensive history from a military perspective. *The Vietnam War: Day by Day*, edited by John S. Bowman (New York: Mallard Books, 1989), is a chronicle of important military and domestic developments.

Another useful work, *Vietnam War Almanac* (New York: Facts on File Publications, 1985), by the military tactician and Vietnam War analyst Colonel Harry G. Summers, provides concise explanations of war topics arranged alphabetically. Summers, one of the last Americans to depart Vietnam on April 30, 1975, also authored *On Strategy: A Critical Analysis of the Vietnam War* (New York: Dell, 1984), which analyzes Vietnam War strategy and considers how to avoid repeating the mistakes made in that war. Myra MacPherson's *Long Time Passing: Vietnam and the Haunted Generation* (Garden City, N.Y.: Doubleday, 1984) examines postwar reactions, including post-traumatic stress disorder.

Vietnam War Memorial: Monument honoring the U.S. servicemen and women who died in the Vietnam War. The memorial, located on the Mall near the Lincoln Memorial in Washington, D.C., lists, etched on its surface, the names of the more than fifty-eight thousand U.S. casualties of the war.

The Vietnam War Memorial, commonly known as "The Wall," actually consists of two walls, each of polished black granite, that meet at a 125-degree angle. The names appear in the order in which the soldiers died, with the height of the memorial corresponding to the rate of deaths. The Wall thus begins virtually at ground level, rises to a height of 10.1 feet, and descends gradually to ground level again. Each wall contains seventy panels, and a nearby alphabetical directory of names identifies the panel on which a specific name is etched.

The individual most responsible for the creation of the memorial was Jan C. Scruggs, a Vietnam veteran who conceived the idea of the memorial and helped to raise about $7 million for the Vietnam Veterans Memorial Fund. A congressional bill set aside two acres for the memorial, and a competition to select a design was held in 1981. The winning entry was submitted by Maya Ying Lin, a twenty-one-year-old Yale University architecture student. Dedicated in 1982, the Wall immediately became a magnet for millions of visitors who came to find the names of loved ones, to honor those who sacrificed their lives in the war, to pay their

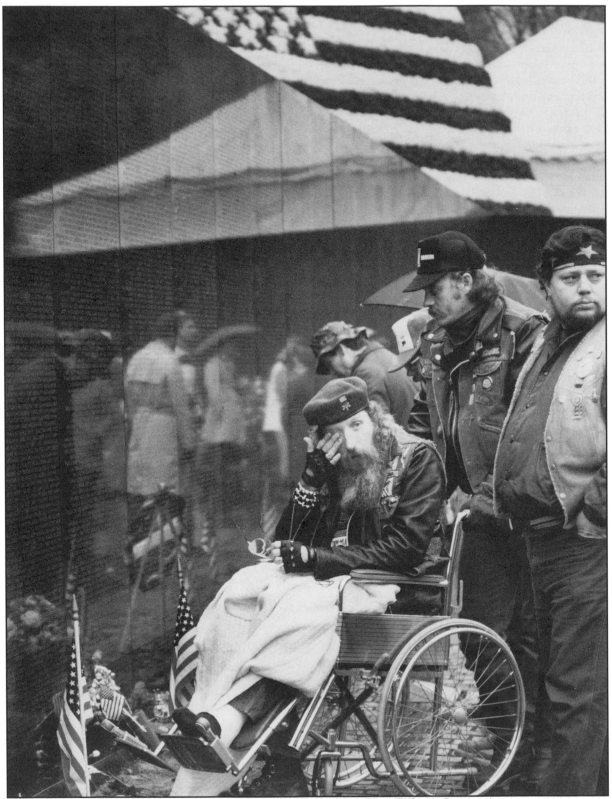

Veterans Day at the Vietnam War Memorial, 1986. (UPI/Corbis-Bettmann)

respect to colleagues in arms, and in many cases to continue their own healing.

The granite memorial is so highly polished that it reflects both the surrounding area and those who gaze at its roster of names, thus bringing visitors into a kind of communion with the men and women who died in Vietnam. Visitors often bring gifts to leave at the Wall: photographs, letters, flowers, articles of clothing, teddy bears, bibles—an almost endless variety of offerings.

Although initially controversial because of its resemblance to a large cemetery monument, the Wall quickly received widespread acceptance. Maya Lin accurately envisioned visiting the memorial as a journey. Walking its length, the visitor follows the progression of the Vietnam War in its most starkly human terms: the enormous cost in lives. The journey also encompasses the cultural heritage of the United States, for captured forever on the surface of the Wall is the ethnic variety of the country—a diversity united in sacrifice.

The Wall itself has been supplemented by three important additions: a flag; a statue of three infantrymen staring in the general direction of the Wall (designed by the architect Frederick E. Hart and dedicated in 1984); and a statue of three women in fatigues, one sitting on sandbags and cradling a wounded soldier (designed by Glenna Goodacre and dedicated in 1993, after a lengthy effort led by Diane Carlson Evans, to honor the women who served during the Vietnam War).

Vigilantism: Attempts by private citizens to take the law into their own hands in order to render punishment to suspected criminal offenders.

Vigilantism typically occurs when citizens do not believe that the criminal justice system is effectively punishing or deterring criminals. Vigilantism has historically been part of American society. In the Old West, prior to the advent of organized law-enforcement

Subway vigilante Bernhard Goetz rides a New York subway in 1987. (Impact Visuals, Bill Biggart)

agencies, citizens often acted on their own to enforce laws and punish offenders; mob violence often resulted in the LYNCHING of perceived troublemakers. The development of modern policing and criminal justice theoretically eliminated the need for vigilantism.

Vigilantism has continued to occur in the United States, but on a smaller scale. Seemingly lax sentences given to offenders, early releases from prison, and failures of law enforcement to apprehend criminals are a few of the causes of frustration that may incite vigilantism. A fear of being victimized or anger at being victimized in the past may also lead to vigilantism.

In recent decades, there have been a number of well-publicized cases of American vigilantism. The best-known case is perhaps that of Bernhard Goetz, a white man who in 1984 was approached by four African American teenagers on a New York City subway. Three of the youths were carrying sharpened screwdrivers, and Goetz testified that they had threatened him; in response, Goetz, who was armed with a handgun, shot the four teenagers. The case caused controversy debating the issue of self-defense versus vigilantism. The first grand jury to consider the Goetz case did not indict him. A second grand jury indicted Goetz, and he was tried and acquitted in 1987 of assault and attempted murder charges. Goetz was later given a one-year jail sentence on a weapons-related charge.

Although most states allow citizens to protect their lives and property to some extent, there are limitations on how people may protect themselves. Use of deadly force is rarely legal unless a person is acting in SELF-DEFENSE in the face of an immediate threat to the person's life. Debate often occurs over what constitutes an immediate threat. Should members of the general public be able to make such life-and-death judgments on their own? Defenders of liberalized self-defense laws argue that such leeway is essential to the protection of law-abiding citizens, while critics of liberalization claim that such policies simply encourage violence and work against the maintenance of public order.

Violence: Exertion of physical force so as to injure or abuse. In modern American society, an act of violence occurs every sixty seconds. Homicide is the leading cause of death among African American males between the ages of fifteen and twenty-four; child abuse is the leading cause of death for children under the age of five. A woman is battered every thirty seconds; a drive-by shooting or random homicide occurs every twenty-four hours. Every child in American society experiences one or more acts of violence before the age of sixteen; these acts include personal and property crimes such as fistfights, stabbings, shootings, verbal assaults, and rape. Such statistics have led many observers to comment that violence is fast becoming a way of life in American culture.

Etiology of Violence. Violence is certainly not new to American society. During the last decades of the twentieth century, however, the United States saw a clear increase in episodes of personal violence experienced by its citizens. An understanding of the formulation and pattern of human behavior is essential to understanding the basis for violence. The study of such factors as family relationships, social environment, race, culture, gender, and economics can provide insight into the origins of violence. Personality disorders related to impulsiveness, judgment, mood swings, and identity problems can also contribute to volatile behaviors in individuals. Environmental stressors such as family dysfunction, oppression, unemployability, and addiction disorders are other contributors to the culture of violence.

On-screen violence in television and film is often said to have reached epidemic proportions. The media's reaction clearly reflects societal fascination; violence sells, and critics charge that the wide dissemination of violent images through movies and television contributes to a broad desensitization to, and a consequent increase in, acts of violence. Critics have also pointed to songs and videos in such popular music genres as gangsta RAP and heavy metal as having contributed to this desensitization. Through the "glorification" and spread of violent images and lyrics, critics charge, individuals are taught that certain violent behaviors are acceptable and will be tolerated.

Analysts also note that society internalizes violent modes of dealing with conflict. Youths in abusive families tend to incorporate abusiveness in their own ways of coping; in much the same way, analysts claim, the broader culture of violence legitimizes and rationalizes the use of violence toward those who are perceived as weak or as threats. When nations use war to settle differences, or when law-enforcement agencies engage in approved acts of violence to control citizens, individuals learn to employ similar violent solutions and behaviors in dealing with their personal problems. According to many observers, society thus reinforces violent tendencies in individuals who are unable to accept limitations on their desires.

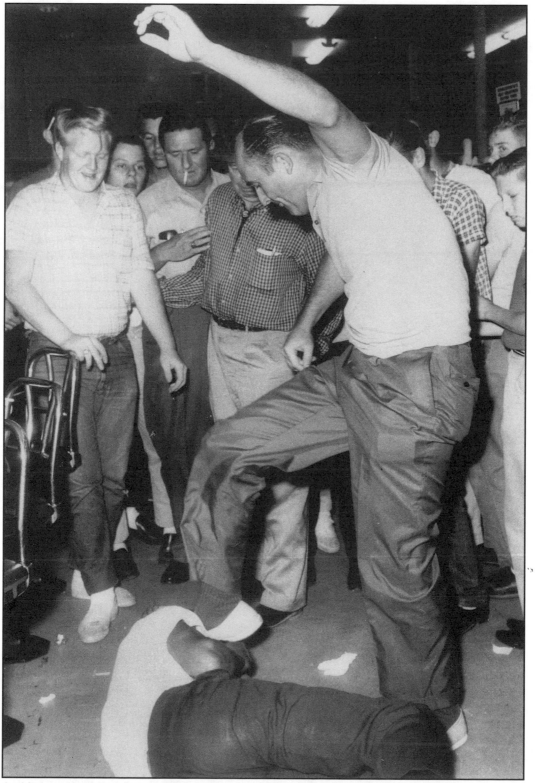

A white crowd watches as an ex-policeman beats a black civil rights protester in Jackson, Mississippi, in 1963. (UPI/Corbis-Bettmann)

Gang-related homicides, such as this New York City shooting, rose in the 1980's and 1990's. (AP/Wide World Photos)

Implications for Society. The link between personal violence and the culture of violence has important social implications. First, critics say, society must rethink policies and values that dictate violence. Antiviolence advocates call for cultural and political leaders to reexamine fundamental assumptions and policies and to revisit nonviolent philosophies and behaviors. For example, some antiviolence crusaders claim, leaders should reexamine the mixture of messages sent and apparent contradictions posed by legislators who call for a ban on assault weapons but who support the manufacture of nuclear bombs. Others challenge the condoning of corporal punishment of children in a society that allows many adult perpetrators of sex crimes to go undisciplined. Many mostly liberal advocates call for a cultural rediscovery and extension of the passionate nonviolent philosophies of the Indian leader Mohandas Gandhi and the civil rights crusader Martin Luther KING, Jr. Others, largely cultural conservatives,

have advocated restrictive measures such as the adoption of regulations on the content of films and recordings and tougher sentencing policies for violent criminal acts as the most appropriate and effective ways to combat the spread of violent tendencies.

Second, many antiviolence crusaders claim, lawmakers have a responsibility to reduce the extreme disparities in income and opportunity between the rich and the poor. Such factors as greed and separatism can help to breed violent behaviors. Hatred between and among ethnic, religious, and racial groups is heightened during periods of scarcity; violence in the United States rose significantly in the 1980's, an era of acquisitive capitalism. In his 1990 work *The Politics of Rich and Poor*, political analyst Kevin Phillips reported that violence in the United States grew to extreme proportions during this period, a time of overt scarcity for many members of the underclass but also a time when greed and insatiable need were blatantly encouraged. Phillips argues that this trend duplicated the behavior of American society during the 1930's, when a shattered economy and a growing population also threatened civil disorder.

The effects of capitalism on the family were memorably analyzed by psychoanalyst Erik Erikson in his 1950 book *Childhood and Society*; Erikson showed a correlation between child-rearing practices in the nuclear family and social attitudes toward the socioeconomic order. In *The True and Only Heaven* (1991), Charles Lasch argued that a society that values greed and devalues equality will support child-rearing practices that reinforce such behaviors in children's personalities. Such factors, these and other scholars have concluded, help to breed the conditions in which violent attitudes and behaviors flourish; children from these families grow up feeling entitled, and they often lack inclinations toward compromise, delayed need gratification, and self-understanding. As a consequence, their impatience with their surroundings often gives rise to confrontational behaviors. This attitude is further exhibited in a search for immediate satisfaction and in anger toward disparities. Many analysts thus conclude that a more equitable distribution of wealth and opportunity is a necessary first step in any effort to curtail the rivalries and violent behaviors caused by social scarcity.

Finally, antiviolence crusaders claim, society must work assertively to teach nonviolent conflict resolution methods such as mediation and interpersonal problem-solving. Ultimately, nonviolent conflict resolution becomes achievable when individuals learn to respect others as separate human beings of equal value who are entitled to equal rights and opportunities regardless of their race, religious beliefs, or social standing. Nonviolence advocates call on lawmakers, cultural leaders, and social systems to play a major role in developing and disseminating such attitudes.

—Narviar Cathcart Barker

SUGGESTED READINGS: The struggle of children to survive the effects of violence is explored in Maria Roy's *Children in the Crossfire: Violence in the Home—How Does It Affect Our Children?* (Deerfield Beach, Fla.: Health Communications, 1988). In *Changing Channels: Living (Sensibly) with Television* (Reading, Mass.: Addison-Wesley, 1983), Peggy Charren and Martin Sandler discuss television viewing and the effects of televised violence. John Monahan examines individual factors leading to violence in *Predicting Violent Behavior: An Assessment of Clinical Techniques* (Beverly Hills, Calif.: Sage, 1981). For information on how to deal with stress and how to cope more effectively with day-to-day pressures, important factors in reducing personal violent tendencies, see Edward Charlesworth and Ronald Nathan's *Stress Management: A Comprehensive Guide to Wellness* (Houston: Biobehavioral Press, 1981).

Violence Against Women Act (1994): Part of Title IV of the VIOLENT CRIME CONTROL AND LAW ENFORCEMENT ACT of 1994. The Violence Against Women Act provides for severe penalties for violent crimes against women. The act provides that such crimes are violations of civil rights and that victims can seek damages on civil rights grounds. The potency of the act and the breadth of its implication has caused considerable controversy, with some experts believing that the allowability of damages for violence will clog the courts and perhaps cause many false accusations. Others counter that the greater deterrence effect will reduce violence and will give victims avenues of compensation formerly denied them.

Violence in schools: Any intentional actions taken while on school property to physically harm or threaten people are defined as school violence. Violence on the grounds of school-sponsored events such as athletic contests and field trips are also considered instances of school violence. This issue is a major dimension in citizen concerns over public education. School violence undermines the level of educational achievement by students; it detracts from student concentration and interest in learning; it produces fear; and it causes physical and emotional damage to thousands of students, teachers, and school administrators each year. Efforts by boards of education to protect persons in schools and expensive school property add hundreds of millions of dollars each year to the cost of financing public schools.

Types of School Violence. Several types of school violence occur with greater frequency than do others. Physical assault, threats of violence, and robbery are the most frequently reported types of violence in schools, but more serious crimes also occur. Sexual harassment sometimes takes the form of stalking victims, attempted rape, RAPE, or beating of victims. Beatings that are not sexually motivated also occur, as do armed robberies and even homicides. Threats of vio-

President Bill Clinton addresses a 1995 meeting on school violence. (AP/Wide World Photos)

lence often endanger students when other students bring guns, knives, or other weapons into schools or when explosive devices such as pipe bombs are brought to schools.

Extent of Violence. To understand how many incidents of violence occur in schools, it is necessary to rely upon social science research, because official crime statistical surveys such as the Uniform Crime Reports (UCR) and National Crime Victimization Survey do not categorize crimes with respect to school settings. Scholars in the United States and Canada began researching school violence in the 1970's and continue to do so. A report titled *Challenge for the Third Century: Education in a Safe Environment* (1977), prepared by the U.S. Senate Subcommittee on Delinquency, helped to focus public attention on school violence. The findings indicated that more than one hundred homicides, nine thousand rapes, and twelve

thousand armed robberies occurred in U.S. schools in 1976. Although students spend approximately 25 percent of their time in school settings, more than 36 percent of reported assaults committed by school-age offenders and 40 percent of reported robberies occurred in school settings. The highest rates of student victimization were found to occur among students ages twelve to fifteen.

In a 1977 report prepared for the Law Enforcement Assistance Administration, Michael McDermott and Michael Hindelang surveyed victimization reports in twenty-eight cities. They found more than 3,760 victimizations in one year in those cities, but this total included thefts at school in addition to violent incidents. Teachers and school administrators were victims in approximately 8 percent of all reported incidents. Assaults and aggravated assault were the most common violent crimes reported in schools; few rob-

A fifteen-year-old is arrested on charges of shooting and killing two classmates at a New York City high school. (AP/Wide World Photos)

beries and rapes were detected in this study.

A 1991 survey conducted by the Bureau of Justice Statistics reported that approximately 400,000 violent victimizations occurred in one school year. A survey of high-school seniors found that of 2,770 seniors in the class of 1993, 3.8 percent of them self-reported incidents of victimization.

Many researchers have found violent school crime to be much higher in large urban schools, particularly those located in economically deteriorating neighborhoods. School staff in California reportedly confiscated 8,539 weapons at public schools in 1988, including 4,408 knives, 2,216 explosives, 1,126 objects that were used or could be used as weapons, and 789 handguns.

Violence in the media: Highly emotional debate centers on the effects that representations of VIOLENCE have on individuals as well as on the culture at large. Many investigations have attempted to prove a direct link between media violence and criminal behavior. The results remain inconclusive.

History. Since before the bloody gladiatorial pageants held in ancient Rome, violence has been central to Western popular culture. "The media," however, typically refers to modern forms of popular culture: print journalism, radio, film, and television. All these forms, or media, have had some degree of violent content at different times in their history. Nineteenth century American newspapers, for example, were filled with sordid accounts of murders, rapes, and executions. The earliest significant American dramatic film, Edwin S. Porter's *The Great Train Robbery* (1903), concerns a violent holdup and its consequences and concludes with a scene in which a character points a gun directly at the camera. In *Gunfighter Nation* (1992), Richard Slotkin argues that the bread and butter of the Hollywood film industry is violence. Slotkin claims that a myth of "regeneration through violence" is inscribed in many of the most famous Hollywood films, from the gangster movies of the 1920's and 1930's such as Howard S. Hawks's *Scarface* (1932) to the Vietnam films of the 1980's such as Sylvester Stallone's *Rambo* series. Many television shows, he also argues—in particular Westerns such as *Gunsmoke* and police shows such as *Miami Vice*—use the same myth. Finally, many pop and rock songs are alleged to have violent, misogynistic, and even Satanic messages. Groups and singers that have been the objects of widely publicized attacks include the rap group 2 Live

Crew, the heavy metal group Guns N' Roses, and the rap singer Ice-T for his song "Cop Killer."

As early as 1908, journal articles appeared criticizing the adverse effects of violence in the media. Such commentary, however, was quite rare in the first half of the twentieth century. In the 1950's, with the rise of television, public concern over media violence greatly intensified. Because of the frequency with which it depicted (and continues to depict) violence and because of its widespread availability, television was viewed as a potential menace to society. A member of the Federal Communications Commission (FCC) spoke for many when he decried the fact that television was pouring an "unending stream of crime, violence, outright murder, brutality, and horror into the living rooms of America." As American society became more violent in the late 1960's and early 1970's, American television (and cinema) became yet more violent, and debates about the causal relationship between media violence and real violence intensified. As neither real nor represented violence diminished, these debates remain intense.

Since the early 1950's, social scientists have spent many years and millions of dollars conducting more than one thousand published studies attempting to demonstrate the harmful effects of violence in the media. In fact, the possible link between television violence and aggressive behavior is the single most-researched aspect of television. Yet scientific opinion remains divided on the reality of this link.

Arguments for Restricting Media Violence. Research on media violence has most often focused on the relationship between TELEVISION AND CHILDREN. One report estimated that the average American child watches eight thousand murders on television by the end of elementary school. After conducting extensive research, a number of psychologists have come to believe that a child who is exposed to a large amount of violent television is more likely to become desensitized to violence. These experts believe that such children are more likely to engage in aggressive or even criminally violent behavior and that this tendency will continue even after the children become adults. Psychologist Leonard Eron of the University of Chicago, who has researched the problem for decades, states that the link is as strong as that between lung cancer and cigarettes. One long-term study measured the amount of violence that eight-year-old boys viewed and then measured their level of aggressive behavior at age nineteen and again at age thirty. The researchers

Illinois senator Paul Simon discusses television violence as a group of network executives look on. (Reuters/Corbis-Bettmann)

found a link between the viewing of violence and aggression that persisted well into adulthood. Some experts see Saturday-morning cartoons as among the worst offenders. These concerns have led some preschools to ban toys and lunch boxes featuring characters from the *Mighty Morphin Power Rangers* television show, which some believe encourages aggressive behavior in youngsters.

Arguments Against Restricting Media Violence. Other experts argue that there is no conclusive proof of the harmful effects of media violence. They say the fact that children view many acts of violence on television is not enough, on its own, to prove that television violence affects behavior in any important way. Instead, for example, children may learn that "bad guys" who commit violence on television are usually punished. (Indeed, many experts argue that television asserts that "bad guys" should be violently punished.)

These experts say that much of the research on the topic is based on laboratory experiments that are a poor imitation of the real world. Other findings may be explained by the fact that more aggressive children tend to seek out more violent television shows to watch rather than by the fact that such television causes children to be aggressive. Skeptical social scientists suggest that others have promoted the idea of a television-aggression link to further their careers or for political reasons. In a 1994 protest of the federal government's attempts to restrict television violence, actor Michael Moriarty quit his role on the popular television series *Law and Order*. Moriarty said that government interference was a violation of the constitutional right to free speech and that parents should be the ones to judge what was appropriate viewing for their children.

Media Violence and Fear of Crime. Instead of looking at whether or not television violence causes aggression, some researchers have taken a different approach: Does violent crime shown in the media lead to an increased fear of crime by the public? Initial research seemed to show such a link; however, a number of follow-up studies did not support these early findings. Other researchers argued instead that the link was explained by people's personalities: Certain people feel that what happens to them is out of their control. In general, these people tend to watch a lot of television and to be afraid of crime. On a related note, many experts have argued that people who complain about their fears of media violence are often articulating deep-seated fears about the role of popular culture as a whole in potentially undermining the morality of society.

Ongoing Controversies. Regardless of scientific disagreement about whether or not violence in the media is harmful, a majority of the public still seems concerned about the issue. For example, a 1993 Times-Mirror poll surveyed 1,516 Americans and found that 72 percent believed that there was too much violence in entertainment television. The issue of television violence has resurfaced periodically; after her eleven-year-old sister was raped and strangled to death, a fourteen-year-old girl from Québec collected 1.3 million signatures for a 1992 petition to the Canadian government asking for new laws to curb television violence. While the resourceful teenager garnered much media attention for the issue, there was no direct evidence that television had played a role in the unsolved killing.

Violence in the media is also a hotly debated political issue, one that is often linked to the issues of PORNOGRAPHY and violence against women. Conservatives often single out violence in the media as emblematic of a general cultural decline. In May, 1995, for example, Republican Senate Majority Leader Robert Dole lashed out against the immorality of violent films such as Quentin Tarantino's *Pulp Fiction* (1995), claiming that they undermined family values. Curiously, however, Dole endorsed James Cameron's spectacularly violent Arnold Schwarznegger vehicle *True Lies* (1995) as embodying those values.

—Aaron Doyle and Kegan Doyle

SUGGESTED READINGS: Richard Slotkin's massive *Gunfighter Nation* (New York: Atheneum, 1992) is an excellent account of the myths of violence in American popular culture of the twentieth century. Ray Surette's *Media, Crime, and Criminal Justice: Images and Realities* (Pacific Grove: Brooks/Cole, 1992) provides a measured account of the research done on the relationship between violence in the media and crime. Guy Cumberbatch and Dennis Howitt's *A Measure of Uncertainty: The Effects of the Mass Media* (London: John Libbey, 1989) provides a strong scientific critique of various research approaches to violence in the media. For a more challenging theoretical account of the relationship between media violence and crime, see Richard Sparks's *Television and the Drama of Crime: Moral Tales and the Place of Crime in Public Life* (Buckingham, England: Open University Press, 1992).

Violent Crime Control and Law Enforcement Act

Violent Crime Control and Law Enforcement Act (1994): U.S. legislation that authorized $30.2 billion for crime prevention and sanctions. In response to concerns about violent crime widely expressed by American voters, President Bill CLINTON proposed a series of initiatives in August, 1993. The president's package included funds to hire 100,000 additional police officers, an expanded list of federal death-penalty crimes, reform of the appeals process available to death-row inmates, a ban on assault weapons, and a waiting period for handgun purchases. In November, 1993, the Senate passed an omnibus crime bill that contained most of the president's program, while the House of Representative approved a series of separate bills that contained similar provisions. The two houses reconciled their legislation in a conference report that passed the House on August 21, 1994, and the Senate four days later. The final law, a carefully crafted compromise, was almost defeated at the last minute by anti-gun-control forces that opposed the assault-weapons ban.

The provision prohibiting the manufacture, transfer, and possession of nineteen types of military-style assault weapons attracted some of the bill's most vocal opposition from the National Rifle Association (NRA) and its supporters in Congress. Protests about infringements on the right to bear arms, however, were outbalanced by reports that semiautomatic weapons were the weapons of choice of drug traffickers and by the support of law-enforcement agencies for the prohibition.

In the area of crime prevention and control, a major initiative involved $13.5 billion for state and local governments to hire more police officers and to encourage COMMUNITY POLICING—the positive and visible presence of police on the beat in neighborhoods. Republicans, in particular, criticized the bill's authorization of funding for recreational and academic programs in high-crime areas. Proponents argued that su-

ESTIMATED VIOLENT VICTIMIZATIONS PER 1,000 U.S. CITIZENS, 1979-1992

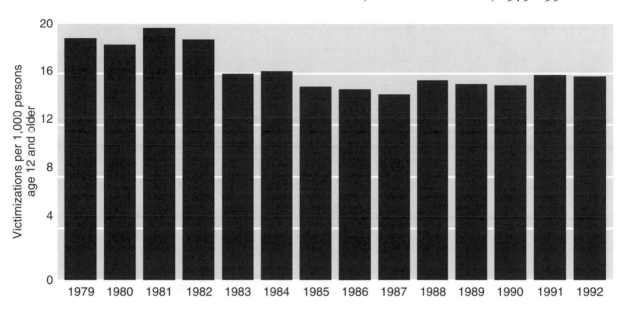

Source: U.S. Department of Justice, Bureau of Justice Statistics, *Sourcebook of Criminal Justice Statistics—1993*. Washington, D.C.: U.S. Government Printing Office, 1994.

Note: Data are from National Crime Victimization Survey and represent victim's reports of violent crime. "Serious violent crimes" include rape, robbery, and aggravated assault.

pervised sports, such as midnight basketball, would offer alternatives to crime and gang activities; critics called the programs "PORK."

The political appeal of a tough approach to crime was apparent in the extension of the death penalty to more than fifty new crimes and in the bill's provision of $9.7 billion for the construction of regional prisons, with incentives for states to implement longer sentences. The act also included a "THREE-STRIKES" component that required life imprisonment for a person convicted on two previous occasions of two serious violent felonies or one serious violent felony and a serious drug offense. To address the potential prison overcrowding that would result from additional life sentences, the bill encouraged state and local governments to explore alternative sentencing such as boot camps, work programs, restitution programs, and weekend incarceration, particularly for young nonviolent offenders.

The Violent Crime Control and Law Enforcement Act also established drug courts to divert offenders into treatment. The VIOLENCE AGAINST WOMEN section of the statute supported RAPE education and pre-vention programs, encouraged the arrest of domestic violence offenders, and funded police, prosecutors, and victims' advocates to address crimes against women.

The final legislation eliminated a proposed section known as the Racial Justice Act, which would have allowed courts to consider statistical evidence of racial discrimination in death sentences. Opposition to the act came from both conservatives who wanted more mandatory sentencing and less "social welfare" and from liberals who objected to the expanded federal death penalty and to the act's emphasis on prison rather than on prevention.

Virginity: Condition of never having engaged in sexual intercourse. The term is applicable to persons of either gender. Virginity is regarded differently by various cultures. In some cultures, the practice of female CIRCUMCISION has been employed to ensure that a woman is a virgin at marriage. The presence of an intact hymen in a woman does not guarantee virginity, however; conversely, the absence of a hymen does not mean that a woman is sexually experienced, as the

Virtual reality

hymen may be broken during exercise or a medical procedure. In contemporary North American society, virginity is typically regarded as being of minimal importance, although ABSTINENCE from sexual intercourse until after marriage is becoming more common as a result of fears about AIDS and other SEXUALLY TRANSMITTED DISEASES.

Virtual reality (VR): Computer-generated artificial worlds that people can enter and control. The technology has potentially revolutionary applications in the military, industry, scientific research, medicine, communications, and entertainment.

VR requires three basic parts. First, it needs a computer or computer network with a large memory and rapid information processor. Second, a software program that holds the details of the artificial world is required. These details include the graphics to create visual action, sounds, and touch; some programs also try to add artificial smells. The third requirement is special interface equipment that covers all or part of the body, connecting the user to the computer and software. The equipment includes gloves for the hands and helmets or goggles with small twin video screens that cover the eyes. Sometimes, a user puts on an entire body suit as well as the gloves. This equipment replaces the keyboard and monitor of a standard computer.

Once a user has donned the interface equipment, the computer creates a visual scene in the eyepieces and sounds in earphones. As the scenery moves, the user has the illusion of being inside the movement, part of the scene. Running through the glove, suit, and helmet are sensors that detect the user's body and head movements. When the user moves, the sensors tell the computer, and it adjusts the scenery to match the move-

A visitor to a virtual reality exhibition uses the technology to "paint" within the software environment. (Archive Photos, Reuters, Jonathan Drake)

ment. If, for example, the user's head turns to the right, the computer changes the scene to show details to the right of the user's viewpoint in the computer images. Furthermore, if something in the computer scenery comes close to the user, impulses may be felt that the computer sends through the sensors in the suit or helmet. A virtual cat may rub against the user's leg, or the texture of bark on a virtual tree may be experienced.

As of the mid-1990's, the images in VR look more like cartoons than life, but as computer power improves and programming becomes more sophisticated, virtual images will come to copy real appearances more faithfully. Potential applications seem endless, with many practical applications already in use. Flight simulators allow pilots and astronauts to practice skills on virtual planes and spacecraft. Surgeons can practice on virtual patients. Scientists can explore normally invisible structures, such as atoms and molecules, with virtual models. People can meet and talk in virtual rooms, each looking at the virtual image of the other. Shoppers can roam a virtual mall and order items that they see there and have them sent directly to them. Architects can inspect the design for new buildings by walking through virtual models of them. Eventually a virtual community may come to exist, where people meet only in "CYBERSPACE," the simulated reality of a communal computer program.

Furthermore, electronic hookups can link people in VR to robots. The user can see through the robot's eyes and can control the robot from a distance by moving his or her hands and arms. Known as telerobotics, the technology allows people to handle dangerous and heavy materials or work in dangerous environments, such as outer space.

Virtue: Moral excellence of character informed by principles of what is right and good. Principles of moral excellence have been expounded and taught for thousands of years, from the Greece of Socrates to the China of Confucius. Articulated lists of these virtues have been influential in defining what is a good person, a good citizen, and a good society. Against a background in which 76 percent of adult Americans in the mid-1990's believed that "the United States is in moral and spiritual decline" (*Newsweek*, June 13, 1994), the success of William Bennett's best-selling *The Book of Virtues* (1993) has demonstrated a resurgence in concern over what virtue is and why it is important.

Identifying Virtue. Matters of morality consist of actions and character based upon generally agreed upon standards of goodness and rightness. It is a hotly debated matter of opinion regarding what those standards are or should be. Moral absolutists contend that there are ideal standards of morality that are cross-cultural and cross-generational. Conversely, moral relativists argue that there are no ideal standards of morality, only matters of personal taste and preferences. These moral preferences, called values, differ from person to person and are largely a matter of personal choice. In contrast, moral absolutists advocate virtues, the morally right choice based on universal principles that transcend individual beliefs. While there is a continuum of thinking on morality between positions of extreme absolutism and extreme relativism, those who emphasize values or virtues in their moral beliefs reflect a tendency toward relativism or absolutism, respectively, in the foundations of their moral thinking.

Virtue is also to be distinguished from vice, morally wrong behavior and character. Vice is thinking and behavior that leads a person away from life promotion, goodness, and perfection of the inner nature. In contrast, virtuous thinking and action lead a person toward life promotion, goodness, and perfection of the human nature. People's choices toward vice or virtue inevitably affect the moral natures of their characters by establishing habits of wrong or good choices. Similarly, societal welfare is determined by the good and bad choices its members choose to engage in. To the proponents of virtue, it is a societal necessity, therefore, that the good choices—the virtues—are identified and taught to the members of that society.

Virtues Across Cultures. Contemporary conceptions of virtue have their birth in ancient writings and have been shaped by different cultural emphases. Different societies stress disparate virtues. One of the problems for modern advocates of virtue is to determine which set of virtues to emphasize. A close inspection of most modern lists of virtues, however, will likely reveal a strong resemblance to four ancient lists of virtues: the teachings of Confucius and Buddha (Siddhartha Gautama) from the Eastern regions of the world, and the principles derived from the ancient Teutons and Greeks (with important additions by St. Augustine) in the Western world.

The Chinese philosopher Confucius, living in the sixth century B.C., taught that there were five primary virtues: charity, righteousness, propriety, wisdom, and sincerity. All of the Confucian virtues are described in great detail in his *Confucian Analects*. Buddha, who lived in India in the sixth century B.C., taught moral principles in works such as the *Eightfold Path* and the *Dhammapada*. Buddhists believe that there are six virtues, or paramitas, that lead to the perfection of character: courage, knowledge, love, meditation, morality (just dealings), and patience.

Conceptions of virtue in Western ideals have been greatly influenced by the Teutonic (inhabitants of Northern Europe) virtues described by the Roman historian Tacitus of the first and second centuries A.D. According to Tacitus in his book *Germania*, the Teutons believed that there were eight signs of the virtuous character: endurance, courage, generosity, hospitality, loyalty, marital purity (abstinence from adultery), modesty, and truthfulness.

Socrates, according to Plato, contends that the ideal state would teach its citizens principles of virtuous character. Socrates believed that nobility of character could be summed up in four qualities: courage, justice, wisdom, and temperance. These qualities are referred to today as the cardinal virtues (from the Latin word cardo, meaning hinge) because all other virtues are seen to be dependent on them. Courage is an inner strength and determination in facing adversity, danger, and fear. Justice is concerned with the qualities of fairness, honesty, rightfulness, and truthfulness in human affairs. Wisdom is the perceptive, discreet, and skillful use of knowledge. The essence of temperance is self-control in finding a balance between the extreme of an excessive or deficient style of life.

St. Augustine (A.D. 354-430) is responsible for integrating the three theological virtues—faith, hope, and love—emphasized in the New Testament (Romans 5:1-5, I Corinthians 13, I Peter 1:21, 22) with the cardinal virtues. Faith is trust and is manifested in a belief in and reliance on others and a transcending belief in and adherence to God's truth. Hope is a forward-looking virtue, a patient waiting for desires to be actualized. The final virtue, love, is a transcending devotion to what is best for someone. Collectively, the four cardinal virtues and the three theological virtues are often referred to as the seven ancient virtues. These seven virtues, with the addition of humility, remain today the criteria by which Catholic sainthood candidates are judged.

The Virtues Synthesized. Detractors of those who would want to promote the message of virtue could easily argue that it would be a sign of cultural bias to emphasize one of these four lists of virtues over the others. Conversely, to try to embrace all four lists of virtues and accommodate other additions would seem to lead to an unwieldy conglomeration of principles. A lengthy list of moral principles loses its impact: Would the "one hundred commandments" carry as much weight as the Ten Commandments? A possible solution to this dilemma is found in comparing the four lists of virtues to one anther.

A number of contemporary, influential moral philosophers, such as Alasdair MacIntyre of the University of Notre Dame and James Q. Wilson of University of California, Los Angeles, have emphasized the seven ancient virtues, or at least the cardinal virtues, in their writings. The strength of the seven ancient virtues is how well other lists of virtues can be reconciled with them. This is particularly demonstrated in comparing the Confucist, Buddhist, and Teutonic lists to the seven ancient virtues. The only virtue of the three prior lists that does not fit in well with the seven ancient virtues is meditation, which may be understood as more of a practice than a character trait. The seven ancient virtues, therefore, provide the modern person with a list that is succinct and has cross-cultural applicability.

Teaching Virtue. Confucius, in *The Great Learning* provided guidance for the teaching of personal and governmental virtue. Conversely, Aristotle, in the *Nichomachean Ethics* indicated that virtues were best acquired through practice, not direct teaching. How to best communicate virtue is a crucial issue for modern proponents of virtue. If what William Bennett, Stephen Carter, Colin Powell, and other contemporary speakers on character have to say is nothing more than talk and has no lasting effect on people's lives, then virtue promotion is destined to be more a societal fad rather than leading to deep changes in the societal fabric.

The 1990's have witnessed efforts to address this communication issue that would have been approved of by both Confucius and Aristotle. At the governmental level, former Vice President Dan Quayle's often-derided campaign for "family values" in the early 1990's can be credited with igniting serious political debate about the role of government and societal institutions in promoting or hindering character development. Many Democrats, such as Hillary Rodham Clinton, and Republicans, such as William Bennett, are strongly in favor of increasing the teaching of character goodness and rightfulness through the power of the government, such as in public schools. At a more personal level, the Aristotelian side of learning virtuous living from the practice of it is greatly dependent upon the availability of virtuous role models to imitate. Where such role models are lacking, stories about virtuous people, such as in Bennett's *The Book of Virtues* (1993) and *The Children's Book of Virtues* (1995) are useful.

Elements of the contemporary virtue movement can be found at many different societal levels, from President Bill Clinton's "politics of meaning" to the Christian Promise Keepers meetings. As an increasing diversity of people concern themselves with the teaching and practice of virtue, there is an increasing reason for believing on the part of the advocates of virtue that the movement of the 1990's will become the societal norm of the next century.   —*Paul J. Chara, Jr.*

SUGGESTED READINGS: The cardinal virtues are first considered to be the standard virtues of the ancient world with the publication of Plato's *Republic*, which can be found in *Five Great Dialogues*, translated and edited by B. Jowett (Roslyn, N.Y.: Walter J. Black, 1969). The most widely read American moral philosophy book of the 1980's, Alasdair MacIntyre's *After Virtue* (Notre Dame, Ind.: University of Notre Dame Press, 1982) discusses the societal impact of virtue. William J. Bennett's *The Book of Virtues* (New York: Simon & Schuster, 1993) and *The Children's Book of*

Virtues (New York: Simon & Schuster, 1995) present stories on virtue for adults and children.

Visas: Government-issued documents. A visa represents official permission, usually signified by a stamp inside a passport, to enter a country. Except for emergency or casual tourist visits to certain localities, travelers must submit passports issued by their country of citizenship to the embassy or consulate of another country before traveling there. Visas are used to regulate cross-border traffic, discourage illegal immigration, and control population growth and also as political instruments reflecting current international relationships.

Vivisection: Invasive research or educational experimentation on living animals. The term is commonly used in a broader sense to include dissection of preserved specimens. In England, antivivisection movements have opposed medical research and school experimentation on animals since the mid-nineteenth century. In the United States, antivivisection forces received little attention until the rise of the ANIMAL

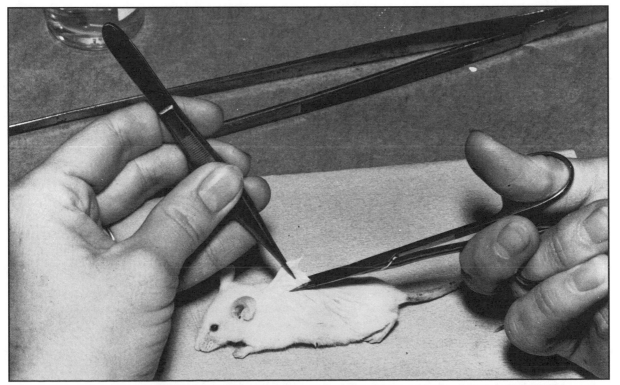

Vivisection of laboratory animals is opposed by many animal rights activists. (UPI/Corbis Bettmann)

RIGHTS movement. Antivivisectionists contend that cell cultures and computer modeling can replace most or all of the need for animal experimentation. In contrast, most of the medical and educational communities contend that the complexity, genuine interactions, and test truthfulness of real labwork are beyond such simulation and that animal experimentation is a necessary part of much scientific and medical research.

Voice of America (VOA): U.S. broadcasting organization created in 1942. A part of the United States Information Agency, the VOA provides news and other information to world listeners. The VOA grew significantly after 1945, as the United States sought to counter communist ideology and the Soviet Union's influence during the Cold War years. Advanced satellite technology has greatly expanded the range and variety of VOA broadcasts. As the Cold War ended and as large federal deficits led to review of various government agencies and programs, however, questions were raised about the justification for the VOA and level of its congressional funding.

Volunteerism: Private, unpaid efforts to respond to societal needs and concerns. Surveys indicate that approximately 80 million Americans engage in some form of volunteer activities, and it has been estimated that volunteer efforts provide the nations's economy with more than $150 billion in annual assistance, services, and resources. Efforts to reduce government budget deficits have heightened interest in volunteer programs as possible means of reducing spending without compromising social services; critics of such proposals, however, allege that most volunteer programs are incapable of fully replacing government services and that such efforts to shift social burdens to the private sector are irresponsible.

Volunteers in Service to America (VISTA): U.S. agency created in 1964 by Congress as a domestic counterpart to the PEACE CORPS. VISTA is administered by ACTION, an independent government agency that oversees volunteer programs within the United States. VISTA volunteers, who must be at least eighteen years of age, are given year-long assignments to work in rural or urban communities in the United States, Puerto Rico, Guam, and the Virgin Islands. In return for a subsistence allowance and health insurance, volunteers live and work among the poor, sharing skills in an effort to combat illiteracy, drug abuse, poverty, and homelessness. Volunteers receive stipends upon completion of service.

Voter apathy: Lack of interest in political issues, often reflected in low voting turnouts. Since the 1960 presidential election, U.S. voter turnout has consistently declined.

History. Although campaigns dominate television and other media for months, nearly half of all eligible voters have failed to vote in recent U.S. presidential elections. The decline in turnout is especially notable because, following legislative changes since 1960, turnout should have increased; instead, it has fallen more than 10 percent. The VOTING RIGHTS ACT of 1965 added large numbers of African Americans to the pool of registered voters. Women have also increased their voting levels to the point where, in recent elections, turnout among women has exceeded that of men. Finally, the U.S. electorate has grown richer and more educated since the 1960's; as wealth and education are related to voting, there should have been an increase, instead of a decrease in voting.

Discussion. A simple explanation for low turnout is that people are simply lazy. A 1980 Gallup Poll revealed that approximately 32 percent of the respondents who did not vote did not either because they did not like the candidates, were not interested in politics, or had no particular reasons. Some people believe that it makes no difference who wins elections, believing that there is no real choice between candidates or parties. They believe that winning candidates and parties fail to carry out their promises and that the same people run the government, no matter who wins.

Other nonvoters claim that the political leaders do not appeal to them. Some of the reasons elections are characterized as unappealing or uninteresting are that the candidates do not offer real choices, are not exciting, or avoid taking positions on the most important issues.

There are, however, institutional and political reasons for lower voter turnout. The 1977 expansion of the U.S. electorate with the Twenty-sixth Amendment diluted the pool of voters with a group of eighteen to twenty-year-old nonvoters. Younger persons have always voted in lower proportions than older citizens. With this addition of some thirty-five million potential

PERCENTAGE OF VOTING-AGE POPULATION VOTING IN U.S. ELECTIONS, 1962-1994

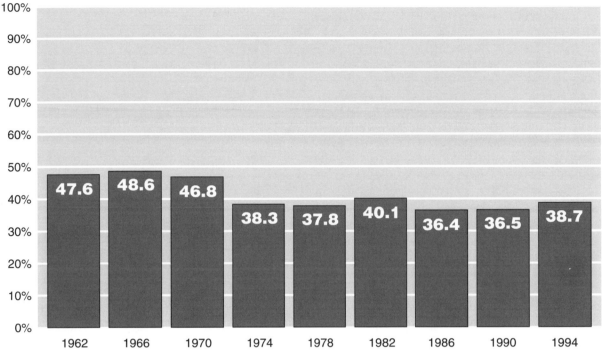

Source: Committee for the Study of the American Electorate.

new voters from less active groups, the total rate of participation was almost certain to decline.

In addition, the Federal Elections Campaign Act of 1971 provided for federal funding of presidential elections, causing candidates to rely less on political party support. The 1971 legislation provided that presidential candidates from the two major political parties might receive federal matching funds. Depending less on the political parties for funding may have caused party workers to be less enthusiastic and to work less hard for their party's candidate.

Voting registration is also often cited as a factor contributing to low voter turnout. The registration process places a responsibility on voters to take an extra step some days or weeks before the election; the process typically involves filling out a form at a county courthouse or with a roving registrar. Other registration-related restrictions, such as the purging of nonvoters' names from registration rolls, also act to reduce voting turnout.

The 1993 National Voter Registration Act, popularly known as the "MOTOR VOTER LAW," allows people to register to vote while applying for a driving license. Despite criticism that the law would lead to registration fraud, within two years, five million eligible voters had been added to the rolls. Supporters of the law hoped that the new registrants would vote in ensuing elections.

Voting Accessibility for the Elderly and Handicapped Act (1984): Law signed by President Ronald Reagan on September 28, 1984, that required states to make all federal polling places accessible to handicapped and elderly voters. States without mail or door-to-door voter registration were also required to provide accessible registration sites. The law was originally to remain in force for ten years and was then to terminate unless Congress voted to retain it.

Voting rights: The right to vote is fundamental to a democratic society. While today these rights are protected for most Americans, this has not always been the case, and the vestiges of past discriminatory voting laws continue to have impact.

History. From Colonial times, voting rights policy was not universal throughout the United States. States independently determined who had the right to vote. Generally, this right was limited to white male landowners, obviously barring political participation for many citizens, including women, blacks, and other ethnic minorities. In a few rare instances, women and blacks had franchise rights in some states. As the states developed, voting rights were generally liberalized to include non-landowners, but states were careful to insert the words "white male" into any new statute. From the early 1800's until the Civil War, all states, with the exception of Maine, restricted the right to vote to whites. By the mid-1800's, even the small percentage of blacks and women who had managed to enjoy franchise rights in the early years of the United States' political development became disfranchised by statutes imposed in the various states.

Women's Vote. The woman SUFFRAGE MOVEMENT, a movement to procure voting rights for women, came on the tail of the abolitionist movement in the late 1800's. Elizabeth Cady Stanton and Susan B. Anthony were well-known leaders of this movement. In June, 1919, after many years of protests and agitation, the Nineteenth Amendment to the Constitution allowing all women the right to vote was passed by Congress. The amendment was finally ratified by the required number of states on August 26, 1920. Many women did not take advantage of this hard-won victory, however. It was not until the 1940's, around the time of World War II, that women began to vote in greater numbers. Women's participation in the electoral process slowly increased, and by 1984 the voter turnout for all women at the presidential election was higher than that of men for the first time in history. African American women have been voting at higher rates than their male counterparts since the 1970's. In fact, since 1984, black women have voted in numbers proportionate to white men and are among the most likely to vote.

Other Minorities. Other minorities have been excluded from voting participation in our country throughout history. It was not until the Indian Citizenship Act of 1924 that Native Americans were considered American citizens by birthright. Citizenship did not ensure franchise rights, however, and states cited various grounds for denying Native Americans the right to vote.

MAJOR EXPANSIONS OF U.S. VOTING RIGHTS

Date	Action	Significance
1870	Fifteenth Amendment	Guaranteed the vote to African Americans.
1920	Nineteenth Amendment	Guaranteed the vote to women.
1961	Twenty-third Amendment	Gave District of Columbia residents right to vote in presidential elections.
1964	Twenty-fourth Amendment	Prohibited use of poll taxes or other taxes to restrict voting rights.
1965	Voting Rights Act	Banned voting tests in the South and some other areas.
1970	Voting Rights Act	Suspended literacy tests for voting.
1971	Twenty-sixth Amendment	Extended vote to eighteen-year-olds.
1972	*Dunn v. Blumstein*	Supreme Court held that long residency requirements for voting were unconstitutional.
1975	Voting Rights Act	Required that voting information be bilingual in parts of twenty-four states.
1982	Voting Rights Act	Extended 1965 act for twenty-five years.

Though Mexicans residing in the Southwest following the Mexican-American War of 1848 were guaranteed full citizenship by the Treaty of Guadalupe, many were shut out of the election process because of the language barrier. This impediment to participation was addressed by Congress in 1975 through passage of amendments to the VOTING RIGHTS ACT of 1965. These new amendments created remedies, including bilingual access to voting. The bilingual provisions were renewed with the creation of the Voting Rights Language Assistance Act of 1992.

For Chinese Americans, the right to vote came with the repeal of the Chinese Exclusion Act in 1943. Even with less restrictive immigration laws, however, the language barrier kept Chinese and other Asian-language minorities out of the political system until the 1975 amendments providing bilingual access were enacted.

Black Vote. After the Civil War, the Thirteenth, Fourteenth, and Fifteenth Amendments were enacted to abolish slavery and establish legal rights for emancipated slaves. The Fifteenth Amendment, finally ratified in 1870, granted the right to vote, regardless of "race, color, or previous condition of servitude." This amendment, however, did not prohibit states from requiring voters to own land, which effectively restricted the voting rights of blacks, most of whom were not property owners at this time. Between 1890 and 1910, states used other methods, racially neutral on their face, to restrict the voting rights of black citizens. POLL TAXES required voters to pay a tax in order to vote, and LITERACY TESTS required the citizens to prove their ability to read. Additionally, local clerks and registrars used their positions to discourage black registration and voting by methods such as applicant disqualification and sometimes through outright intimidation. GERRYMANDERING, a practice of redrafting voting district boundaries to manipulate the number of minority voters in a given district, was a widely used method of diffusing the power of the black vote.

Political activism over voting rights, in conjunction with other social pressure brought to bear by the CIVIL RIGHTS MOVEMENT in general, paved the way for more powerful voting rights laws for African Americans and other minorities. In March of 1965, an attack by Alabama state troopers and police on demonstrators preparing to march for voter registration brought national attention to the need for improved voting rights laws. Soon after this event, the Voting Rights Act of 1965 was passed, and significant changes were made in the law.

Voting Rights Act of 1965. The Voting Rights Act of 1965 is considered the first major legislation to impact voting rights for African Americans and other minorities. This act targeted certain states with particularly discriminatory practices and covered Alabama, Georgia, Louisiana, Mississippi, South Carolina, Virginia, and half of North Carolina. A key piece of this legislation banned poll taxes and literacy tests as voting requirements. It also took control over local elections out of the hands of clerks and registrars and put it into the hands of the federal government. In some counties, federal examiners were sent to register voters themselves. The legislation shifted power from local courts to Washington by providing that all new voting practices in the jurisdictions covered by the act must be "precleared" by the U.S. attorney general or the fed-

Black voters newly protected by the 1965 Voting Rights Act go to the polls in Mississippi. (UPI/Corbis-Bettmann)

eral courts. As a result of the act, African Americans after 1965 were registered to vote in greater numbers than ever before. For example, in 1965, Mississippi had a 7 percent black voter-registration rate; by 1985, the rate had shot up to 86 percent, the second-highest in the nation. In several of the states covered by the act, there were more blacks than whites registered by 1985.

Originally designed to expire after five years, the act has been renewed and expanded. A 1975 extension gave non-English-speaking voters language assistance to aid with registration and voting. Amendments in 1970 reduced the voting age to eighteen.

In 1980, a coalition of 185 national organizations pushed again for extension and expansion of the Voting Rights Act, which was set to expire in 1982. These efforts were successful, and the act was extended for another twenty years, with the exception of the bilingual provisions, which were extended for ten years. One of the key components to the expansion of the act at this time was the implementation of a "results test," which established that if election practices could be shown to affect minorities adversely, they were discriminatory, whether or not an intent to discriminate was established.

Voter Participation. In a country founded on democracy, the right to vote is exercised by surprisingly few of its citizens. In 1992, a presidential election year, only 55 percent of the voting-age population cast their ballots in the national election. Efforts to increase voter registration and voter turnout have been successful in some states. In Alaska, voter registration increased by 20 percent, and voter turnout by more than 9 percent, when postcard registration was allowed. Some states allow election-day registration as well. While opponents of this procedure fear election fraud, no substantial evidence has developed to support this fear. Voter participation in three states using same-day registration ranked first, second, and fourth in the nation.

It is not only access to voter registration that prevents citizens from voting. Studies show that primary determinants to voting patterns for both men and women of all races are: education, income, and occupation. Those who are economically marginalized or racially isolated often have a sense that the political system has no relevance for them, and they are thus disconnected. Women and minorities remain underrepresented in politics. In the early 1990's, African Americans constituted 13 percent of the population of the United States but less than 4 percent of the members of Congress. In 1988, less than 5 percent of the members

of Congress were women, though women make up more than 50 percent of the American population. Studies show that women and minorities tend to support different policies than the policies of white males. Thus, greater voter participation by these and other economically marginalized groups could dramatically alter the face of politics in the United States of America.

—*Lorriane D. Baker*

SUGGESTED READINGS: Relevant legislation is analyzed by various scholars in *Voting Rights in America: Continuing the Quest for Full Participation* (Washington, D.C.: Leadership Conference Education Fund Joint Center for Political and Economic Studies, 1992), edited by Karen McGill Arrington and William L. Taylor. The history of women's suffrage is outlined in Eleanor Flexner's *Century of Struggle: The Woman's Rights Movement in the United States* (Cambridge, Mass.: The Belknap Press of Harvard University Press, 1959). *Controversies in Minority Voting* (Washington, D.C.: The Brookings Institution, 1992), edited by Bernard Grofman and Chandler Davidson, is an in-depth look at the effect of the Voting Rights Act on minorities.

Voting Rights Act (1965): U.S. federal civil rights law passed to eliminate LITERACY TESTS and discriminatory registration tactics that had earlier denied African Americans access to the voting process. The Voting Rights Act of 1965 also fulfilled President Lyndon B. Johnson's hope, announced in his 1965 State of the Union Address, that Congress would eliminate "every remaining obstacle to the right and the opportunity to vote."

Public sentiment would neither support nor oppose voting-rights legislation until evidence of racial violence in the Southern states hit home. As members of the STUDENT NONVIOLENT COORDINATING COMMITTEE (SNCC) conducted a series of voter-registration drives among disfranchised blacks, the Reverend Martin Luther KING, Jr., and the SOUTHERN CHRISTIAN LEADERSHIP CONFERENCE (SCLC) prepared nonviolent strategies that would capture the nation's attention and accelerate the passage of voting-rights legislation. Despite differences of opinion between established SCLC members and younger, more militant members of SNCC, the two came together in January, 1965, to organize a series of nonviolent protests and marches in Dallas County, Alabama.

None was more successful in capturing public attention than the march from Selma, Alabama, to the state

President Lyndon B. Johnson signs the 1965 Voting Rights Act into law. (AP/Wide World Photos)

capitol in Montgomery planned for Sunday, March 7, 1965. Alabama state police intercepted nearly six hundred demonstrators just outside Selma and halted their progress with tear gas and physical violence. Civil rights advocates retreating from the attack faced equally intense violence at the hands of local authorities and segregationist whites. Meanwhile, television sets around the country reported on this "BLOODY SUNDAY" in Selma. Subsequent efforts to overcome racial injustices in and around Selma were more successful, but few carried the impact of the first march on Montgomery.

Eight days after the melee in Dallas County, President Johnson appeared before Congress and a national television audience to urge the passage of the Voting Rights Act. The bill authorized federal intervention in any state or county that had employed literacy tests and recorded fewer than half of its voting-age residents as registered voters. Congress did not cast a con-

clusive vote on the measure until language was added empowering the U.S. attorney general to intervene in areas where discriminatory practices had occurred and to order federal examiners to run voter-registration drives. Another late addition to the bill aided Spanish-speaking Americans, who had formerly been subject to English reading tests at the polls.

The final version of the bill made its way through Congress with relative ease and became law on August 6, 1965. Johnson applauded its passage and admired the obstacles contributors to the civil rights effort had overcome. The time for rejoicing, however, was brief. Less than a week after the landmark bill became law, racial violence erupted in the Watts section of Los Angeles, California. In a five-day riot ending August 16, 1965, agitated African Americans engaged federal, state, and local authorities in a conflagration that took twenty-eight lives and destroyed more than $200 million in property. While

Voucher programs for schooling

"Bloody Sunday" had won many allies for the CIVIL RIGHTS MOVEMENT, violent scenes from Watts alienated many more and shattered the uneasy peace between militant blacks, moderate protesters, and American society at large.

Voucher programs for schooling: Provision of public funds for private spending on education. In voucher programs, parents of a school-age child receive a voucher, or promissory note, for the amount that the state normally provides for that child's education. For example, under a voucher plan, parents may elect not to send their child to the public school in their area; rather, they may request a voucher for the amount the state spends on the child's education and use that money for a private school's tuition. Currently, parents in the United States who wish for their children to attend private school do not receive such a subsidy from the government.

Voucher programs began to be discussed seriously in the 1980's, although the idea was not new. Proponents of voucher programs, including Christian fundamentalists and many other cultural conservatives, praised the voucher system as a way to revitalize the deteriorating U.S. public-school system. Vouchers promised to bring a degree of competition to schools, since schools would be forced to compete for students. Better schools would receive more parental approval and thus more money.

Opponents of the voucher system, including teachers' unions, public-school officials, and some representatives of low-income and minority groups, argued that the voucher system would in practice amount to a subsidy for middle-class parents to send their children to private schools; poor areas, they argued, could not expect a great increase in private development of schools. Many citizens also objected to the idea of using state money to finance religious education (in the case of a voucher's being used to pay for a student's attendance at a religious school). Opponents pointed out that the competition model is not always the best. Many basic social-welfare tasks, such as fire control, police, and schools, they argued, are not improved by being privatized and made subject to market forces.

Both sides agreed that the school system in the United States needed improvement. Calls for vouchers as a means of improvement, however, dwindled in the early 1990's. In some cases, courts struck down the implementation of voucher programs in view of the legal standard of SEPARATION OF CHURCH AND STATE. According to one 1995 poll, the majority of Americans opposed vouchers but supported school prayer.

W

Wage discrimination: Employment issue. Wage discrimination refers to differences in average levels of pay for groups of workers, with the differences not reflecting productivity or labor cost differences. Past and present discrimination based on race and gender contributes to earnings disparities observed among white, African American, and Hispanic workers. Earnings disparities according to race, in many instances, reflect a combination of current DISCRIMINATION and enduring consequences of discrimination practiced generations before. The effects of discrimination are circular and cumulative in nature.

African Americans and Hispanics typically earn 25 percent to 30 percent less than do white workers in similar jobs. Although typically women earn less than men, the percentage depends on age and occupation.

The mechanisms by which the political process and the market economy enforce wage discrimination against women and minorities are complex. Some are rooted in expectations, social customs, and beliefs and institutions of society; others are based on economic factors such as education, training, and work experience.

Employment Discrimination. Title VII of the CIVIL RIGHTS ACT OF 1964 outlawed discrimination on the basis of race, color, religion, gender, or national origin. A typical legal case involving what is called adverse impact and lack of business necessity involves employment practices that exclude members of protected groups at a higher rate than their counterparts (for example, 25 percent of female job applicants are hired, whereas 50 percent of male applicants are hired). The case may result in a ruling of illegal discrimination if the employer is unable to show that employment practices and hiring criteria are job related and result from business necessity. This principle was established by the Supreme Court decision in *Griggs v. Duke Power Company* (1971). The case concerned whether the issue of discriminatory intent had to be shown in Title VII cases. The Court ruled that practices with disparate impacts on different groups were illegal even if there was no intent to discriminate.

Affirmative Action, Comparable Worth, and Quotas. The purpose of AFFIRMATIVE ACTION programs is to increase the representation of protected groups in job categories traditionally dominated by white men. Public opinion shifted on affirmative action from its beginnings in the 1960's. Some politicians became openly opposed to affirmative action and all race- or gender-based preferences, arguing that they were another form of discrimination. Analysts contend that women in general and white women in particular have benefited most from affirmative action programs.

COMPARABLE WORTH is a new approach, introduced in the mid-1980's, to reduce the male-female wage gap. The concept goes beyond "equal pay for equal work" to "equal pay for comparable worth." Although the courts sometimes have ruled that comparable worth is an appropriate remedy for persistent male-female wage gaps, the approach lacks strong support based on economic analysis. A basic problem is reaching agreement on which jobs or skills are comparable.

Quotas, as numerical targets designed to remedy past discrimination and increase employment of members of particular groups in specific instances, lack public support. Quotas and other race- or gender-based preferences have triggered a political backlash, again because they are perceived as a form of REVERSE DISCRIMINATION. Corporate DOWNSIZING and economic uncertainty pose the most serious threat to public support for affirmative action programs, because job reductions impose stronger competition among workers.

Many factors account for wage discrimination. In some cases, differences in earnings reflect differences in skills, education, or experience. These differences might be based on discrimination by earlier employers or in the educational system. Social expectations also play a role. Women, for example, typically have been perceived as second earners in households, so that they did not "need" to earn as much as men. The most important factor in wage discrimination may be the formation of noncompeting groups, whether through conscious discrimination or indirectly through past discrimination and social expectations. If labor markets are segmented, reserving managerial positions for white men while relegating women and minorities to menial and dead-end jobs, chronic wage gaps may persist for decades.

WAGE GAPS BY AGE, GENDER, AND ETHNIC GROUP

U.S. Workers Ages Thirty and Older

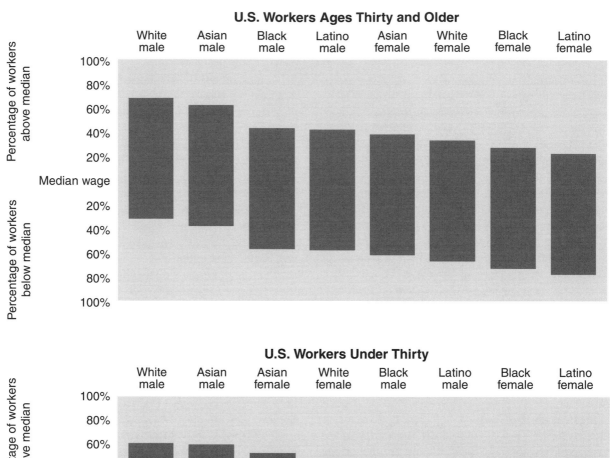

U.S. Workers Under Thirty

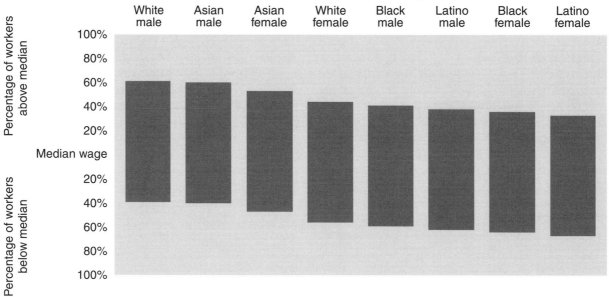

Wage gaps persist but have narrowed in recent years.

Source: Los Angeles Times. Primary source: U.S. Census Bureau.

SUGGESTED READINGS: For data on wage disparities, see the Bureau of Labor Statistics' *Employment
and Earnings* (Washington, D.C.: Bureau of Labor
Statistics, 1994). For a sound economic analysis, see
Paul Samuelson and William D. Nordhaus' *Economics*, 14th ed. (New York: McGraw-Hill, 1992).

War Brides Act (1945): U.S. legislation that allowed
120,000 alien wives, husbands, and children of members of the U.S. armed services who fought in World
War II to enter the United States as nonquota immigrants. Under the National Origins Act of 1924 then in
effect, IMMIGRATION QUOTAS for Southern and Eastern
European countries were small, and the waiting list for
those qualified was years long. Until passage of the
War Brides Act, soldiers' dependents born in countries
such as Italy or Poland faced long waits before they
were able to obtain immigrant visas.

War crimes: Only three times in the twentieth century has the international community come together to
consider establishing a tribunal to adjudicate war
crimes. The first time was after World War I, when the
Treaty of Versailles called for the establishment of
such a court to try accused German war criminals; for
political reasons, however, the Versailles Treaty provisions were never enforced. The second tribunal, the
famous Nuremberg Trials, was held to try the major
Nazi war criminals of the Third Reich. The most recent
attempt to establish an international war-crimes tribunal occurred in 1993, when the UNITED NATIONS established an international tribunal in an effort to prose-

Women entering the United States under the War Brides Act arrive in New York in 1946. (UPI/Bettmann Newsphotos)

cute people suspected of war crimes in the BALKANS WAR.

World War II. The London Agreement and the Charter of the International Military Tribunal signed August 8, 1945, established the legal foundation for the series of war-crime trials in Germany known collectively as the Nuremberg Trials. The victorious Allied powers (principally the United States, Great Britain, France, and the Soviet Union) were signatories to the London Agreement and to the charter. The charter set forth three separate crimes charged against individual Nazi defendants and Nazi organizations. These were war crimes, crimes against peace, and crimes against humanity. In 1945, "crimes against peace" and "crimes against humanity" were totally novel concepts in international law. The prosecution and conviction of the major Nazi defendants under these two charges still raise some serious questions about their legal legitimacy.

The International Military Tribunal (IMT) convened on November 20, 1945, at the Palace of Justice in the Nuremberg suburb of Fürth. Sir Geoffrey Lawrence of Great Britain opened the first of 403 public sessions of the trial. Twelve additional series of trials of lesser Nazi officials were held between 1946 and 1949.

The most significant trial, however, was the first, held in the Palace of Justice. There were four permanent judges and four alternates. The four permanent jurists were Lord Justice Sir Geoffrey Lawrence, president of the tribunal, and his alternate, Justice Norman Birkett (Great Britain); Francis Biddle and his alternate, Judge John J. Parker (United States); Professeur Donnediue de Vabres and his alternate, Le Conseiller Robert Falco (France); and Major General I. T. Nikitchenko and his alternate, Lieutenant Colonel A. F. Volchkov (Soviet Union).

The chief prosecutors were Sir Hartley Shawcross (Great Britain); Robert H. Jackson (United States); François de Menthon and Auguste Champetier De Ribes (France); and General R. A. Rudenko (Soviet Union). Defendants were allowed either appointed or assigned counsel, and some retained the ablest defense lawyers in Germany. The trial was conducted under Anglo-American accusatorial practice.

The opening of the Nuremberg war-crimes trials in 1945. (AP/Wide World Photos)

Of the twenty-four German defendants charged, sixteen were convicted of committing war crimes and crimes against humanity; twelve were convicted of committing crimes against peace; and eight were convicted of conspiring to commit crimes against peace. Of the nineteen defendants convicted, twelve were sentenced to hang; eleven of these twelve were executed in the prison gymnasium on October 16, 1946. One defendant, Hermann Goering, committed suicide before he was executed. Three defendants were acquitted. Martin Bormann, head of the Nazi Party Chancery in Berlin, was charged, tried, and convicted *in absentia*. Gustav Krupp von Bohlen und Halbach, a German armaments manufacturer, was adjudged too ill and infirm to stand trial. Three of the six accused organizations were found to be criminal: the notorious *Schutzstaffel*, or SS, the Gestapo, and the Leadership Corps of the Nazi Party.

The prosecutors presented their case against each of the twenty-one defendants and charged organizations, largely from voluminous written and photographic documentation. Several international law precedents were established at Nuremberg that remain in effect. First, the principle of a fair trial and DUE PROCESS of law was applied to individuals charged with international war crimes; second, the conspiracy to wage and the actual initiation of aggressive warfare were legally recognized as international criminal acts; and third, it was recognized that individuals and certain state-sponsored organizations could be held accountable for war crimes, crimes against humanity, and crimes against peace. Finally, individuals could be held criminally accountable for offenses committed by them pursuant to superior military or civilian orders.

The trials of the major Japanese war criminals began later and lasted longer than the Nuremberg proceedings. Known officially as the International Military Tribunal for the Far East (IMTFE), the trials were planned and discussed as early as the Cairo Declaration of December 1, 1943. The tribunal was established by General Douglas MacArthur in his capacity as the Supreme Allied Commander in Japan. MacArthur had sole authority to select the judges submitted to him by the United States, Great Britain, China, the Soviet Union, Canada, Australia, The Netherlands, France, and New Zealand. On April 29, 1946, the tribunal was officially organized, and twenty-eight Japanese were indicted. The trial commenced on June 3, 1946, and concluded on November 4, 1948. In all, 419 witnesses testified, with an additional 779 witnesses represented by both deposition and affidavit.

The tribunal consisted of eleven judges and no alternates. The jurists were Sir William F. Webb, the presiding judge (Australia); John P. Higgins, who was later replaced by Major General Myron C. Cramer (United States); Lord Patrick (Great Britain); E. Stuart McDougall (Canada); Henri Bernard (France); I. M. Zaryanov (Soviet Union); Ju-Ao Mei (China); Delfin Jaranilla (Philippines); Bernard Victor A. Roling (Netherlands); Erima Harvey Northcroft (New Zealand); and R. M. Pal (India).

The defendants were charged on a total of fifty-five counts, including thirty-six counts of crimes against peace, sixteen counts of murder, and three counts of conventional war crimes and crimes against peace. Unlike in Nuremberg, no "organizational criminality" charges were preferred against the Japanese. The general defenses raised by the accused took the same legal stance as those raised at Nuremberg.

Seven defendants were sentenced to death by hanging, and all were executed on December 23, 1948, in Sugamo Prison in Tokyo. Sixteen of the accused were given sentences of life imprisonment; one received a twenty-year prison term, and one a seven-year term. Related war-crime tribunals sat in judgment of lesser Japanese military and civilian officials through the year 1951.

Vietnam War. From March 16 to March 19, 1968, an American combat operation took place in Quang Ngai Province in South Vietnam. In that operation, numerous noncombatant elderly men, women, and children were killed by the men of C Company, 1st Battalion, 20th Infantry Regiment, 11th Infantry Brigade of the American Division. The most notorious killing of unarmed civilians occurred in the hamlet of My Lai. In November, 1970, U.S. Army investigators searched the area and estimated that between four hundred and five hundred people had died at My Lai.

The case attracting the most attention involved Lieutenant William Calley, who was charged with murdering twenty-two Vietnamese civilians at My Lai. Under international law, the killing of noncombatant civilians is a war crime.

On March 29, 1971, Calley was convicted in the longest court-martial in American military history. His defense attorneys ultimately removed the case to the federal courts. In *Calley v. Callaway* (1974), a district court in Georgia ruled that a military judge at Fort Benning, Georgia, had violated Calley's Fifth and Sixth Amendment rights and granted a writ of *HABEAS*

Accused war criminal Ivan Demjanjuk denies allegations that he is the war criminal known as "Ivan the Terrible."
(Archive Photos/Reuters/Jim Hollander)

CORPUS in Calley's favor. The government appealed, and on September 10, 1975, the U.S. Circuit Court of Appeals for the Fifth Circuit in New Orleans reversed the federal district court order and reinstated the judgment of the military court-martial, which had found Calley guilty of having acted with murderous criminal intent. By the time the case had reached the Fifth Circuit Court of Appeals in 1975, however, the Army had paroled Calley.

Bosnia. In 1993, the UNITED NATIONS established the International Tribunal for the Prosecution of Persons Responsible for Serious Violations of International Humanitarian Law Committed in the Territory of the Former Yugoslavia Since 1991. The statute of the tribunal contained five articles and empowered that body to bring to justice individuals charged with violating numerous international treaties and conventions. The terms of the peace agreement that brought an end to the conflict in late 1995, however, did not provide for the extradition of suspected war criminals. Moreover, NATO troops enforcing the settlement were enjoined by their superiors from pursuing war-crimes suspects; NATO commanders and their civilian leaders were concerned that such efforts could spark renewed fighting and endanger the fragile peace. As a result, a number of suspected war criminals indicted by the U.N. tribunal in The Hague, The Netherlands, remained at large, particularly in the Serb Republic; although many Serbian leaders were implicated in the mass killing of Bosnian Muslim civilians, the political and military will to pursue them did not appear to exist.

—John Cumming Watkins, Jr.

SUGGESTED READINGS: An excellent overview of war crimes can be found in Jay W. Baird's *From Nuremberg to My Lai* (Lexington, Mass.: D.C. Heath, 1972). A detailed account of the My Lai case and the

Nuremberg precedent is Joseph Goldstein, Burke Marshall, and Jack Schwartz's *The My Lai Massacre and Its Cover-Up: Beyond the Reach of Law?* (New York: The Free Press, 1976). The Institute for World Order's *War Criminals: War Victims: Andersonville, Nuremberg, Hiroshima, My Lai* (New York: Random House, 1974) is also a valuable source. More recent coverage of war crimes in Bosnia and their aftermath can be found in "The Dead Cry Out" (*Newsweek*, February 5, 1996).

War on Drugs: Series of U.S. federal anitidrug initiatives begun during the Ronald REAGAN and George BUSH administrations. The "War on Drugs" took legal shape in such legislation as the Omnibus Drug Enforcement, Education, and Control Act of 1986 and the Anti-Drug Abuse Act of 1988, which created new federal agencies and programs to combat illegal drug use and heightened penalties for drug-related crimes. Supporters of the War on Drugs have called such initiatives necessary responses to a crisis brought on by escalating drug use. Critics of such efforts dismiss talk of a drug crisis as unfounded and politically motivated; moreover, they assert that stiffer sentencing laws, particularly "ZERO TOLERANCE" policies, have caused a massive overburdening of the court and prison systems and have frequently led to the application of inappropriately harsh and counterproductive penalties to defendants convicted of minor drug crimes.

War Refugee Board: U.S. agency established by President Franklin D. Roosevelt in 1944 by executive order as the dimensions of the Nazi Holocaust in Europe became known. The board itself did not bring any refugees to the United States during the war; only a token group of fewer than a thousand European Jews were admitted as temporary residents under presidential parole. The activity of the board, however, did prepare the way for the DISPLACED PERSONS ACT of 1948 and the REFUGEE RELIEF ACT of 1953, which together admitted more than 500,000 war refugees to the United States.

Wards Cove Packing Company v. Atonio (1989): U.S. Supreme Court case. Jobs in some Alaskan salmon canneries were of two general types: Unskilled jobs were filled mostly by nonwhites, and skilled jobs were filled mostly by whites. In reviewing a suit based on the "disparate impact" of HIRING PRACTICES, the Court voted five to four to retreat from the strict standards of *Griggs v. Duke Power Co.* (1971) and to require plaintiffs to prove that a specific hiring practice discriminated against a class of people. In the Civil Rights Act of 1991, however, Congress returned to employers the burden of defending any hiring practice that resulted in a significant statistical disparity.

Water pollution: Any change in the physical, chemical, or biological properties of water that may adversely affect the health, survival, or life activities of organisms. Pollutants may be caused by the natural environment or from human action.

Causes. Water is one of the most abundant natural resources on the planet, but 97 percent of it is salty, oceanic water. Of the remaining 3 percent, less than 1 percent occurs in lakes, ponds, rivers, and streams and in underground aquifers, which are porous, water-bearing geological formations.

The greatest amounts of noxious and toxic water pollutants originate in human activities: nitrates and phosphates in runoff from heavily fertilized agricultural lands, golf courses, and suburban lawns, and human and animal feces. The human waste in cities is treated in municipal wastewater systems that discharge a nutrient-rich liquid into nearby waterways. Some fecal matter in city-street runoff is from pets and feral animals. Rural pastures, feed lots, and stables also contribute large amounts of waste to runoff.

The large volumes of nitrates and phosphates in waterways result in eutrophication, overenrichment that causes excessive growth of algae and aquatic plants. The growth tends to shade out desirable plants, reducing the amount of dissolved oxygen in the water. In turn, habitats for fish and other aquatic organisms are diminished.

Chemicals used in agriculture and golf-course and lawn maintenance—including the pesticide dichloro-diphenyl-trichloroethane (DDT), banned in the U.S. but still used in other countries, add to water pollution. In aquatic food chains, DDT concentrations increase through the phenomenon of biological magnification. Concentrations of DDT in fish eaten by humans have caused many people to acquire a high body-levels of DDT.

Industrial sources of water pollutants are heavy metals, including zinc, cadmium, lead, and mercury. Petroleum products enter waterways mostly from urban street runoff.

A widely disputed water pollutant is heat from steam-powered electric plants. The plants take in hundreds of thousands of gallons of water per day (sometimes millions of gallons, depending on the generating capacity of the plant) as coolant. The water is drawn into the plant and then discharged, but is heated an additional ten to fifteen degrees in the process. The water is otherwise virtually unchanged. Proponents claim the water enhances the growth of aquatic organisms. Critics maintain that the heat negatively changes the natural ECOSYSTEM receiving the heated effluent.

Groundwater pollution frequently affects shallow aquifers when the source of contamination is nearby. Deep aquifers, however, may be polluted by sources hundreds of miles away. The pollutants include chemical-laden leachate from landfills, gasoline and diesel fuel from leaking, underground storage tanks, nutrients and biocides from agricultural areas, and salt spread on roads to melt snow and ice in cold-climate areas.

Trends. Water-pollution problems have increased as a result of the growth of human population. In the United States, the per-capita consumption of water averages one hundred gallons per day. This water is used once and then discharged either to a municipal wastewater system or into an in-ground disposal system (septic tank or cesspool). In the home, the water picks up a load of human waste and household chemicals, including detergents, and kitchen wastes. As the population grows, the total volume of used water grows.

Although many of the wastes are treated in wastewater treatment facilities, many of these facilities are old, inefficient, and frequently overloaded. It is not unusual when treatment plants are overwhelmed after a heavy rainstorm for raw, untreated sewage to be dis-

Workers clean spilled oil from a California beach in 1969. (UPI/Bettmann Newsphotos)

A science-fair exhibit demonstrates causes and effects of water pollution. (Don Franklin)

charged into the nearest waterway. In some municipalities, such as Boston and New York City, wastewater facilities date back to the nineteenth century. The rising costs of construction result in taxpayer revolts against building new plants.

The increasing human population in developed nations such as the United States, Great Britain, Japan, and Germany has caused a shift in LAND USE. In many areas, what had been prime agricultural land now supports housing tracts, shopping centers, and roadways to serve the expanding populace. Marginal agricultural land has been put to the plow. Such lands, however, require more fertilizer, PESTICIDES, and water for irrigation, all of which eventually enter surface and groundwater supplies. The larger population also means more garbage and solid waste to be buried in landfills and more automobiles dripping petroleum products onto roadways.

Health Effects. The most direct impact on human health from water pollution comes from the microorganisms, bacteria, viruses, and parasites in sewage. A variety of these organisms exist in the human stomach, in a generally harmless, ecological relationship. Large numbers of them leave the body in feces. It is when organisms enter the upper digestive tract that they cause disease. The illness may be simply a case of diarrhea and vomiting followed by complete recovery. The causative organism usually is the very common bacterium, *Escherichia coli* (often known simply as *E. coli*).

More serious are typhoid fever and cholera, both caused by fecal bacteria. Viruses common in human feces include those that cause poliomyelitis and hepatitis. Unfortunately, even the highest form of wastewater treatment, including chlorination, does not result in 100 percent elimination of the microorganisms.

In less-developed nations, parasitic worms are common in human feces and affect large segments of the population. It is not unusual in some remote areas for a stream to be used for cooking and drinking water, for bathing and laundry, and for sewage disposal. A common parasite in such places is the worm that causes

Water pollution can cause massive destruction of marine life. (UPI/Bettmann Newsphotos)

schistosomiasis, also known as bilharzia. An aquatic snail acts as the worm's intermediate host. The worm larvae penetrate human skin from the water and, during the course of their life cycle, produce large masses of eggs in the human host's blood vessels, where they interfere with the flow of blood to the kidneys, lungs, liver, and other vital organs. Brain damage and death may result.

In North America, hikers and campers often are dismayed to find a pristine-looking mountain stream or lake with a sign warning about drinking the water. Despite the appealing look of the streams, the water usually harbors the protozoan *Giardia intestinalis*. The source of the contamination is improper disposal of feces by earlier hikers and campers. The resulting disease, giardiasis, causes diarrhea, nausea, and fatigue.

Some chemical water pollutants are especially troublesome, particularly those that are not retained by soil particles but instead percolate down into the groundwater. Heavy metals such as lead and mercury in drinking water can attack the nervous system, causing mental retardation and physical deformities. Fetuses carried by pregnant women are often seriously harmed when the women drink water containing heavy metals.

Nitrates in drinking water from fertilizers and sewage effluent can often cause a fatal reaction in newborns called "blue-baby disease." The nitrates in the infants' blood can cause oxygen depletion, which leads to death.

The role of DDT and other pesticides in human health is not clearly understood. However, these complex organic compounds may be linked to certain types of human CANCERS.

Legislation. The role of contaminants in water pollution was not recognized until modern science became more sophisticated. All manner of wastes were dumped into the nearest waterway in the belief that nature was resilient and could absorb the wastes indefinitely. Conventional wisdom erroneously held that running water "cleanses itself every one hundred feet," and that "the solution to pollution is dilution."

The first federal legislation to reduce water pollution was the 1899 Rivers and Harbors Act. This law, also known as the "Refuse Act," prohibited the dumping of "trash" into rivers and harbors. Unfortunately, it was silent on the dumping of sewage into navigable waterways and was rarely enforced. A more effective piece of legislation was the 1972 Water Pollution Control Act. This law, with amendments, controlled a variety of noxious and toxic pollutants. Sometimes called the CLEAN WATER ACT, its principal focus was to make surface water in the United States "fishable and swimmable." Water quality was further enhanced with passage in 1974 of the Safe Drinking Water Act. This act empowered the U.S. Environmental Protection Agency to set standards in drinking water for levels of metals, pesticides, nitrates, and radioactivity. In addition, municipal drinking-water systems must be able to filter and disinfect the water to remove *Giardia* and intestinal viruses. Each state must establish rules that at least meet the requirements of the federal act.

—*Albert C. Jensen*

SUGGESTED READINGS: The world's supply of water and the vital role it plays in making life function is described in Elizabeth K. Berner and Robert A. Berner's *The Global Water Cycle* (Englewood Cliffs, N.J.: Prentice-Hall, 1987). Fumio Matsumura warns of the dangers of agricultural chemicals in *Toxicology of Insecticides*, 2d ed. (New York: Plenum Press, 1985). Frank Graham, Jr., presents an environmentalist's views on water pollution and water management in "Gambling on Water" (*Audubon*, July/August, 1992).

Water rights: Differing interpretations concerning the fair distribution of water have long been the basis of disputes between individuals, municipalities, states, and nations. Especially sensitive in areas where water is scarce, water allocation represents an important social, economic, and political issue.

Types of Water Rights. One system of water allocation is riparian rights. Generally speaking, where a waterway is unnavigable, the property owners along its shores own the land underneath the water up to the halfway point and are allowed to use the water that flows on or stands on their property. Most governments allow their citizens riparian rights as long as usage does not drastically impair stream flow or water level.

Another method used to distribute water is the doctrine of prior appropriation. Prior appropriation is basically practiced as "first in time, first in right": the first individuals or groups of individuals who utilize the water in a river or lake have primary rights to that water.

Areas of Conflict. Because water is an essential component of the life cycle, it can be rightly assumed that the more arid the climate, the more avid the competition for existing resources.

In the Southwestern United States, the most notable

conflict concerns California and Arizona and the water in the Colorado River. The need for large-scale irrigation in both states and the growing need for drinking water in Los Angeles and Phoenix have resulted in heated political struggles between the two states. On several occasions, the tension has approached the point of violence. Attempts by the two states to jointly administer water have eased tensions somewhat, but continuing population growth threatens future harmony.

The problem between Mexico and the United States is related to the California-Arizona dispute because it concerns the same river systems. Attempts by the two governments to regulate fairly scarce water supplies have complicated international relations. The first treaty, signed in 1906, dealt only with dividing the upper Rio Grande. The next treaty, signed in 1944, while including the lower Rio Grande and other major rivers, left such problems as population increases to the future.

Most nations in the Middle East face water shortages, and shared water systems only complicate an already politically volatile area. With some of the greatest population increases on earth, the Middle East is becoming more reliant than ever on irrigation to feed its people.

Israel and Jordan, which have been enemies for many reasons, must share the water in the Jordan River basin. Israel alone exceeds the renewable water supply by 300 million cubic meters per year, or about 15 percent. If no agreement can be achieved between the two, or if population growth does not decline, Middle East tensions will only increase.

SUGGESTED READINGS: Water rights and international ramifications of water usage are explored in Norris Hundley's *Dividing the Waters: A Century of Controversy Between the United States and Mexico* (Berkeley: University of California Press, 1966) and in *Last Oasis: Facing Water Scarcity* (New York: W.W. Norton, 1992), by Sandra Postel. In *America's Water: Federal Roles and Responsibilities* (Cambridge, Mass.: MIT Press, 1993), Peter Rogers offers solutions to decreasing water supply.

Watergate scandal (June 17, 1972-August 9, 1974): Major American constitutional crisis. The Watergate scandal was resolved when the U.S. SUPREME COURT ordered President Richard M. NIXON to comply with a court subpoena to turn over relevant tapes. Proof of Nixon's obstruction of justice forced him to resign from the presidency.

The scandal began when several members of the Committee to Reelect the President decided to break into the national headquarters of the DEMOCRATIC PARTY in Washington's Watergate Hotel on June 17, 1972. Although three of the seven burglars arrested worked for the Committee to Reelect the President, it was not then known that Nixon had been involved in paying money to the defendants to remain quiet. Two years later, it was proved that on June 23, 1972, Nixon himself had ordered the CENTRAL INTELLIGENCE AGENCY to interfere with the investigation of the crime and that his main assistants, John Erlichman and Bob Haldeman, approved the secret payment of large sums of money to the seven defendants.

The conspiracy appeared to have succeeded, and Nixon was reelected in November, 1972. In March, 1973, however, the coverup began to unravel. Judge John Sirica suspected that he had been lied to by the defendants when they denied the existence of a coverup. As he was preparing to sentence the convicted felons to prison, he offered them a choice: If they cooperated with prosecutors, they would receive lenient prison terms; if they failed to cooperate, he would sentence them to forty-five years in prison. The pressure succeeded. James McCord told Judge Sirica that he and his fellow criminals had been paid money to perjure themselves. Soon, Archibald Cox was appointed as special prosecutor to investigate the Watergate scandal, and a Senate committee chaired by Senator Sam Ervin of North Carolina began to hold hearings.

When it was revealed during the Senate hearings that all conversations in the Oval Office had been recorded, Cox obtained from Judge Sirica a subpoena for the relevant tapes. Nixon resisted this court order, citing the claim of NATIONAL SECURITY. In an obvious attempt to end the judicial examination of his actions, Nixon fired Cox on October 20, 1973, but public opinion forced Nixon to appoint a new special prosecutor, Leon Jaworski.

Eventually, the U.S. Supreme Court voted unanimously that Nixon had to comply with the subpoena from Judge Sirica. The tapes proved Nixon's guilt. The Judiciary Committee of the U.S. House of Representatives voted to impeach Nixon, who chose to resign on August 9, 1974, when he realized that Republican senators would no longer support him. Although the political corruption of Richard Nixon scandalized most Americans, the judicial branch of the U.S. government reaffirmed that not even a president is above the law.

Sam Ervin (below map) chairs a meeting of the Senate committee investigating the Watergate scandal. (UPI/Corbis-Bettmann)

SUGGESTED READINGS: Theodore H. White's *Breach of Faith: The Fall of Richard Nixon* (New York: Atheneum Press, 1975) provides a clear history of the Watergate scandal. Sam Ervin expressed his views on the Watergate scandal in *The Whole Truth: The Watergate Conspiracy* (New York: Random House, 1980).

Wealth, distribution of: Cultures and individuals vary in their understanding of wealth. While theorists broadly generalize that items both essential and rare constitute the wealth that members of a culture strive to acquire, people often cherish idiosyncratic notions. A mother's "wealth," for example, might stem from her children's love and appreciation. A gardener might feel "rich" the year his roses produce especially vibrant blooms. Unique definitions of wealth often permit those in otherwise impoverished circumstances to survive and flourish. Yet they do not yield to statistical analysis.

To understand the distribution of wealth in a nation, more readily accessible measures are used. In developing nations, landholdings often serve as proxies for wealth. In developed nations, the wealth of an average citizen might consist of a home and a pension, while the minority possess wealth in the form of stocks, bonds, and other capital goods. Many studies of wealth rely on estate tax returns, which have a necessarily retrospective character.

Although income dynamics roughly parallel the distribution of wealth, the United States has greater inequality in the concentration of wealth than of income. So, while the top 1.0 percent of families owned approximately one-fourth of the country's net wealth in 1991, the same group received only 11 percent of all money income. Using another measure, Daphne T. Greenwood reported in 1987 that 1 percent of all families in the United States owned 60.3 percent of all corporate stock in the country. Finally, in his 1991 book, *The Rich Get Richer*, Denny Braun reported that 10 percent of U.S. families controlled 70 percent of the nation's net wealth.

Classic theories of CAPITALISM view accumulated wealth as the result of personal initiative, hard work, and talent. Under this view, unequal distribution of wealth is desirable, both as a reward for effort and as

A 1991 demonstration protesting cuts in government spending for the poor. (Jim West)

an incentive to achieve. When accumulated wealth reflects unequal opportunity, rather than personal accomplishment, the basic premises of capitalism are violated, and the efficiencies of the free market are lost.

In the United States, race, marital status, and age all influence access to wealth. The Census Bureau issues a report on household wealth, based on its Survey of Income and Program Participation. The 1991 results suggested that the median value of white households in the nation was ten times that of African American and Hispanic households. The wealth of married couples was six times that of single households. Finally, the wealth accumulated by households headed by the elderly was substantially higher than that of younger adults.

International Comparisons of Income Distribution. Among industrialized nations, the United States is distinguished by above-average income inequality and unusually high rates of POVERTY. Several studies have overcome the difficulties of securing comparable figures, using data from the WORLD BANK and the Lux-

embourg Income Study. Economists typically compare national income distributions using a global measure called the "gini coefficient." In these studies, Australia, France, Canada, and the United States typically have the highest coefficients, reflecting above-average inequality in distribution of income. Comparable data for wealth (as opposed to income) have not been developed.

Data from the Luxembourg Income Study of ten Western industrialized nations have been used as the basis of international comparisons of poverty. Results indicate the United States has by far the highest overall rate. Canada and Australia also reported above-average poverty rates. The United States reports the highest poverty rates for single people, single parents with children, and single elderly people, and below-average poverty rates for older couples.

Although the United States fares relatively poorly by comparison with other industrialized nations, developing nations report much higher rates of income inequality. Brazil, for example, typically has the highest rate of inequality, with more than half the nation's income concentrated in the top 10 percent. In the United States and Canada the top 10 percent receive just under a quarter of the nation's income.

International data have also been used to compare the compensation packages offered to executives of major corporations. For example, David Kirkpatrick reported in a 1988 issue of *Fortune* magazine that CEOs in West Germany and Japan make only 65 percent of what CEOs of comparable companies make in the United States.

Recent Trends: Greater Inequality. Economic trends in recent decades have resulted in greater income inequality in the United States. This change is dramatic when viewed against the post-World War II backdrop of relatively stable income dynamics. Children have been most dramatically affected by declining resources available to disadvantaged families. In 1991, Braun reported that the share of national income going to U.S. families with children declined by nearly 20 percent between 1973 and 1984.

Although some attribute rising inequality to erosion of the SAFETY NET under the Ronald REAGAN Admini-

A well-to-do pedestrian passes a panhandler in New York City. (UPI/Corbis-Bettmann)

Weathermen

stration, most analysts note that the United States has
lost highly paid, unionized manufacturing jobs, replacing them with underpaid jobs in the service sector. An
emerging concern in today's global economy is the
extent to which major manufacturers export factories
to developing nations to take advantage of a less demanding work force and fewer government regulations.

Inequality and Democracy: Incompatible Forces?
Plato suggested that the ideal ratio between the wealth
of the richest citizen and that of the poorest be four to
one. Aristotle suggested a ratio of five to one. Contemporary theorists void such clear pronouncements, arguing simply that extreme inequality and political democracy are incompatible. A modicum of inequality
may increase work incentive, but an excessive amount
leads to hopelessness and desperation, with social un-
rest the result. In support of this view, Edward Muller
analyzed income inequality in more than fifty countries and discovered that the death rate from political
violence in countries goes up as income inequality increases. He also observed that democracies fail in conditions of extreme inequality.

In the United States, emerging arguments over campaign financing and lobbying reform have noted the
strong association between wealth and political power.
At a minimum, the very wealthy have greater access to
elected officials. At most, special interests control officials through campaign contributions. This is incompatible with democratic values favoring equal access
by all members of the electorate.

Redistribution Efforts: The Role of Government.
U.S. government policies do not include redistribution
of income or wealth as an explicit goal. Yet redistribution is often an indirect result of both tax and expenditure policies. The United States has a progressive IN-
COME TAX, which requires proportionately higher
contributions from those with high incomes. This has a
mild redistributive effect by slightly reducing the resources available to the wealthy. To increase the resources of the disadvantaged, government programs
provide cash payments and goods. Federal assistance
programs such as AID TO FAMILIES WITH DEPENDENT
CHILDREN (AFDC) and Supplemental Security Income
(SSI) provide monthly income to the needy. In-kind
programs like FOOD STAMPS provide access to goods.
TAXATION and government expenditures do little to redistribute the nation's income, although transfer programs to some extent alleviate the effects of POVERTY.

Perhaps the most powerful redistributive program in
the United States is its public EDUCATION system. In-

tended as a great "leveler," the public education system was designed to prepare children from a wide
range of backgrounds to participate effectively in
democratic society. Jonathan Kozol's 1991 book *Savage Inequalities* persuasively documents the failure of
public education to serve low-income children. Con-
currently, growing numbers of wealthy families have
removed their children from the system, providing
them the training necessary to sustain a privileged
status.

Despite growing concerns about HOMELESSNESS and
deteriorating conditions in low-income households,
Americans generally resist the idea of using government power to redistribute wealth. This violates the
nation's long-standing concern for protection of private property. Indeed, deliberate mandatory redistribution is seldom publicly advocated. Americans seem
willing to tolerate redistribution as an indirect effect of
government policies and programs. Voluntary redistribution in the form of private charity and volunteer service such as George BUSH's "thousand points of light"
are widely accepted.   —*Amanda Smith Barusch*

SUGGESTED READINGS: Classic capitalist theory is
available in the 1976 printing of Adam Smith's difficult book *An Inquiry into the Nature and Causes of the
Wealth of Nations* (New York: Oxford University
Press). For in-depth examination of the emerging underclass in America, see Michael Harrington's *The
New American Poverty* (New York: Holt, Rinehart,
and Winston, 1984). Consideration of the educational
system and low-income children is provided in
Jonathan Kozol's *Savage Inequalities: Children in
America's Schools* (New York: Crown Publishers,
1991). Examination of life histories of the poor can be
found in Amanda Smith Barusch's *Older Women in
Poverty: Private Lives and Public Policies* (New York:
Springer Publishing, 1994). For a radical view on the
treatment of wealth, see Sam Pizzigati's volume *The
Maximum Wage: A Common-Sense Prescription for
Revitalizing America—By Taxing the Very Rich* (New
York: Apex Press, 1992).

Weathermen: Revolutionary branch of the 1960's
U.S. political group STUDENTS FOR A DEMOCRATIC
SOCIETY (SDS). In June of 1969, Bernardine Dohrn
and Jim Mellen signaled a break with the broader SDS
movement when they announced their manifesto, "You
don't need a weatherman to know which way the wind
blows," a quotation from a Bob Dylan song. Weather-

Members of the Weathermen outside a federal court during a 1970 conspiracy trial. (UPI/Bettmann)

men (and women) targeted young people in northern cities with their revolutionary rhetoric and terrorized numerous college and high-school campuses. The group's violent tactics—including bombings, robberies, and murders—drew broad condemnation and led to its virtual eradication by the FEDERAL BUREAU OF INVESTIGATION (FBI) and other law-enforcement agencies.

Webster v. Reproductive Health Services (1989): U.S. SUPREME COURT case. In *Webster*, the Supreme Court upheld the Tenth Amendment right of the state of Missouri to place several restrictions upon patients' access to ABORTION and to declare as a matter of state statute that human life begins at conception. The Court, though, also upheld the basic Ninth Amendment abortion right established sixteen years earlier in *ROE V. WADE* (1973).

When the Supreme Court originally established the fundamental right to abortion in *Roe v. Wade*, the main restrictions placed upon this right were based on the stage of the pregnancy. In the stormy aftermath of *Roe*, a number of states, including Missouri, investigated the strategy of placing additional statutory restrictions upon abortion without directly challenging *Roe*. As one of the states that went furthest in that direction, Missouri gained the attention of the Supreme Court and of the entire nation with its 1986 law, which prohibited publicly funded abortions and required a viability test for fetuses conceived more than twenty weeks prior to the abortion, rather than relying on the trimester scheme suggested by *Roe*. The Missouri statute also restricted the communications of publicly funded medical practitioners with their patients about abortion and declared that human life begins at conception. So the Supreme Court's consideration of the constitutionality of these extremely controversial legislative items became an important legal precedent in the ongoing debate over abortion.

In the majority opinion by Chief Justice William REHNQUIST, the Court decided that the state of Missouri acted within its sovereign legislative authority in passing a statute of this general sort. But the Court stopped short of the wholesale overthrow of *Roe* that some observers had predicted. Comparing the *Webster* verdict with other closely related cases, it is now clear that the states may restrict abortion rights provided that they do so in a manner that the Supreme Court finds reasonable and proper. For example, in a later case, it

emerged that requiring a juvenile patient to have the consent of a parent or guardian prior to the abortion would be considered reasonable by the Court, while requiring an adult patient to consult with her husband would not.

In his dissenting opinion in the *Webster* case Justice Harry Blackmun, author of the majority opinion in *Roe*, displayed a rare level of acrimony. Blackmun's dissenting opinion was joined by Justices William Brennan and Thurgood MARSHALL. PRO-CHOICE advocates such as Blackmun probably felt some degree of vindication in the fact that *Roe* remained the law of the land, while many PRO-LIFE advocates have turned to the state legislatures to do further battle against *Roe*. It is clear that the Supreme Court will give the states considerable latitude in this arena, but the moderately conservative coalition on the Court led by Justice Sandra Day O'CONNOR has worked to balance STATES' RIGHTS against abortion rights while preventing the total overthrow of *Roe*.

Welfare system and reform: Government assistance to poor citizens to guarantee them access to decent housing, food, and medical care, and efforts to cut or eliminate such assistance. In the United States, welfare includes both federal- and state-funded programs. In the 1990's, critics of welfare spending attacked programs as badly administered, riddled with corruption and FRAUD, and, worst of all, ineffective at helping poor people escape the cycle of POVERTY. Following the 1994 federal elections, Republican politicians pushed hard for a complete restructuring of the welfare system. Democrats responded by accusing Republicans of using poverty programs to distract attention from other areas of the federal budget, such as excessive spending on defense programs, that also needed reform. In July, 1996, however, Democratic president Bill Clinton signed Republican-sponsored legislation that promised far-reaching changes to the U.S. welfare system.

History. Government ENTITLEMENT PROGRAMS designed to help the poor are a fairly recent development. Although charity has been recognized as a virtue for hundreds of years, large-scale organized assistance by a national government to the poor was unknown until the nineteenth century.

In the United States, for example, prior to the 1930's, help for the poor was organized on a local or state level. Counties operated ORPHANAGES for children whose parents were either deceased or too poor to provide basic necessities. The counties also operated workhouses and poor farms for the indigent. People who were elderly, poor, and had no family nearby with whom to live during their declining years found themselves relegated to the county poor farm or, in urban areas, the workhouse. Transients unable to provide proof of income, tramps and hoboes caught panhandling on public streets, poor people found on the streets late at night—all often found themselves sentenced by a local magistrate to stay at the county poor farm or workhouse. The poor farms, workhouses, and orphanages were designed to be self-sufficient. Residents tilled gardens, tended livestock, or worked at various industries in exchange for a place to live.

This system of poor farms and workhouses had its roots in Europe. In many European countries, a system of workhouses had developed to manage both the underclass—that is, people born into poverty with little hope of advancement—and middle-class debtors. In early nineteenth century England, people who were unable to pay debts were considered criminals and sentenced to workhouses. As industrialization spread throughout England, conditions for the poor deteriorated. Workhouses were filthy and overcrowded, but conditions in general in urban areas were not much better. Novels such as the works of Charles Dickens drew public attention to the horrific conditions the poor endured. England, like France, had instituted an old-age annuity for government employees early in the nineteenth century, so the notion that the nation had an obligation to care for its citizens was not entirely new. By the end of the century, Great Britain had begun welfare programs, such as subsidizing housing developments, designed to ensure that all citizens would enjoy a decent place to live.

In the United States, the national government was slower than those of European countries in becoming involved in welfare issues. During the Progressive Era, from 1896 to 1920, public attention was focused on the problems of the poor, both the urban and the rural underclass, but responsibilities for action were seen as lying with the states or with private agencies. The city of New York, for example, strove to improve living conditions for the poor following exposés by journalist and photographer Jacob Riis in the 1890's. Settlement houses organized by private groups such as the Junior League or individual philanthropists and activists appeared in many urban areas. The goal of settlement-house volunteers and workers was to lift the urban

poor, many of whom were recent immigrants to the United States who neither spoke nor read English fluently, out of poverty through education. By teaching the poor proper nutrition, housekeeping, and fundamentals of American government, settlement-house workers hoped to produce productive citizens.

As the twentieth century progressed, states passed social-welfare legislation ranging from TRUANCY laws mandating that children under the age of sixteen attend school to housing codes regulating sanitation and safety, and many activities begun by settlement houses were taken over by health inspectors and social workers. Still, it was not until the GREAT DEPRESSION of the 1930's devastated the country that the federal government began to play an active role in providing welfare assistance for the U.S. populace. Following the crash of the STOCK MARKET in October, 1929, economic conditions throughout the United States rapidly worsened. Within a few years, 25 percent of the workforce was unemployed. Soup kitchens became common sights in urban areas. Under Republican president Herbert Hoover, the government passed legislation such as the Emergency Relief and Construction Act of 1932 in an attempt to reverse the economic downturn. Despite this, public perception that the Hoover Administration had done too little too late contributed to Democrat Franklin D. Roosevelt's election in 1932.

Roosevelt promised a "NEW DEAL" and quickly set in motion a wide range of social-welfare programs, in the form of both direct relief and work relief. Programs created under the Works Progress Administration (WPA), such as the Civilian Conservation Corps (CCC), provided food and housing, training, and a small wage to thousands of unemployed young men. CCC workers worked in state and national parks and forest reserves building thousands of miles of road to make formerly inaccessible areas available to the public. The CCC is often cited as an example of a successful social-welfare program; it served as a model for similar state and federal programs, such as the JOB CORPS, but it has never been replicated on as large a scale as in the 1930's.

In addition to work-relief programs, New Deal legislation included the SOCIAL SECURITY ACT of 1935. Although it is often perceived as applying only to the elderly, the Social Security Act actually formed a comprehensive social-welfare program designed to protect all U.S. residents from the ill effects of economic hardship. The act included twenty different titles, or subject areas, that would assist people in times of sickness, disability, UNEMPLOYMENT, and RETIREMENT. Legislators have amended the Social Security Act a number of times. Some of the original titles were eliminated, while new titles were added. Congress added disability benefits in 1956 and MEDICARE benefits in 1965. In the 1990's, programs funded and administered under the Social Security Act included Supplemental Security Income, AID TO FAMILIES WITH DEPENDENT CHILDREN (AFDC), Medicaid, Old-Age, Survivors', and Disability Insurance (OASDI), and Medicare.

World War II and the economic boom that followed diverted public attention from welfare issues until the 1960's. After the war ended, there was a brief interest in instituting a national health plan similar to the one the British government developed, but U.S. citizens failed to support the idea. It was not until the administration of President Lyndon B. Johnson that the federal government again took an interest in fighting POVERTY. Under Johnson's leadership, programs such as the Work Incentive Training Act, or WIN, provided training allowances and paid child-care expenses for welfare recipients attending school or receiving on-the-job training, while the federal FOOD STAMPS program administered by the Department of Agriculture helped ensure that poor people would enjoy adequate nutrition.

Sources of Controversy. Most U.S. citizens have always held ambivalent attitudes toward providing welfare benefits to the poor. The history of the United States is laced with stories of entrepreneurs born into poverty who through determination and individual ingenuity rose above their origins and became millionaires. There is a strong national belief that all people have an equal opportunity to succeed and that, therefore, people who are poor are poor by choice. That is, many people believe that welfare recipients remain on welfare because they are too lazy to work.

This belief that welfare recipients are lazy is often coupled with a misperception of what welfare entails. Many people, for example, assume that anyone using food stamps to purchase groceries is unemployed. The truth is that eligibility for food stamps is based on family income. A person can be working full-time, but if wages earned fall below certain guidelines, that person is eligible for food stamps.

Sensational stories in the news media spotlighting abuses of the welfare system also contributed to public dissatisfaction with assistance programs. Although statistics indicated most recipients of public aid were on welfare less than three years, stories highlighting families that had been on welfare for multiple generations led many people to believe too many recipients had chosen welfare for a way of life. Similarly, stories of deliberate FRAUD served to emphasize weaknesses in the system. During congressional hearings investigating welfare reform, for example, congressmen heard testimony describing fraudulent Aid to Families with Dependent Children (AFDC) claims that had cost the government hundreds of thousands of dollars.

Finally, in any political climate where taxpayers were clamoring for budget reform, welfare made a convenient target for politicians. By the mid-1990's, the United States government was facing harsh budget realities. The national debt was growing, and taxpayers had indicated they would likely vote out of office anyone who proposed tax increases, but most items in the federal budget were considered politically untouchable. The one area where political LOBBYING was weakest was poverty programs; poor people did not vote.

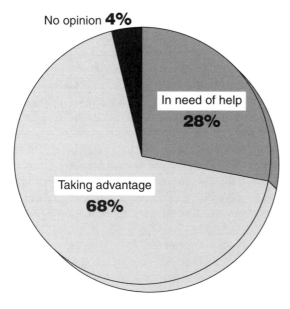

**PUBLIC OPINION, 1994:
ARE MOST PEOPLE ON WELFARE
TRULY IN NEED OF HELP,
OR TAKING ADVANTAGE
OF THE SYSTEM?**

No opinion **4%**

In need of help
28%

Taking advantage
68%

Source: George Gallup, Jr., ed., *The Gallup Poll: Public Opinion, 1994* (Wilmington, Del.: Scholarly Resources, 1995).

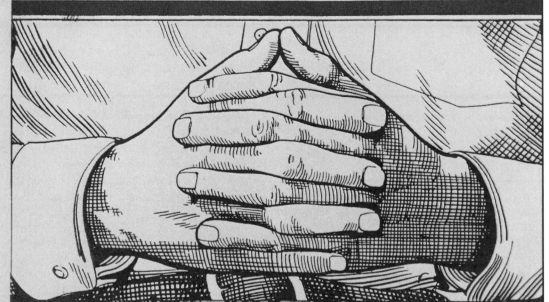

SUSPECT WELFARE FRAUD?

DON'T JUST SIT THERE

REPORT IT!

WRITE: **FRAUD INVESTIGATOR**
Grant Co. D.S.S.
P.O. Box 111
Lancaster, WI 53813

OR CALL: **(608) 723-2136** OR 723-6743

Instances of fraud have led to many calls for reform of the welfare system. (James L. Shaffer)

U.S. WELFARE SPENDING, 1989
(IN MILLIONS OF DOLLARS)

Program Categories	Federal	State and Local
Social insurance	387,290	80,765
Public aid	79,852	47,623
Health and medical programs	24,215	32,651
Veterans programs	29,638	466
Education	18,520	220,111
Housing	15,184	2,943
Other social welfare	8,492	8,117
Total	**563,191**	**392,676**

Source: U.S. Department of Commerce, Bureau of the Census, *Statistical Abstract of the United States, 1992.* Washington, D.C.: U.S. Government Printing Office, 1992.

Note: "Social insurance" includes Social Security, Medicare, public employee retirement, and workers' compensation; "Public aid" includes Medicaid, Supplemental Security Income (SSI), and food stamps.

Proposed Reforms. Prior to the 1994 elections, the REPUBLICAN PARTY proposed a program for budget reform they called a "CONTRACT WITH AMERICA." In 1995, with the power of the new Republican congressional majority behind him, Speaker of the House Newt GINGRICH introduced a number of reforms to the existing welfare system drawn from the "contract." These reforms included giving more authority to individual states to determine how federal funds for programs such as AFDC would be administered and instituting a requirement that no welfare recipient could receive benefits for more than two years. Gingrich believed that limiting benefits would force recipients to go to work. Gingrich also proposed discouraging teenagers from becoming pregnant and collecting welfare checks by prohibiting payment of benefits to minors. Finally, he suggested that one solution for poor families trying to raise children on inadequate incomes would be to bring back ORPHANAGES. Rather than allowing children to grow up in a CULTURE OF POVERTY and welfare dependency, Gingrich argued, children would be better served by being placed in group homes administered by private charities.

In response to the Republicans' draconian suggestions, the Democratic administration of President Bill CLINTON argued that what was needed were not harsh measures such as penalizing families for poverty by removing their children from their homes, but instead improved administration of existing programs and increased funding for programs that had been shown to work. In July, 1996, however, in what many observers saw as a politically inspired election-year move, Clinton agreed to sign a Republican-sponsored reform bill that radically revamped the U.S. welfare system. The legislation ended federal support for such welfare staples as AFDC, replacing it with "block grants" of money to the individual states to fund their own independent relief programs. Many liberals decried Clinton's act as a betrayal of the poor, while many conservatives exulted over the apparent demise of a system they had long assailed. Commentators from across the political spectrum, however, admitted that the effects of such sweeping reform were bound to be unpredictable.

Areas of Agreement. Both Republicans and Democrats agreed, however, that the individual states should be granted more freedom in designing programs for administering welfare funds. Several states had obtained special permission from the federal government to experiment with welfare administration in the 1990's.

Wisconsin, for example, linked AFDC payments to school attendance. If a child living in an AFDC household missed school, the family was penalized through a reduction in its AFDC grant. Although the program was sharply criticized as placing an unreasonable burden on parents, some analysts argued that it had multiple positive effects. Parents were forced to become more involved in their children's lives, and the children themselves benefited by being more likely to succeed in school. Under Republican governor Tommy Thompson, Wisconsin made completing high school mandatory for all AFDC recipients.

Michigan, New Jersey, and other states also moved to reform their welfare programs. Michigan completely eliminated its general assistance program in 1990 and made significant changes to its AFDC programs. General assistance is relief paid to childless, indigent adults. In Michigan, if an adult was unemployed and had no income, he or she had to qualify as disabled and unable to work for that reason in order to receive any government financial assistance. Michigan's elimination of general assistance met with considerable criticism and was blamed for rising rates of HOMELESSNESS in urban areas. Critics noted that many of the adults receiving general assistance prior to its elimination had actually been eligible for disability, but that state social-services workers had chosen not to complete the proper paperwork, as it was faster and easier to process the general assistance forms. Thus, the supposed savings provided by the elimination of general assistance were an illusion, because the majority of the recipients simply transferred from one program to another.

A reform that many states instituted was a form of WORKFARE: The recipients were required to earn their AFDC checks or food stamps through their participation in JOB-TRAINING PROGRAMS or public service. Recipients not enrolled in school had to perform a certain number of hours of work for nonprofit or government agencies in their communities. Recipients received a modest travel allowance or subsidized CHILD CARE to offset their expenses. Workfare was based in part on the belief that one problem many welfare recipients had in finding and holding a job was a lack of acceptable work habits. Participants in many workfare programs were required to attend regular meetings where they were counseled on interviewing skills, preparing résumés, and looking for work.

Finally, states such as New Jersey began penalizing welfare mothers who had additional children while receiving AFDC. Rather than seeing an increase in the monthly welfare check, a woman having an additional child while on welfare would either receive no increased allowance or might even have her monthly check reduced.

Roadblocks to Reform. Although few people would argue that the welfare system did not need reform, serious impediments existed. While both Democrats and Republicans debated which measures would be most effective in terms of cost cutting, both sides, like the general public, ignored many of the realities of poverty in the United States.

As a number of social critics and reformers have noted, poverty has multiple causes. The standard of living in rural areas often tends to be lower than in urban regions through factors such as lack of opportunity: There are fewer employers, and little industry; what work there is tends to be either low paying or seasonal in nature. Rural resort areas often depend on a seasonal labor force that ekes out a living by relying on forms of social welfare such as food stamps, unem-

Demonstrators in Philadelphia call for welfare reform. (Impact Visuals, Harvey Finkle)

ployment compensation, and AFDC during the months when tourism is slow or nonexistent. Similarly, welfare recipients residing in an inner-city ghetto often are trapped by a combination of a lack of jobs in the immediate community and poor public transportation to allow them to reach employers in the suburbs. A study of the public transit system in the Washington, D.C., area, for example, revealed that the system was set up in such a way as to make commuting out of the city to employers locating in the rapidly growing suburbs almost impossible.

Critics of the welfare system also frequently discount or ignore the economic disincentive to work that exists in areas where the only employment available is MINIMUM WAGE or part-time with few fringe benefits. It makes no economic sense for a single parent to incur the hardships of procuring child care in order to work at a job that does not pay enough to meet daily expenses, particularly when accepting employment would mean losing Medicaid coverage. Welfare recipients have little motivation to take jobs that reduce their already low standard of living.

Lack of educational opportunities is also an important factor. To demand that a welfare recipient find a job when that recipient is functionally illiterate because of a childhood spent in overcrowded, underfunded, substandard public schools is both unrealistic and cruel. Despite a national ideology that emphasizes equal opportunity, the sad truth is that the quality of the education available to children in the United States varies widely from state to state, city to city, and even neighborhood to neighborhood. School districts with large minority populations often suffer from lack of funding and decaying infrastructures. Many critics of efforts to reform welfare have suggested that the United States would do better if it instead concentrated on reforming the educational system. Children who are encouraged to remain in school and pursue worthwhile careers are not likely to end up on welfare.

By suggesting that welfare recipients should be willing to work or else lose their benefits, welfare critics also ignored the fact that the majority of persons receiving welfare funds were children. It is an obvious truism that if a child must be present in the home for a family to receive AID TO FAMILIES WITH DEPENDENT CHILDREN, then children are receiving welfare. Critics of the suggestion that all able-bodied adults should work argue that instituting such a requirement without providing for adequate day care for their children will create more problems than it solves.

Finally, advocates of harsh measures of welfare reform ignore the fact that in any population there will always be some people who simply are unable to play a truly productive role. Despite the best efforts of social workers and educators, there will always be some individuals who are so socially inept or lacking in skills that it is not possible for them to keep a job. Studies of work-training programs conducted among welfare recipients have indicated that the simple truth is that some welfare recipients are on welfare not because they do not want to work but because they are incapable of working. Scholars assessing the data were undecided as to whether this resulted from being raised in a "CULTURE OF POVERTY" that was isolated from mainstream American VALUES or from a lack of basic intelligence, but agreed that some welfare recipients simply did not respond to job-skills training. The question then becomes one of a society's moral responsibilities to the disadvantaged: Is it ethical to penalize the poor for their own misfortune?

The United States has a tradition of rugged INDIVIDUALISM. U.S. citizens are not comfortable with the notion that the government has an obligation to provide a social SAFETY NET for everyone. While other countries have experimented with providing CHILD-CARE allowances, comprehensive medical benefits, and other social-welfare programs to every citizen regardless of need, the United States has provided social welfare only grudgingly, and then in piecemeal fashion. Where other countries such as Canada, Sweden, and Portugal have national health-care programs that apply to every citizen, the United States limits national HEALTH INSURANCE to two populations: the elderly, through MEDICARE, and the poor, through Medicaid. In a similarly contradictory fashion, where the Scandinavian countries treat children as a valued resource and provide a paid leave to all new parents to ensure that children are given a good start in life, the United States applies a needs test and provides financial assistance only to those desperate enough to apply for help.

Nevertheless, most U.S. citizens are still willing to accept various forms of government aid and, indeed, see it as a right if it is not, in their minds, labeled as welfare. Workers who are injured on the job may receive disability payments funded through the SOCIAL SECURITY ACT, the same act that regulates Aid to Families with Dependent Children, and they firmly believe that their disability checks are not welfare but that AFDC checks are. The true challenge in welfare reform may thus lie not in reforming the administration of social-welfare programs but instead in changing societal attitudes. —*Nancy Farm Mannikko*

SUGGESTED READINGS: *Teen Mothers—Citizens or Dependents?* (Chicago: University of Chicago Press, 1995), by Ruth Horowitz, is a fascinating examination of a government program intended to help teenage mothers complete high school and get jobs. Desmond King's *Actively Seeking Work?* (Chicago: University of Chicago Press, 1995) compares unemployment and welfare policy in the United States and Great Britain.

Lawrence H. Summers' *Understanding Unemployment* (Cambridge, Mass.: MIT Press, 1990) provides an economic analysis of theories of joblessness, while Harvey Green's *The Uncertainty of Everyday Life, 1915-1945* (New York: Harper Collins, 1992) gives a historical context for many twentieth century social policies. Both an anthology edited by Judith A. Chafel, *Child Poverty and Public Policy* (Washington, D.C.: Urban Institute Press, 1993), which analyzes child poverty in the United States, and William Julius Wilson's *The Ghetto Underclass* (Newbury Park, Calif.: Sage, 1993), a study of problems in urban areas, provide readers with a wealth of information regarding the relationships between government intervention and continuing poverty in the United States.

Wellness: Positive physical, emotional, mental, or spiritual health achieved through conscious and careful living. The concept of wellness is central to many "NEW AGE" health philosophies. Wellness practices focus on prevention and can include both conventional medical approaches and such alternatives as vegetarian and macrobiotic diets, YOGA, TAI CHI, imagery and visualization techniques, dream therapy, meditation, positive thinking, stress and anger management, ecological awareness, massage and other types of body manipulation, and special breathing techniques. Wellness advocates assert that health states are affected by one's thoughts, feelings, and relationships and by one's overall outlook and spiritual values. Detractors argue that the benefits of such approaches are largely unproven and that many wellness techniques amount to little more than quackery.

West, Cornel (b. June 2, 1953, Tulsa, Okla.): African American educator and philosopher. The Harvard and Princeton-educated West became director of Prince-

ton's Afro-American Studies Department in 1986 following a controversial tenure at Yale, during which he clashed with administrators over the university's failure to divest itself of South African investments. His books include *Prophesy Deliverance!: An Afro-American Revolutionary Christianity* (1982) and *The Ethical Dimensions of Marxist Thought* (1991).

West Bank: Section of Palestine that lies between Israel and the Jordan River. More than two thousand square miles in area, it includes East Jerusalem, the Latrun Salient, and the northwest quarter of the Dead Sea. Control of the area has been bitterly contested by Israelis, who occupied it in 1967, and Palestinian nationalists, who view it as a crucial remnant of their "lost garden." In 1993, Israel agreed to extend autonomous status to the West Bank and the GAZA STRIP. Israeli-Palestinian relations have been complicated by the status of East Jerusalem, which is claimed by Israel, and by the presence of Jewish settlements in Palestinian territory.

Westmoreland v. CBS (1985): U.S. district court case. In 1982, the Columbia Broadcasting System (CBS) broadcast a ninety-minute documentary charging that General William C. Westmoreland had fabricated and suppressed intelligence information about the VIETNAM WAR in order to deceive the American government and people. Westmoreland sued for LIBEL. Evidence showed that Westmoreland had not suppressed or distorted intelligence and that CBS had fabricated some of its broadcast. Nevertheless, the realities of U.S. libel law—in particular, the "reckless disregard of the truth" standard—caused Westmoreland to withdraw his suit before the case actually went to the jury.

Wetlands: Land areas that are flooded or saturated with water part or all of the year. Freshwater wetlands are called marshes, bogs, or swamps. Saltwater wetlands are called tidal wetlands or coastal marshes. Each type supports distinctive vegetation and animals adapted to wet conditions. Some persons view wetlands as waste areas that should be drained, filled in, and used for growing crops or for building. Other persons see wetlands as valuable resting, feeding, and breeding areas for a variety of wildlife. Wetlands also function to filter out sediments, nutrients, and bacteria from surface runoff waters.

Whaling: The hunting, killing, and processing of large marine mammals, usually on the high seas. The animals' flesh is eaten in many countries, but fears about the conservation of several whale species caused international concern and dissension.

For centuries, whaling was conducted from sailing ships and with handheld harpoons. In the late nineteenth century, steam (and, later, diesel) ships and cannon-fired harpoons greatly increased the whalers' efficiency. Populations of blue, sperm, right, bowhead, and other large whales quickly declined to dangerously low numbers. In 1946, the International Whaling Commission (IWC) was established to manage the whale stocks. The IWC could only make recommendations; it had no regulatory authority.

Member nations of IWC approved a five-year moratorium on whaling to begin in 1985. The ban was renewed in 1990. The Soviet Union, Iceland, Norway, and Japan opposed the moratorium, and the latter three nations began whaling for "scientific" research. After the carcasses were examined, the meat was sold. The exploited species was the minke whale, a smaller animal. All of the great whales, except the minke, are on the endangered species list. Biologists examining the DNA of whale meat sold in Japan have found humpback and fin whale (protected species) in the markets and restaurants. Japan, Iceland, and Norway announced that they intended to continue whaling for research but also because their people enjoyed and needed whale meat in their diets.

In 1995, Japan killed about 300 minke whales for research in the Southern Ocean Sanctuary. Estimates of the minke population in the sanctuary suggested 760,000 individuals. Japan argued this research could

Activists protest the White House visit of Japan's prime minister following the 1988 departure of the Japanese whaling fleet to kill whales in the Antarctic. (UPI/Corbis-Bettmann)

add important information about the biology of the species and the effect of oceanic pollution on their health. Once the research was completed, the whale meat was sold to help defray research expenses.

Norway and Iceland conducted their research on minke whales in the North Atlantic Ocean. The catch in 1992 was ninety-seven animals out of a population estimated at 87,000. An adviser to the Norwegian Ministry of Foreign Affairs pointed out that consuming whale meat was a cultural affair in that country. Further, natives of Iceland, Norway, and Japan depended on the whale resource for subsistence. Proponents of whaling saw it as a sustainable use of a natural resource. Opponents viewed it as an archaic activity and a violation of ANIMAL RIGHTS.

The effects of moratoria on whale populations are not well understood. The Pacific gray whale was removed from the endangered species list in 1995 after a forty-year moratorium, but other species face possible extinction. Further decline of whales as the result of continued whaling, but also damage to the whales' environment, may seriously impair oceanic biodiversity.

Environmental impacts damaging to whale populations include noise from ships that may drive whales from calving grounds or disrupt whale sounds essential to communication. Fertilizer and PESTICIDE runoff from farms and sewage can poison fish eaten by whales. In addition, whales have been killed in collisions with ships or when entangled in discarded fishing gear.

Whistleblowing: Exposure by employees of organizational crimes or abuses. Whistleblowing often involves exposing some aspect of a company or other organization's policies, beliefs, or informal practices in an attempt to bring about change. Whistleblowers may risk being fired and may also encounter ostracism from coworkers. In response, many governments have adopted statutes protecting whistleblowers from retaliation. Examples of situations that might lead to whistleblowing include knowledge about dangerous or faulty technology, job-based health hazards, pay irregularities, and other forms of FRAUD.

White-collar crime: Information on the variety of white-collar crimes is not as carefully collected and routinely reported as that on "street" crimes such as burglary and robbery. Nevertheless, experts estimate that white-collar crime annually costs taxpayers billions of dollars. Cost, however, must be estimated in more than dollars, as white-collar crimes may be committed by those in high positions of trust in business and government. When trust in important decision-makers and institutions is violated, people lose confidence in investing, voting, and other basic social activities.

Definition. The first major scholarly work on white-collar crime was published by Edwin H. Sutherland in 1949. Even more than today, it was then generally assumed that CRIME was mostly committed by those of low social standing. If crime were in fact committed as much by those of high as low social status, however, criminological theory would have to be revised. To examine this possibility, Sutherland defined white-collar crime as acts committed by people of respect and high social standing in the course of their occupations.

After Sutherland, scholarly interest in white-collar crime waned until the 1960's and 1970's. In 1970, Herbert Edelhertz questioned the generality of Sutherland's definition. White-collar crime, he said, was "democratic," something committed by people from all walks of life. To Edelhertz, white-collar crime refers to illegal acts committed by nonphysical means such as craftiness and deception to obtain something (for example, profit or gain) or avoid something (for example, the payment of a bill or taxes). All white-collar crime, according to Edelhertz, has the following elements: an intent to commit an illegal act; an intent to disguise; reliance on victim carelessness and unwitting cooperation; and concealment of illegality. In contrast to Sutherland, then, Edelhertz encouraged the study of white-collar crime as a certain type of offense rather than a type of crime committed by a certain type of offender.

Types of White-Collar Crime. There are three basic types of white-collar crime: ad hoc individual crimes, occupational crimes, and organizational crime. Ad hoc individual white-collar crime includes offenses committed by individuals independent of their occupations. An important source on crime is the Uniform Crime Reports published annually by the FEDERAL BUREAU OF INVESTIGATION. Arrest data are provided on three types of white-collar crime: embezzlement, FRAUD, and forgery and counterfeiting. Unfortunately, no effort is made to distinguish the arrests of those who committed an offense in the course of their occupations from those who did not. Generally, arrests for these offenses account for about 4 percent of all those arrested annually.

Of these crimes, arrests for fraud are the most numerous (more than three-fourths of the annual total). Fraud is "the intentional misrepresentation of fact to unlawfully deprive a person of his or her property or legal rights, without damage to property or actual or threatened injury to persons."

Arrests for forgery and counterfeiting (counted as a single category) generally account for less than 20 percent of the total for all three. Forgery is "the alteration of something written by another person or writing something that purports to be either the act of another or to have been executed at a time or place other than was in fact the case." Counterfeiting is "the manufacture or attempted manufacture of a copy or imitation of a negotiable instrument with value set by law or convention, or possession of such copy without authorization and with intent to defraud by claiming the genuineness of the copy."

Embezzlement arrests represent about 2 percent of the total for these offenses. Embezzlement is "the misappropriation, misapplication, or illegal disposal of property entrusted to an individual with intent to defraud the legal owner or intended beneficiary."

Occupational white-collar crime includes illegalities committed by individuals in the course of their occupations. In 1986, eleven Boston-area policemen were indicted for illegally obtaining and selling police examinations over an eight-year period. In 1988, two executives were convicted of fraudulently marketing and selling alleged apple juice for babies that was in fact a mixture of water, sugar, and chemicals. In 1988, *Time* magazine reported a variety of cases. A New York congressman was found guilty of extorting fifty thousand dollars in exchange for influencing procurement of a defense contract; a Medicaid case concerned a New York physician and his father who bought blood from poor people at fifty cents a sample and then billed Medicaid as much as two thousand dollars for the cost of testing the blood of alleged Medicaid patients; a "Pentagon payola" case involved eighty-nine employees of a computer firm who were charged with procurement fraud and bid-rigging (colluding with competitors before each was to bid on the purchase of equipment); and an insider-trading case involved the selling of prepublication copies of *Business Magazine* to a stockbroker who wished to buy stocks recommended in a column before the price increased.

"INSIDER TRADING" became a national scandal during the 1980's. Insider trading is the illegal exchange of investment information between colluding parties. Two of the more infamous examples are Ivan Boesky and Michael MILKEN. Boesky was said to control $3 billion worth of stock-purchasing power, and Milken was regarded as the most powerful man in American financial circles. The two developed a close relationship, one that eventually included violation of SECURITIES AND EXCHANGE COMMISSION (SEC) prohibitions against insider trading.

Boesky pleaded guilty to a charge of conspiring to file false claims with the SEC. He was fined $100 million, barred from the investment business for life, and sentenced to three years in prison. In 1988, a news agency released an article entitled "Boesky in Country Club Jail." The federal minimum-security California facility in question was described as having "open air television so prisoners can watch and work on their suntans at the same time."

Milken later pleaded guilty to six felony counts involving fraud and the filing of a false tax return. He was fined $600 million and sentenced to ten years in prison. On appeal, his sentence was reduced to two years. He was released after serving twenty-two months.

Organizational white-collar crime entails illegal acts committed by companies and agencies. Because of limited means and obstacles surrounding the ability to study high-ranking decision-makers in business and government, Sutherland examined the illegal activities of the nation's seventy largest nonfinancial companies from criminal court records and the records of regulatory bodies such as the SEC and the FEDERAL TRADE COMMISSION. He found that the seventy organizations had close to one thousand decisions rendered against them. They averaged fourteen each, and the range was from one to fifty. Forty-two firms had criminal courts convictions, and they averaged four each. Sutherland believed that such evidence was sufficient to indicate the fallacy of assuming that crime was essentially the result of POVERTY and underprivilege.

After Sutherland, the next major study of organizational crime was led by Marshall B. Clinard in 1979. The study examined the record of illegality (as indicated by the records of federal regulatory agencies) for the years 1975 and 1976 of 582 of the nation's largest publicly owned companies. Nearly 60 percent of the firms were found to have an enforcement action rendered against them. The companies had a record of 1,860 violations, with an average of more than three each.

In 1985, *Time* magazine reported that General Electric had pleaded guilty to a charge of defrauding the U.S. Air Force of $800,000. General Dynamics was found to have overcharged the PENTAGON by $75 million for items such as country-club fees and transportation. At the time, forty-five of the one hundred largest U.S. military suppliers were reported to be under criminal investigation.

In 1990, General Electric settled claims with the federal government for overcharges involving military equipment. In 1991, the Unisys Corporation pleaded guilty to a number of felony and civil charges concerning procurement fraud and manner of bidding on Pentagon contracts.

Sentencing White-collar Offenders. Generally, white-collar offenses receive relatively light penalties. Seldom is a lengthy sentence imposed on a major corporate offender such as Michael Milken. When high-ranking white-collar offenders are sentenced to jail or prison, they are typically assigned to minimum-security institutions with more than the usual basic amenities and personal freedom. Mostly, firms are fined and the amount is seldom sufficient to deter future illegality. It is still the case that judges and the public find it difficult to regard the well-dressed, well-educated white-collar offender as a criminal in the class of a burglar.   —*Calvin J. Larson*

SUGGESTED READINGS: Basic information on the nature, variety, and costs of white-collar crime, as well as the sentencing of white-collar offenders, can be obtained from Edwin H. Sutherland's *White Collar Crime* (New York: Holt, Rinehart and Winston, 1949), James W. Coleman's *The Criminal Elite* (New York: St. Martin's Press, 1993), and Jeffrey Reiman's *The Rich Get Richer and the Poor Get Prison* (Needham Heights, Mass.: Allyn & Bacon, 1995). Important works on insider trading include Dennis B. Levine's *Inside Out: An Insider's Account of Wall Street* (New York: Putnam's, 1991) and James B. Stewart's *Den of Thieves* (New York: Simon & Schuster, 1991).

White flight: Movement of an area's white population from cities to suburbs or other outlying regions when the number of minority residents increases in a neighborhood. The most common motivating factors for white flight are a loss of jobs, an unwillingness to put children in desegregated schools, the search for higher paying jobs, and a fear of crime. White flight is not limited to moves to the suburbs but may also include the crossing of state lines.

White flight was first observed in association with court-mandated school desegregation, as many whites in affected areas moved to avoid the busing of their children to integrated schools. White flight seems to occur in waves, pushing these individuals further and further away from the cities. Threatened by the influx of immigrants and black professionals to the suburbs, affluent whites moved further away from the old suburbs to new, more expensive housing. One often-noted effect of the phenomenon has been the impetus it has given to the development of public transportation systems such as subways and trains.

Another type of white flight is attributed to poor whites who flee central cities to states that have low immigrant populations, fewer minorities, lower costs of living, and greater job availability. Northern industrial states and the Farm Belt have thus lost many whites to Southern and Western states; however, college-educated whites have tended to stay in the cities, perhaps as a result of the availability of jobs for the well educated in urban settings. Poorer whites have also cited such reasons as rising taxes, overcrowded schools, language barriers, rising crime rates, and a fear of immigrants and people of other races.

The final major group that contributes to the phenomenon of white flight is the elderly. As a group, the elderly are motivated to leave central cities for many of the same reasons cited by others; in addition, many elderly whites move to find favorable weather. Many elderly white people have thus left Northern industrial states, the Farm Belt, and the Frost Belt for the Sunbelt and Northwestern states. Many real-estate companies build new houses, condominiums, and resort areas to encourage the elderly to relocate; such developers are often accused of preventing African Americans and other minorities from relocating to these areas by creating de facto racial barriers such as high prices.

White Ribbon Campaign: Antiviolence movement. In 1989, at the University of Québec at Montreal, fourteen women were shot to death during a rampage by a disturbed gunman, Marc Lepine, whose suicide note expressed antifeminist rage. This tragic event inspired a wave of attempts across Canada to address issues of male violence. The White Ribbon Campaign is a national effort to remind the public of the incident by encouraging the wearing of emblematic white lapel ribbons. In the United States, the movement may have

The Ku Klux Klan and neo-Nazi groups adhere to the philosophy of white supremacy. (AP/Wide World Photos)

inspired the "White Ribbons Against Pornography" campaign run by the group Morality in Media.

White supremacist movements: Racist organizations promoting the superiority of whites. Contemporary white supremacist movements developed in the late 1960's and early 1970's in reaction to the CIVIL RIGHTS MOVEMENT. Estimates suggest that there are from ten thousand to twenty-five thousand core activists in a variety of white racist organizations in the United States, almost double the membership of the late 1970's.

Scholars suggest that the growing membership of white supremacist groups in the 1990's is directly related to the dramatic social change in the American culture and the shift of the American population toward greater diversity. White supremacist associations in the United States include the Aryan National Front, the National Socialist Liberation Front, the White Aryan Resistance, the Order, the Christian Defense League, the KU KLUX KLAN, the Posse Comitatus, and the Christian Vanguard. The movement's literature attacks African Americans, Jewish Americans, and other ethnic minorities, portrays women as weak and subservient, and seeks to restore America to its "pure" Anglo-Saxon past.

The most radical members of such groups claim that their goal will be realized in a violent racial war that will result in the "purification" of the United States and the unity of all white Christians. In 1979, members of a neo-Nazi group and the Ku Klux Klan killed five demonstrators at an anti-Klan rally in Greensboro, North Carolina. In 1984, two members of the American Nazi Party were convicted of civil rights violations in the murder of a Jewish radio talk-show host in Denver, Colorado. In 1988, Kenneth Menske and Kyle Brewster, members of a "skinhead" group in Portland, Oregon, were arrested for the beating death of a black man, Mulugeta Seraw. Finally, the 1995 bombing of a federal building in Oklahoma City, Oklahoma, was traced to members of a paramilitary organization thought to have ties to white supremacist organizations. These events and others served to dramatize the racial divisions in American culture and have forced citizens to take notice of a growing racist presence in the United States.

Whitewater investigation: In 1977, Arkansas attorney general, gubernatorial candidate, and future U.S. president Bill CLINTON, along with his wife, Hillary Rodham CLINTON, obtained an unsecured $20,000 loan to invest in a real-estate venture in northern Arkansas. The Clintons' involvement in the failed Whitewater Development Company—named after the Whitewater River that the land to be developed bordered—resulted in a number of allegations involving financial corruption and ethical misconduct.

During the 1992 presidential campaign, reports of the Clintons' investments in a failed Arkansas real-estate venture began to surface. What made the reports interesting to the media at the time were the Clintons' partners in the venture, James and Susan McDougal. Bill Clinton had befriended James McDougal in the 1960's, and together they had made a small profit on a 1977 land deal. Press reports alleged that the Clintons had used the investment for improper tax deductions and that James McDougal may have diverted money from Madison Guaranty, a failed Arkansas thrift he headed, to the Whitewater development. It was also alleged that Hillary Clinton, a partner in the law firm that represented Madison Guaranty, may have used her relationship as the first lady of Arkansas to protect the thrift from state banking regulators. Clinton denied any wrongdoing and claimed that he and his wife had lost $68,900 in the Whitewater development, even though the loss had never been reflected in their tax returns.

In December, 1992, the Clintons sold their share in Whitewater to James McDougal for $1,000. Political opponents and journalists still had suspicions about the Clintons' relationship with James McDougal and Madison Guaranty, which was taken over by regulators after it was declared insolvent. On July 20, 1993, Deputy White House Counsel Vincent Foster was found dead in a Washington-area park, the victim of an apparent suicide. Foster, a former law partner with Hillary Clinton, had represented the Clintons in their relationship to McDougal and Whitewater Development.

In October, 1993, *The Washington Post* reported that federal regulators had begun a criminal investigation into the conduct of Madison Guaranty. Both Bill and Hillary Clinton were named as possible witnesses in the investigation. By January, 1994, Whitewater was no longer merely a failed real-estate investment; murky reports of document shredding and the removal of Whitewater-related documents from Foster's office after his suicide led Republicans to call for a special prosecutor. Under increasing political pressure, Clinton was forced to approve the appointment of special

Whitewater investigation

President Bill Clinton addresses reporters on the subject of the Whitewater investigation. (Archive Photos, Reuters, Win McNamee)

prosecutor Robert Fisk to investigate the Clintons' involvement in Whitewater and the circumstances surrounding Foster's death.

In February, 1994, allegations of a Watergate-style coverup began to plague the Clinton Administration. It was alleged that White House Counsel Bernard Nussbaum and other officials had attempted to influence federal banking regulators' investigation of Madison

Guaranty and possible links to the Whitewater development. On March 3, Clinton ordered his staff to "bend over backwards" to avoid interference in any investigation of Whitewater. On March 4, Nussbaum was fired by Clinton. On March 10, Fiske convened a grand jury and subpoenaed ten White House and Treasury Department officials to testify. Surveys taken in March indicated that more than half of Americans thought that the Clintons were hiding something about Whitewater. Fiske's preliminary report, released in July, 1994, suggested that while further investigation was required, there was no evidence to suggest that the Clintons' involvement in Whitewater had been illegal. Fiske also reported that "the evidence is insufficient to establish that anyone within the White House or Treasury acted with the intent to corruptly influence" the investigation. In August, Fiske was replaced as special prosecutor by Kenneth Starr.

Starr and his staff spent the next year collecting documents and taking depositions. Eager to capitalize on Whitewater, the Republican-led Congress held House and Senate hearings on Whitewater in the summer and fall of 1995. The hearings failed to uncover any dramatic revelations about the Whitewater development or the conduct of Clinton Administration officials. A report prepared by former Republican prosecutor Jay Stevens in August, 1995, for federal banking officials investigating Madison Guaranty confirmed that the Clintons had lost $42,192 in connection with Whitewater and failed to provide any evidence to suggest that the Clintons were aware of misconduct by McDougal. While questions remained about the legality of some of the Clintons' tax deductions and about

Hillary Clinton's role in protecting Madison Guaranty from bank regulators, Whitewater did not develop into the sort of political scandal that Republicans had desired and the Clinton Administration had feared.

Wiesel, Elie (b. Sept. 30, 1928, Sighet, Romania): Writer and human rights activist. A victim of Nazi persecution of the Jews during World War II, Wiesel was confined in both the Auschwitz and Buchenwald concentration camps before he was liberated by U.S. troops in April, 1945. Uncertain about how to verbalize his traumatic experiences, Wiesel maintained a self-imposed silence on the subject until 1954, when he decided it was his responsibility to bear witness to the horrors of history. In extensive writings and lectures about the Holocaust and the human condition, he has explored the themes of madness, murder, suffering, evil, God, apathy, suicide, and faith. An outspoken advocate for civil rights in South Africa, Soviet Jewry, and nuclear disarmament, he was awarded the Congressional Gold Medal of Achievement in 1985 and the Nobel Peace Prize in 1986.

Holocaust survivor Elie Wiesel. (UPI/Corbis-Bettmann)

Wilderness Act (1964): U.S. environmental legislation. Signed into law on September 3, 1964, by President Lyndon B. Johnson, the act set aside nine million acres of national forests as the National Wilderness Preservation System, with 51.9 million acres of other lands to follow. Development was prohibited in these areas "where man himself is a visitor who does not remain." With the law's passage, environmentalists scored a major victory over mining and lumber interests. The act, the preeminent legislation of the modern environmental movement, reflected a shift in environmental philosophy from conservation of resources for future use to preservation of nature for its own sake.

Wildlife Refuges. *See* **Zoos and Wildlife Refuges.**

Willke, Jack (b. John Charles Willke, April 5, 1925, Maria Stein, Ohio): Pro-life author and leader. Willke is the coauthor (with wife Barbara) of a variety of pro-life educational materials,

Political columnist George F. Will in 1977. (UPI/Corbis-Bettmann)

including *Handbook on Abortion* (1971) and *Abortion: Questions and Answers* (1985). He has played a major role in the development of right-to-life organizations at the local, state, national, and international levels. He served as president of the NATIONAL RIGHT TO LIFE COMMITTEE (NRLC) from 1980 to 1983 and again from 1984 to 1991 and as president of the International Right to Life Federation beginning in 1985. Under his leadership, the NRLC expanded significantly. In 1991, he founded the Life Issues Institute.

Will, George (b. May 4, 1941, Champaign, Ill.): Conservative columnist and political commentator. Will attended Trinity College in Connecticut and Oxford University before obtaining a doctorate in political science from Princeton University in 1964. He taught political science at Michigan University and the University of Toronto but left academia in 1970. From 1973 to 1975, he served as the Washington editor of the conservative journal *National Review* and soon earned a national reputation as a syndicated columnist. In 1977, he won a Pulitzer Prize; his many books include *Statecraft as Soulcraft: What Government Does* (New York: Simon & Schuster, 1983).

Wills: Written, videotaped, or oral instructions outlining how people wish to influence others' behaviors before and after death. Each of the basic types—legal testaments or wills, living wills, and ethical wills—fulfills three functions: to bring order out of the chaos created by death and dying, to provide survivors with support, and to allow individuals to vent opinions.

Testators are persons who make legal wills; executors are persons or organizations named by testators who, after paying from the estate all burial and legal debts, inheritance taxes, outstanding income taxes, estate management costs, and creditors, then distribute bequests. When persons die intestate (without leaving wills), without naming executors, or with executors who refuse the role, the courts appoint administrators, who, following the laws of descent, make decisions about the estate regarding bank accounts, real-estate property, bonds, life-insurance policies, shares of stock, or any other personal property.

PROBATE is the court process by which legal wills are confirmed as genuine and properties are officially turned over to beneficiaries. Wills and codicils (will supplements), as well as their revocation, must demon-

strate the testators' intent and free will. Though not required, legal experts suggest wills be dated and photocopied to replace lost or unintentinally destroyed originals. A will may be revoked by written statement or physical act such as tearing or burning the document, crossing out each page, or writing either "void," "cancel," or "null" on each page.

To reduce claims against the estate, all children, including those who may be disinherited, are named in the will. Contestors of last testaments argue that wills were fraudulent, witnesses were incompetent (that is, emotionally unstable, acting under duress, or a beneficiary), testators were of unsound mind or were coerced, makers revoked the will, or wills were written by testators under eighteen years of age who had never been married or had served as members of the armed forces. In the United States, courts have held that fingerprints, rubber stamp inscriptions, nicknames, initials, illegible signatures, and proxy signatures are valid as signatures.

Though most legal wills are typed documents, some are handwritten or videotaped, in part or in their entirety. Persons in imminent mortal danger resulting from illness or accident and persons on active military duty during time of war may make holographic (oral) wills.

In 1977, California became the first state to pass natural-death legislation, which grants individuals' written requests that no "heroic measures" be used on them when recuperation is unlikely. These "living wills" (or dying-with-dignity or right-to-die wills), as well as legal wills and revocations, are subject to state guidelines.

Ethical wills, which bequeath a spiritual and moral legacy—in the form of family history or folklore to surviving children and grandchildren—via tape-recorded, videotaped, handwritten, or typed messages, are based on traditional authority or a desire to return to cultural roots.

SUGGESTED READINGS: Jack Riemer and Nathaniel Stampfer's *So That Your Values Live On: Ethical Wills and How to Prepare Them* (Woodstock, Vt.: Jewish Lights Publishing, 1991) provides instruction and examples of living wills, while Hannelore Wass and Robert A. Neimeyer's *Dying: Facing the Facts*, 3d ed. (Washington, D.C.: Taylor & Francis, 1995), describes will substitutes and rights of the terminally ill and offers other legal perspectives.

Wilson, Pete (b. Aug. 23, 1933, Lake Forest, Ill.): U.S. politician. Wilson served in the California Assem-

Pete Wilson casts a ballot in 1990. (UPI/Corbis-Bettmann)

bly, as the mayor of San Diego, and as a U.S. senator before becoming governor of California in 1991. He won a second term as governor in 1994. Hoping to gain the Republican nomination for the presidency in the 1996 elections, Wilson opposed affirmative action programs and called for deep cuts in government spending, especially in social programs such as welfare. He cited limited campaign finances as the reason for his withdrawal from the presidential race in September, 1995.

Winfrey, Oprah (b. Jan. 29, 1954, Kosciusko, Miss.): Television talk-show host and actress. The first African American woman to host a successful nationally syndicated television show, Winfrey began her broadcasting career in 1971 on a Nashville radio station. After working as a television news anchor in Baltimore in the 1970's, Winfrey eventually became the host of a local Chicago daily talk show. By 1986, the show had gone into national syndication, and Winfrey soon became one of the best-known and most powerful figures in television. Although she has drawn praise for her groundbreaking success as both a woman and an African American, she has also drawn criticism for focusing on sensational topics in her syndicated programs.

Wiretapping: Clandestine interception of telephone or other electronic communications. In earlier times, this practice was usually accomplished by "tapping" telephone lines to eavesdrop on phone calls. The practice is almost always illegal except when conducted by law-enforcement agencies, and it is then legal only with a warrant or other judicial authorization. Wiretapping now involves many media in addition to telephone wires, such as cellular telephone transmissions, computer data, satellite and microwave data links, and other electronic and digital communications. With new technologies, wiretapping and its related activities make the interception of information easier than ever to accomplish and equally easy to conceal.

Wise use: Doctrine regarding the conservation of natural resources. Wise-use philosophy asserts that nature should be judiciously harnessed for the benefit of humans and not left in a pristine, undisturbed state. Wise-use policies also prescribe that nonrenewable resources not be depleted too rapidly and that renewable

resources be culled wisely to allow sufficient time for regeneration. Inherent in the doctrine of the wise use of nonrenewable resources is the process of recycling reclaimable materials before they are irretrievably dispersed into landfills. The doctrine of wise use is part of a continuum of environmental policies spanning the extreme positions of total economic development and complete preservation.

Women: Women in U.S. and Canadian cultures face similar issues. These include aspects of personal relationships and families, single-parent households, poverty, homelessness, employment opportunities, sexual harassment, family caregiving responsibilities, child care, reproductive choices, AIDS and other health problems, access to health care, and personal safety.

The number of couples who cohabited instead of marrying increased markedly in the latter half of the twentieth century. Societal norms became more accepting of cohabitation. As a result, in part, of cohabitation, by the 1990's, one out of four births occurred out of wedlock.

The marriages that do occur do not necessarily last. One of every two marriages in the United States ends in DIVORCE, and the rate does not seem to be affected by whether couples cohabit before marriage. The high rates of cohabitation and divorce mean that more children are spending at least some part of their youth in a single-parent household, most often headed by the mother. In Canada, approximately 75 percent of divorced women had custody of their children during the 1990's. It has been estimated that 50 percent of white children and 90 percent of black children in the United States will live in a single-parent family headed by the mother.

Issues of single-parent families also tie into issues of economics. Women typically suffer a reduction in their available household income of about 30 percent during the year following a divorce. Much of this is the result of the fact that women tend to earn less than men for performing the same jobs. Single-parent families are far more likely than dual-parent families to be in poverty. In the United States, medical and dental services often are too costly for families in or near POVERTY, so women and children go without preventive services. In Canada, access to medical services is guaranteed through a universal health-care system.

American women who have to resort to public assistance benefits for housing, medical care, and food costs receive only about three-fourths of the amount deemed appropriate to live at the poverty level. The cost of child care is more than $3,000 per year on average for each child of preschool age, presenting a dilemma for single parents. They may have to work to support their children, but if they work, they may have to pay for child care, which can be a substantial proportion of their income; in addition, if they work, they may lose entitlements to public assistance. Competing financial demands often result in single parents being unable to pay rent, then becoming homeless. It is estimated that 35 to 45 percent of homeless families with children are single-mother families. Child-care obligations and limited economic opportunities thus have led to what has been called the "feminization of poverty."

Employment Issues. As more women have entered the labor force, attention has focused on the disparities between men and women in regard to pay, chances for promotion, fringe and medical benefits, and occupa-

tional stereotyping. Legally, men and women are entitled to equal pay for equal work, yet two-thirds of workers receiving the minimum wage are women. Men average one full-time job, whereas women often hold two or more part-time or temporary jobs to receive the same pay. In addition, their jobs may have no benefits because they are not full-time.

SEXUAL HARASSMENT is any unwanted sexual attention, experienced by a woman or by a man. Most often, women are the victims of harassment. Patting, pinching, and other touching; sexual comments and suggestions; and pressure to go on dates or engage in sexual activity are examples of sexual harassment. Attention has focused on sexual harassment in the workplace, but harassers may be neighbors, acquaintances, or clients. Typically, harassers have some authority or power over the persons they may have harass.

Harassment causes anxiety, embarrassment, and fear. It also threatens a woman's employment if the

Participants in a Take Back the Night Program rally against sexual harassment, date rape, and other forms of mistreatment of women. (Impact Visuals/Carolina Kroon)

harasser is her boss or supervisor. Experts believe that the majority of women will experience some form of sexual harassment during their lives.

Family Issues. A comparatively new women's social issue is that of women holding multiple roles and responsibilities within their families. Women are expected to maintain the home and fulfill various obligations to their spouses and children, as in traditional families. In addition, they are increasingly likely to work outside the home to assist the family financially, go to school to increase employability, and provide caregiving services to parents or other family members as they age and need assistance in their daily decisions and tasks. All these obligations take time from women and exact an emotional toll, affecting physical health and mental well-being. Societal norms have not yet adjusted to the fact that women often have careers as demanding as those of men; women still are expected to enact their traditional roles even though they may have new increased responsibilities.

Both in the United States and in Canada, INFANT MORTALITY is an important health concern. According to the WORLD HEALTH ORGANIZATION, Canada has the seventh-lowest infant mortality rate among nations, whereas the United States ranks twenty-first. This difference points up the fact that American women may have more difficulty obtaining prenatal and infant care. The various pressures of family life, particularly for single mothers, may lead them to be less healthy during pregnancy, causing health problems for their children. ABORTION, the voluntary expulsion of a fetus before full-term delivery, presents ethical dilemmas and issues involving moral, religious, legal, emotional, and political considerations. No matter what law or policy is formulated, reproductive choices will always be individual decisions. After the 1973 *ROE V. WADE* Supreme Court decision that legalized abortion in the United States, the number of abortions rose sharply, but the number stabilized after 1980. The number of illegal abortions and rates of maternal mortality declined dramatically.

Health. Women are thought to be healthier than men because, on average, they live longer. The life expectancy of American women is about seven years longer than that of men. The changing social roles of women, women's own expectations, and familial responsibilities affect the health of women. Various roles and attempts to fill them contribute to stress-induced behavior, deficiencies in the immune system, and susceptibility to lifestyle diseases including heart disease.

Within the United States and Canada, the rate of infection with HUMAN IMMUNODEFICIENCY VIRUS (HIV), the virus that leads to ACQUIRED IMMUNE DEFICIENCY SYNDROME (AIDS), rose rapidly among women during the 1980's and 1990's. Black women and Latinas more often are infected with HIV than are white women.

The initial symptoms of HIV infection are different in men and women, resulting in many missed diagnoses and frequent late diagnosis of HIV related illnesses in women. Once infected with HIV, women tend to die of AIDS-related illnesses much more quickly than do men. By the mid-1990's, AIDS was the leading cause of death among black and Hispanic women in New York and New Jersey, and it was the leading cause of death for all women aged twenty to twenty-nine years in New York City. It was the seventh leading cause of death among women aged twenty-five to thirty-four years.

Women are different from men in several ways that affect their health status. Biologically, females are meant to have more fat than males during puberty. Media messages, however, promote slimness; to meet that expectation, many adolescent females reduce their food intake to unhealthy levels or develop eating disorders. Such unhealthy behaviors may develop into patterns that last into adulthood.

Women's health also is affected by economic status. Some physicians have biases concerning women on public assistance, and it is a fact that reimbursement for services rendered to such women is slow. Poor women thus are less likely to receive adequate health care and preventive procedures. Economic status also affects the health of men, but women are more likely to be poor than are men.

Ethnicity also is linked to women's health. Ethnicity often is intertwined with poverty, which is linked to poor health. In addition, some members of ethnic minorities may not speak English fluently, limiting their access to health care because they cannot adequately explain their problems to physicians or are not able to read about how to obtain health care and because their limited proficiency in English keeps them out of jobs that offer health-care benefits.

Women face different health problems as they age. Physicians tend to prescribe mood-altering drugs more often to middle-aged women with depression than to men. With the advent of MENOPAUSE, women become more susceptible to some diseases and health conditions.

Women campaign for the right to vote in New York City circa 1912. (Corbis-Bettmann)

Women's Rights. Personal violations against women are rampant. In Canada, women are approximately seven times as likely to be assaulted as men. HOMI-CIDE, RAPE, sexual assault, and harassment are the types of violence most often reported against women. The elderly, the poor, and women of racial or ethnic minorities report more often than men that fear often curtails their activities.

Violence in the home is common, and women are most often the victims. In the United States, every fifteen seconds a woman is beaten by her husband or boyfriend, and every six minutes a woman is forcibly raped. Nearly one-third of female homicide victims are killed by their husbands or boyfriends, and one in three women is sexually assaulted in her lifetime.

History documents women's long, arduous struggle for equality with men in various benefits, activities, and behaviors. Works of literature, political records, personal journals, and even the Bible record descrip-

tions of restrictions on women's acceptable behavior and lack of equality with men.

One of the most vigorously fought struggles for women's rights concerned the right to vote. This right, taken for granted by many men, was first seriously proposed for American women by suffragists Elizabeth Cady Stanton and Lucretia Mott at a women's rights convention in Seneca Falls, New York, in 1848. These women and other suffragists began a seventy-year struggle to obtain the right to vote, culminating in 1920 in the passage of the Nineteenth Amendment to the U.S. Constitution.

Women also became involved in the temperance movement. Part of their interest concerned the link between use of alcohol and violence against women and children. During the nineteenth century and into the early twentieth, husbands had the legal right to abuse their wives and children physically. It also was a husband's legal right to use both his and his wife's wages to buy alcohol before meeting his family's basic needs of food, clothing, and shelter. The WOMEN'S CHRISTIAN TEMPERANCE UNION (WCTU), founded in the 1870's, worked toward protecting women and children by attempting to outlaw the use of liquor, opium, and tobacco, as well as by campaigning against gambling. The WCTU opposed the women's SUFFRAGE MOVEMENT until, after numerous legal failures, it realized that the women's vote would be necessary for it to achieve its goals.

Various groups formed in Canada during the first half of the twentieth century to achieve rights for women. Among these were the Women's Liberal Federation of Canada (WLF), under the influence of Cairine Wilson and her "respectable feminism"; the Calgary Labour Women, influenced by Amelia Turner; and the Women's International League for Peace and Freedom (WILPF), influenced by Laura Hughes and Gertrude Richardson's antiwar activities. These groups and others worked to have women-supported representatives on city councils, send delegates to national conventions, and submit resolutions for discussion and nominations for executive positions. They received and disseminated information concerning political, peace, and labor issues, election procedures, and campaign tactics. Women in most of Canada were granted the right to vote in 1921, but women in Québec did not receive that right until 1949.

Women often were declared as candidates but rarely were elected. After World War II, women became more active as "watchdogs" of Canadian political decisions and policy concerning women, gender inequality, labor barriers, and peace and freedom. Most women in Canadian governmental positions are with the cultural, social welfare, educational, and women's issues ministries.

Women's Liberation. Prior to the 1960's and the WOMEN'S LIBERATION MOVEMENT, being "feminine" had particular social connotations. A feminine woman was expected to be loving, pretty, kind, and selflessly giving to those in need. She was dependent on a man's beneficence and protection for her present and future well-being. She was emotionally sensitive and nurturing toward children and families, but she did not understand economic or political issues. She was delicate and lightly muscled, and therefore incapable of performing strenuous physical work, yet she was capable of doing extensive housework. Although aspects of this social definition remain in many people's concepts of femininity and womanhood, few people subscribe

to the traditional view of femininity in its totality. The women's liberation movement developed throughout the 1960's and 1970's under such leaders as Betty FRIEDAN (author of *The Feminine Mystique*, 1963, and first president of the NATIONAL ORGANIZATION FOR WOMEN), Gloria STEINEM (outspoken editor of *Ms.* magazine), and Diane Harkin (Canadian founder of the Women for the Survival of Agriculture). The Canadian Voice of Women/Voix des Femmes (VOW) initially served to train politically inexperienced women to become effective activists.

Various groups of women worked independently on numerous issues and goals of interest to women. For example, women worked to stop sex-segregated advertisements for jobs. Others worked to increase traditional and continuing educational opportunities for women. Still others worked to eliminate war and violence. Others worked toward resolving gender issues, such as the ability to work in jobs considered not traditional for women. These are only a few of the social problems recognized during the 1960's. The women's rights movement at first consisted of older, professional women fighting broad gender discrimination in the political, economic, and legislative arenas. The women's liberation movement consisted of younger, college-aged, more radical women pursuing definitive equalization and feminist issues. The women's liberation movement began when women decided that being "feminine" denied them the rights, jobs, income, and benefits of men. They used the term "feminist" to indicate a staunch advocate of social, political, and economic freedoms for women.

The CIVIL RIGHTS MOVEMENT, occurring at about the same time, seemed to bring separate women's groups together in the United States. Racial inequality, and all that it entailed both politically and socially, appeared to be similar to sexual inequality as experienced by women. The Civil Rights movement had organizers and leaders willing to be arrested and even die for what they believed to be just causes. Women from around the United States began assisting black women in the South. Soon, women across the nation realized that they should unite their efforts, talents, and skills; form social connections and networks; articulate ideologies; and organize communities and causes.

The National Organization for Women (NOW) was a natural outcome of all these events in the late 1960's. The women's liberation movement was influential in identifying, modifying, and solving women's problems. It also had what some saw as a negative influence on women's issues and causes. Feminists insisted that women were discriminated against in all aspects of American society. The socially accepted and expected female subservience in the home, family, job, and political environments was not tolerable to them. Feminists would leave their homes and families to demonstrate, and many risked breaking the law to bring issues into the public eye. Many nonfeminists believed that the women's liberation movement consisted only of young, belligerent, risk-taking women with what appeared to be a traditionally masculine drive to succeed. The media portrayed feminists as women who would stop at nothing to pursue their cause. Many traditional men and women felt personally threatened and wanted to disassociate themselves from these aggressive female radicals. As a result, although feminists had some success in their efforts concerning issues of women's equality, they also acquired an insinuated "masculine" label as a result of their militant, contentious methods and behavior, and many felt alienated from the gender they were trying to protect.

During the 1980's and 1990's, additional discrimination issues arose concerning violence against women, reproductive rights, child-care responsibilities, and employment opportunities. As feminists fought for rights concerning these decidedly female issues, and as society became more accustomed to women asserting their rights, the tendency to stigmatize feminists as overly masculine abated.

Social Issues of the Future. The primary issues for women include access to personal health care, medical research (currently biased toward spending on issues of men's health), inequality in employment, family caregiving obligations, multiple role responsibilities, reproductive choice, AIDS-infected women and children, sexual harassment in the workplace, violence and safety in the home and community, child care, homelessness and poverty, and single-mother households.

Technology offers hope for alleviation of a few such problems. With the spread of the computer and its capabilities, more women are able to work from their homes. This has the potential to reduce the stress of child care, as these women do not have to be absent from the home. In addition, with workers' identities blurred by distance from the workplace, perhaps women will be treated more equitably as employees, judged and rewarded based on their productivity rather than their gender. Nevertheless, women will still doubtless have to fight for their rights in various arenas, and some problems will remain particularly theirs.

—Kathleen J. Hunter

SUGGESTED READINGS: Sherri Matteo, as editor of *American Women in the Nineties: Today's Critical Issues* (Boston: Northeastern University Press, 1993), has compiled a set of chapters focusing on women's issues central to current research and with policy implications for women. Johanna Kerr, as editor of *Ours by Right: Women's Rights as Human Rights* (Ottawa, Ontario, Canada: North-South Institute, 1993), investigates the male-dominated development agencies and their continued denial of women's inherent human rights and lack of response to their concerns, especially in poor countries.

Beverly J. McElmurry, Kathleen F. Norr, and Randy Spreen Parker's *Women's Health and Development: A Global Challenge* (Boston: Jones and Bartlett, 1993), with contributions from the World Health Organization's Collaborative Centres, provides reports on the status of women's health and development in various countries, including the United States and Canada. Patricia Aburdene and John Naisbitt's *Megatrends for Women* (New York: Villard, 1992) reviews numerous issues and trends women should know about in order to be empowered now and in the future. Linda Kealey and Joan Sangster, as editors of *Beyond the Vote: Canadian Women and Politics* (Toronto: University of Toronto Press, 1989), have compiled essays about women's politics and activism.

Harriet Hyman Alonso's *Peace as a Women's Issue: A History of the U.S. Movement for World Peace and Women's Rights* (Syracuse, N.Y.: Syracuse University Press, 1993) reviews the lives of feminists and examines issues associated with the connection between responsible female citizens, women's issues, suffragist organizations, and peace. Steven M. Buechler's *Women's Movements in the United States: Woman Suffrage, Equal Rights, and Beyond* (New Brunswick, N.J.: Rutgers University Press, 1990) explores and reviews the roots and ideologies of the feminist movement while identifying recurring themes across historical periods.

Women, ordination of: Religions with the formal office of an ordained priesthood struggle with the issue of whether or not to include women in a traditionally male role. The issue of women's ordination is a major conflict in Roman Catholicism. Since many religions

One of the first women ordained by the Episcopal church celebrates the tenth anniversary of her 1974 ordination. (UPI/Corbis-Bettmann)

ordain women and Catholicism does not, this issue is a barrier to church unity among Christians. Many people also consider women's ordination to be part of the struggle for women's equality.

Most organized religious denominations, such as the Episcopal, Presbyterian, and Methodist churches, allow the ordination of women. Religions that do not have ordained ministers (for example, the Quakers) usually include women in leadership positions. Conservative and Reformed Judaism allow women to be rabbis. Many Roman Catholic women believe that they have little or no voice in the church because they cannot be priests. Only priests can hold the top leadership positions in the church, such as bishop, cardinal, and pope. Ordination by a bishop empowers a person to perform certain rituals and sacraments, such as hearing confessions, celebrating mass, and blessing marriages. For believers, the priest is an authority figure and acts in the person of Jesus Christ.

Influenced by Vatican II (1963-1965), which modernized and liberalized the Catholic church, groups such as the Women's Ordination Conference, founded in 1975, were formed to work for the greater participation of women in church life. A Gallup Poll taken in 1993 showed that 64 percent of American Catholics believe women should be ordained. Many people support the ordination of women to the priesthood because there is an extreme shortage of priests in the Catholic church. Many Catholics are deprived of sacraments and the mass because they must be performed by a priest. In some parts of the United States, mass is celebrated only weekly or even monthly, especially in rural areas. In some parts of the world, Catholics may see priests only on an annual basis.

More and more lay women and men are stepping into some of the roles that used to belong only to priests. Laity are running parishes and distributing Holy Communion during prayer services over which they preside. These practices increase support for the ordination of women. In 1976, however, the leadership of the Catholic church declared that women cannot be ordained because Jesus did not ordain any women. Also, since Jesus was a man, only men can represent him in religious rituals. Pope John Paul II repeated the ban in 1995. Many Catholics continue to support women's ordination. They believe that because some bishops support women's ordination, eventually women may be ordained.

SUGGESTED READINGS: Leonard and Arlene Swidler's *Women Priests: A Catholic Commentary on the Vatican Declaration* (New York: Paulist Press, 1977) contains the Vatican's declaration against women priests, with responses and analyses from theologians and scholars. *Women Clergy: Breaking Through Barriers* (New Brunswick, N.J.: Transaction Press, 1985) by Edward Lehman is a study of ordained women in Protestant Christian denominations.

Women's Christian Temperance Union (WCTU): Voluntary society founded in Ohio in 1874 to discourage alcohol sale and consumption. In Canada, local WCTU's were founded in 1874, and a national organization was in place by the early 1880's. Support for temperance broadened during World War I and provided the impetus for both the United States and Canada to introduce prohibition laws.

Women's Educational Equality Act (WEEA, 1974): U.S. federal legislation. The WEEA was drafted to authorize funds to support educational programs designed to counter traditional sexist stereotyping, especially in public education and in textbooks. The act's passage was spurred by calls for stricter enforcement of Title IX of the EDUCATION AMENDMENTS ACT of 1972, which barred sex discrimination in any education program or activity receiving federal funding. After the passage of the WEEA, several women's groups filed suits against the Department of Health, Education, and Welfare for nonenforcement of the requirements of Title IX. The act, supported by President Gerald R. Ford, was renewed in 1978.

Women's health: Important issues involving women's health at the end of the twentieth century include such physical problems as HEART DISEASE, CANCER, and osteoporosis and such questions as what women should do to maintain a high quality of life.

History. Women make up more than half of the world's population; nevertheless, most health research was long conducted principally on men and focused mostly on male issues. By the latter half of the twentieth century, however, research about specifically women's health issues had increased substantially; women had also been broadly added as subjects in studies concerning such unisex health concerns as heart disease and cancer. Many of these more recent studies were designed to determine whether women reacted differently from men to similar treatments and whether there are inherent differences that make women react differently from men.

During the twentieth century, there has been a long-term shift in causes of death from infections to life-style-related diseases. The leading cause of death in women in the 1990's is cardiovascular disease, which kills almost 500,000 American women a year—more than ten times the number killed annually by breast cancer, and greater than the annual toll from all forms of cancer combined. The top cancer killer of women is lung cancer, which causes more than sixty thousand deaths per year.

Heart Disease. The myth that men are the only ones at risk of cardiovascular disease has been put to rest. Prior to MENOPAUSE, women are at lower risk of such diseases; after age fifty, however, their risk increases, and by age seventy-five, their risk is equal to that of men. By the year 2000, experts say, women can expect to live at least one-third of their lives after menopause, when they no longer have the protective effect of estrogen to counter cardiovascular problems.

Cardiovascular risk factors are similar for men and women, but some such factors have a specific gender relationship. About 65 percent of heart attacks in pre-menopausal women occur in smokers, with a direct correlation between the number of cigarettes smoked and the level of risk. High cholesterol is not as great a risk in women as in men. Some women, moreover, are protected by their fat distribution; fat accumulated in the abdomen, where men tend to accumulate it, causes an increased risk of cardiovascular disease, while fat accumulated in the hips and thighs, where women tend to, does not seem to increase risk.

There are also race differences. Obesity is a minor modifiable risk factor. Half of all African American

First Lady Hillary Clinton addresses a 1995 World Health Organization panel discussion on women's health. (Archive Photos/Reuters/Win McNamee)

women are obese, compared to only one-third of white women. Hypertension is a major modifiable risk factor. After age forty-five, 60 percent of white women are diagnosed with mild hypertension, compared to 79 percent of African American women; African American women also tend to become hypertensive much earlier. Hypertension is one area that experts believe needs further research using female subjects; treatment guidelines are presently based mostly on studies using only male subjects.

Several studies have found that physicians treat heart disease in women less aggressively than in men, especially in women under fifty. Doctors often assume that chest pains in women are caused by factors other than heart disease, and they are not as likely to use by-pass surgery as a treatment. Experts thus suggest that women with cardiovascular concerns need to become proactive in their own health care and refuse to settle for unequal care.

Cancer. Although heart disease is the number-one killer of women, cancer also exacts a heavy toll. Many high-profile cases of women with BREAST CANCER have generated enormous publicity about the disease; the National Breast Cancer Coalition, a lobbying group, has increased the visibility of breast cancer and has been successful in directing research funds toward its prevention, diagnosis, and treatment.

Despite such measures, breast cancer is increasing, with more than 180,000 cases diagnosed annually in the United States. Improved diagnostic tools, better self-examinations, and more successful treatments have lowered the death rate from the disease to 46,000 annually. The majority of new cases are slow-growing tumors occurring in women over the age of fifty; such cases are among those which have the highest survival rate with early detection. In 1994, a breast cancer gene was discovered, raising hopes that the discovery might benefit the relatively small percentage (5 to 10 percent) of women with a genetic predisposition-to breast cancer. The majority of victims, however, still need to rely on early detection and aggressive treatment to improve their survival odds.

Cervical cancer has declined since the development of the Pap test in the 1940's. Internationally, cervical cancer deaths have been reduced by 70 percent. In North America, where Pap tests are a regular part of medical care, death from the disease has become relatively rare.

Lung cancer is the major cancer killer of women, accounting for the deaths of about sixty thousand American women annually. The incidence rate for men has declined slightly, but the incidence rate for women is still rising; this trend is largely the result of the increased number of women smokers after World War II, many of whom are now being diagnosed. SMOKING causes 85 percent of lung cancers, making the disease one of the most preventable cancers, yet the number of teenage smokers is still on the rise.

Ovarian cancer is one of the deadliest forms in women, because detection is difficult; the disease is usually diagnosed only in the advanced stages. Knowing family history may be an extremely important risk-reduction factor. AGING and never having had children dramatically increase risk, while the use of oral contraceptives, even for a short time, and the process of tubal ligation both significantly reduce risk for this form of cancer.

Menopause and Osteoporosis. Average life expectancy has steadily increased since 1900, causing greater risk for two related syndromes. At about the age of fifty, most women experience MENOPAUSE, a gradual decline in the production of sex hormones followed by a decrease in ovulation and, eventually, menstruation. The process takes three to five years; the absence of menstruation for one year is generally considered the criterion for menopause. The longer a woman lives past menopause, the greater her risk for developing osteoporosis, a gradual decline in bone density that often leads to fractures, the most common sites being the hip, wrist, and vertebrae. Bone density changes throughout life. During puberty and into the early twenties, bone density increases; during the next two to three decades, density remains fairly constant. Past the age of fifty, decline in density begins. This is thought to be normal aging, but for women loss is more rapid after menopause because of the lack of estrogen. Men and women can experience osteoporosis, but women usually precede men by ten to fifteen years.

The prevention of or prolonging the onset of osteoporosis is a function of three things: diet, physical activity, and hormones. Calcium is needed to increase bone density. The recommended daily requirement is from 800 to 1200 milligrams per day but may need to be as high as 1500 milligrams per day for teenagers and post-menopausal women. Preventive exercise should be weight-bearing and site-specific. Walking is beneficial for the hip; additional strength work is needed for the wrist and vertebrae. Research suggests that isometric exercises (constant contraction with no shortening of the muscle) may be the best form of strength exercise to increase or maintain density. Hormone replacement therapy is the only way for women to maintain estrogen after menopause. This possibility should be discussed with a physician to weigh the risks (increases in some cancers) and benefits (prevention of osteoporosis and reduction in heart disease) to determine whether this is a viable treatment. The best way to prevent osteoporosis is to gain the greatest bone density in the growing years and then maintain it as long as possible.

Quality of Life. Physicians commonly offer the following suggestions to women who wish to maintain WELLNESS and reduce their risk of most female health concerns: Do not smoke; eat fruits, vegetables, and grains; use alcohol only in moderation; maintain a healthy weight; exercise regularly, for both endurance and strength; avoid overexposure to the sun; take advantage of regular health screenings; and, above all, take charge of one's own health. A positive mental attitude, physicians say, may be the best medicine to guarantee a lifetime of wellness.   —*Wendy E. S. Repovich*

SUGGESTED READINGS: A thorough presentation of women's health issues in the 1990's can be found in *Women's Health 1995*, edited by Sheldon Margen, Joyce C. Lashof, and Patricia A. Buffler (New York: Health Letter Associates, 1995). *How and Why We Age*, by Leonard Hayflick (New York: Ballantine Books, 1994), discusses aging issues as they pertain to both men and women and also addresses the question of why women live longer than men.

Women's liberation movement: Movement for the social equality of the sexes and against patriarchy and SEXISM. The movement was active in the 1800's and early 1900's and received new vitality in the social-action environment of the 1960's.

Sexism and Patriarchy. "Sexism" is the belief that one sex is innately superior or inferior to the other. It is often considered to be similar to racism in its damaging impact. Sexism is the basis of patriarchy, a form of social organization in which males dominate females. Patriarchy appears to be universal; that is, it seems to be the pattern in every known society, past or present. There are families, businesses, and occupations that are obviously matriarchal (dominated by women), such as nursing and kindergarten teaching; matriarchy, however, is nowhere extended to an entire society. In several of the Iroquois tribes, the women decided which male would be the leader of the group, and they

had the power of impeachment; nonetheless, it was the men who made all other major decisions in the life of the tribe.

One result of sexism and patriarchy is unequal pay for women and men in the same occupations. Women in the United States earn about 64 percent of what men earn in identical occupations. Women are also more likely than men to live in POVERTY. Other aspects of sexism and patriarchy include SEXUAL HARASSMENT, woman-battering, RAPE, and other forms of violence against women. It is estimated that 25 to 50 percent of wives in the United States are physically assaulted by their husbands; a woman is more likely to be injured by a family member or close friend than in an automobile accident.

Goals of the Movement. Early goals of the women's liberation movement included the abolition of SLAVERY, women's suffrage (the right to vote), and the prohibition of alcoholic beverages. The first two have been accomplished, and the third seems to be a hopeless cause. Women also campaigned for equality of educational opportunity, and today more women than men are attending colleges in the United States.

More recently, the goals of the movement have centered around such issues as reproductive choice, improving the status of women, and the sharing of both breadwinning and household tasks. Further goals include equal pay for equal worth and challenging gender-based inequality in every major aspect of society: the family, organized religion, the military, politics, the economy, education, health care, journalism, entertainment, and the law.

Beginnings of the Movement. Saint Paul is reported to have written in A.D. 55, "In Christ there is neither Jew nor Greek, neither male nor female." In 1696, Mary Astell, in "An Essay in Defence of the Female Sex," declared that "souls are equal," insisting that women's minds should be developed as well as those of men. A woman identifying herself as "Sophia" wrote in a 1739 book, *Woman Not Inferior to Man*, that the differences between the sexes are only the result of education, custom, and circumstances. She proposed that no woman should be denied access to EDUCATION or entry into any profession, including the military.

The political philosopher Davie Hume opposed confining women to the domestic sphere. John Stuart Mill held similar views. In 1792, Mary Wollstonecraft published the most influential early feminist publication, *Vindication of the Rights of Women*, which called for the complete equality of men and women, particu-

Supporters of the Equal Rights Amendment march through Springfield, Illinois, in 1976. (UPI/Corbis-Bettmann)

larly in the area of education.

In the United States, the first sizable gathering of feminists was organized by Elizabeth Cady Stanton. It was known as the Women's Rights Convention and was held at Seneca Falls, New York, in 1848. Two years later, another women's rights activist, Lucy Stone, organized a similar convention with the support of Julia Ward Howe. These groups combined in 1863 to form the Women's National Loyal League under the leadership of Susan B. ANTHONY. This organization proposed a women's suffrage constitutional amendment in 1878, which Congress rejected.

In 1890, the National American Women's Suffrage Association was formed. Before the year's end, Wyoming became the first state to give women the right to vote. Carrie Chapman Catt was elected president of the organization in 1900 and led the movement, staging large marches and demonstrations throughout the country. Finally, in 1920, the Nineteenth Amendment became law, giving all women age twenty-one or over the right to vote in the United States. Women in England received the right to vote in 1918, if they were aged thirty or older; in 1928, the voting age for women was lowered to twenty-one.

The Canadian experience with regard to women's suffrage was similar; it was granted in 1916 in Manitoba, Saskatchewan, and Alberta. The other provinces were slower to give women the right to vote, with Québec holding out until 1940.

Recent Developments. In 1953, the French feminist Simone de Beauvoir published *The Second Sex*, which became a catalyst for a second wave of feminist activism in the 1960's. Influential to the movement in the United States was *The Feminine Mystique*, written by Betty FRIEDAN and published in 1963. The decade of the 1960's was a period of widespread progress in many areas of CIVIL RIGHTS, putting the country in a favorable mood for considering the demands of women.

The NATIONAL ORGANIZATION FOR WOMEN (NOW), founded by Friedan in 1966, continues to be the most outspoken and influential organization involved in the fight for women's rights. The National Women's Political Caucus began in 1971. Leaders of this association, which addresses women's issues in the government realm, have included Shirley Chisholm, Bella Abzug, and Gloria STEINEM, the politically active publisher of *Ms.* magazine.

These and other groups led the attempt in the early 1970's to amend the Constitution of the United States with a simple statement called the EQUAL RIGHTS AMENDMENT. The wording was as follows: "Equality of rights under the law shall not be denied or abridged by the United States or by any State on account of sex." It was approved by the House of Representatives in 1971 and by the U.S. Senate in 1972 but failed to gain the necessary ratification by the states.

The Movement in the 1990's. It is generally recognized that there are three major types of feminists. The first classification, sometimes referred to as "liberal FEMINISM," includes the mainstream organizations and advocates the availability of maternity leave and CHILD CARE for working women. Liberal feminists further seek equality in the workplace, in education, and in the political realm. They have persistently urged Congress to consider renewing the passage of the Equal Rights Amendment. Though there is a marginal group called "Feminists for Life," most liberal feminists favor legalized ABORTION.

"Socialist feminists" tend to link the social disadvantages of women largely to the capitalist economic system. CAPITALISM tends to benefit certain categories of people much more than others. Socialist feminists view social reform, the goal of liberal feminists, as inadequate. They advocate a socialist revolution as the only way to ensure equality for all men and women.

"Radical feminism" tends to seek a gender-free society or even a matriarchal society. Radical feminists argue that men have run the world long enough and have not eliminated wars or poverty and that perhaps it is time to give women a chance. Some groups advocate escaping from male domination through LESBIANISM. Others promote goddess worship as a rejection of traditional religions, which they often view as patriarchal. One radical feminist group calls itself the Society for Cutting up Men (SCUM). Another has taken on the acronym WITCH, for the Women's International Terrorist Conspiracy from Hell.

The UNITED NATIONS sponsored large gatherings of women in Egypt in 1994 and in China in 1995, opening women's rights issues for international debate. The U.S. Senate's nomination hearings for Supreme Court Justice Clarence THOMAS in 1991 drew national attention to the problem of SEXUAL HARASSMENT. Thomas was approved, despite the harassment accusations of University of Oklahoma law professor Anita HILL. The murder trial and subsequent acquittal of former football player O. J. SIMPSON in 1995 likewise brought the issue of VIOLENCE against women into public focus.

—Calvin Henry Easterling

SUGGESTED READINGS: A solidly researched book

An opponent of women's liberation in New York City, 1973. (UPI/Corbis-Bettmann)

that raises issues about the education of women is Jane Gaskell's *Gender Matters from School to Work* (Philadelphia: Open University Press, 1992). Judith Lorber has written a brilliant and detailed argument for gender differences as being cultural rather than biological, *Paradoxes of Gender* (New Haven, Conn.: Yale University Press, 1994). For a brief and clear analysis of wage and workplace differences for men and women, see Barbara F. Reskin and Irene Padavic's *Women and Men at Work* (Thousand Oaks, Calif.: Pine Forge Press, 1994). An excellent overview of sexism in society can be found in Nijole V. Benokraitis and Joe R. Feagin's *Modern Sexism: Blatant, Subtle, and Covert Discrimination* (Englewood Cliffs, N.J.: Prentice-Hall, 1986).

Woodstock I and II (1969, 1994): Music festivals. The original Woodstock festival, promoted as "three days of peace, love, and music," took place on a dairy farm in Bethel, New York, August 15-17, 1969; admission was six dollars per day. Twenty-seven musical acts performed, among them many that are still widely recognized by music fans: Jimi Hendrix, the Grateful Dead, the Jefferson Airplane, the Who, Creedence Clearwater Revival, Crosby, Stills, and Nash, and Joan Baez. A few of the original acts returned to the stage in 1994, either to play at Woodstock '94 (such as Santana, Joe Cocker, and Crosby, Stills, and Nash) or at the smaller Bethel '94 concert (such as Richie Havens, Country Joe McDonald, and Melanie).

The 1969 Woodstock festival came to represent for young people of the time a "last outpost on the free world." Within a few years, idols Janis Joplin and Hendrix had died of drug overdoses, a number of bands had either disbanded or lost members, and the reigning peace of rock and roll was disrupted by a stabbing at a Rolling Stones concert at Altamont, California, in

Fans at Woodstock '94. (AP/Wide World Photos)

1970. The free love and abundant drug use of the first Woodstock festival were overshadowed at Woodstock '94 by the threats of AIDS and the presence of more potent drugs than were in wide use in 1969. (HEROIN, which ran as low as 2 percent pure in 1969, was often more than 60 percent pure in 1994.) Moreover, many of the tenets of the alternative mindset of the Woodstock generation have become so commonplace that they had little value for the young people of 1994.

Woodstock '94 was criticized by some who had attended the original festival as blatantly commercial. Some bands reportedly received up to $350,000 for their gigs; the alternative band Nine Inch Nails was paid $250,000 for a ninety-minute set. A pay-per-view television broadcast was available for $49.95; run-of-the-mill rock concert souvenirs and a CD-ROM, album, and video of the festival were also produced for young consumers. Instead of recapturing the spirit of the first Woodstock, the 1994 version resembled the original mainly in that a huge number of young people came together again in pursuit of a common goal: a good time. Besides the returning original artists, the 1994 lineup included acts such as MTV favorites Aerosmith, Melissa Etheridge, Cypress Hill, and Green Day. Tributes to the original festival were provided: Etheridge performed Janis Joplin's classic "Piece of My Heart," and John Popper of the band Blues Traveler did a harmonica rendition of "The Star Spangled Banner" that harked back to Hendrix's memorable electric-guitar version at the original festival. Woodstock '94 took place in Saugerties, New York, a few miles away from the original site, August 12-14; tickets were $135.

Work ethic: Commitment to work for its intrinsic values, such as character-building, personal discipline, and the contributions work makes to general prosperity, as well as for its potential to enhance one's personal wealth. The term was made prominent by the German sociologist Max Weber (1864-1920) in *The Protestant Ethic and the Spirit of Capitalism* (1905). Weber argued that Methodism, Pietism, Baptism, Calvinism, and other "ascetic branches of Protestantism" caused Europe and North America to adopt new and positive attitudes to work and wealth after the seventeenth century. According to Weber, these attitudes are prerequisites for a modern society anywhere in the world.

After World War II, this thesis spawned a large body of literature on "modernization" that looked for equivalents to the "Protestant ethic" in the indigenous cultures of former colonial nations. In the 1960's and 1970's, this literature came under sharp criticism for imposing the values of the developed world on the struggling populations of the developing world and for imposing a single model of culture and development on the world as a whole.

More recently, the presumed role of the work ethic in creating prosperity in North America has come under debate. Those sectors of the labor force exhibiting the highest UNEMPLOYMENT rates, especially the "underclass," are often said to suffer from a decline in their work ethic. Policies requiring work from people who receive welfare benefits are predicated on this view. Critics of this view, however, suggest that labor market opportunities are extremely restricted or least meaningful for these groups, and that explaining unemployment by reference to a demise of the work ethic blames the victims of changing social trends. Among the changes that explain unemployment better than the demise of the work ethic, they say, are the steady decrease in high-wage manufacturing jobs with medical and other benefits alongside the increase in low-wage retail and service jobs (such as jobs in the fast-food industry) that provide few if any benefits.

Others who are occasionally said to exhibit a declining work ethic are financial speculators, including stock traders, real-estate investors, and those with some degree of wealth who want to "get rich quick." Insider trading scandals on Wall Street and the savings-and-loan scandals of the 1980's gave prominence to many members of this group and highlighted their alleged ethical shortcomings.

The criticisms of both lower-class and upper-class groups for their weak commitment to work can be understood as coming from those in the older middle classes (such as retailers and small businessmen) and newer middle classes (professionals with credentials achieved from a higher education). These latter groups generally benefited from the kinds of economic and occupational trends that marked the twentieth century until the 1970's. Since then, however, they have felt threatened by the pace and unpredictability of social change, as it becomes increasingly globalized.

SUGGESTED READINGS: Christopher Jencks provides a balanced overview of the evidence regarding attitudes to work among the "underclass" in *Rethinking Social Policy: Race, Poverty, and the Underclass* (Cambridge, Mass.: Harvard University Press, 1992).

Michael Hughey analyzes the popularity of the work ethic among the middle classes in "The New Conservatism: Political Ideology and Class Structure in America" (*Social Research*, Autumn, 1982). Charles Derber compares the causes and consequences of lack of restraint among the lower and upper classes in *Money, Murder, and the American Dream: Wilding from Wall Street to Main Street* (Boston, Mass.: Faber and Faber, 1992).

Workers' compensation: Laws designed to protect employees and their families from economic losses resulting from accidental personal injury arising out of and in the course of employment. Workers' compensation laws are enacted by individual states. All states provide for prompt, adequate, and guaranteed payment of medical expenses and partial replacement of lost wages after an employee suffers a work-related injury or illness. Death benefits are provided to the dependents of deceased employees. Rates of compensation and duration of benefits are set by each state.

Before workers' compensation laws were enacted in the United States in the early 1900's, an injured employee's only recourse to collecting damages resulting from a work-related injury was to sue the employer. Existing laws maintained that an employer was responsible only for injuries or death resulting from a negligent act by the employer. The existing legal system placed the burden of proof on injured employees or their survivors to show that the injury or death was a direct result of employer negligence. For most people, this was an economic impossibility.

States began adopting workers' compensation laws in 1911. These laws began to set aside the requirement that an employee prove negligence on the part of the employer. By 1948, every state had enacted a workers' compensation law. Federal regulations provide workers' compensation to certain groups of employees not covered by state laws.

Contemporary workers' compensation laws have adopted a "no-fault" approach to injuries that occur on the job: Employers are liable for injuries sustained by their employees in the course of employment, regardless of fault or where the injury occurs. Employers are also responsible for all injuries that occur on their premises. In exchange, employees have given up the right to sue employers, even if an injury is directly related to employer negligence. Benefits are awarded on a statutory schedule, without requiring recourse to courts for each work-related injury.

A major premise of workers' compensation legislation is that the employer should consider the expense of workers' compensation insurance as a production cost. Employees are not required to subsidize expenses associated with work injuries. Workers' compensation costs are added to the price of a product or service and passed on to the consumer, on the theory that society as a whole benefits and, therefore, any increased costs should be borne by the entire population.

Work-related injury benefits generally cover losses incurred as a result of medical expenses, lost wages, rehabilitation expenses, permanent disability, and death but do not provide for any pain and suffering experienced by a work-accident victim. Most states require each private-sector employer to provide some type of security to ensure that they can meet the financial obligations of workers' compensation laws.

Compliance with statutory requirements is managed by a state's workers' compensation agency, commission, or board. Compliance activities include monitoring active and canceled policies, investigating the qualifications of self-insured companies, hearing contested compensation claims, and prosecuting viola-

U.S. WORKERS' COMPENSATION BENEFITS PAID IN 1989

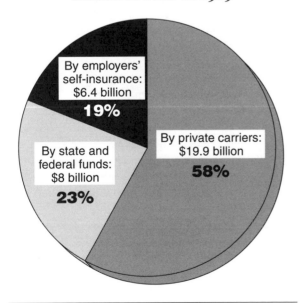

Source: Data are from U.S. Department of Commerce, Bureau of the Census, *Statistical Abstract of the United States, 1992.* Washington, D.C.: U.S. Government Printing Office, 1992.

tions.

Workers' compensation policy premiums are affected by two factors: job-classification rates and the accident experience of the employer. Job-classification rates are based on the historic and actuarial degree of hazard for a given occupation. The other factor is the loss or accident experience of the employer. Job-classification rates are based on industry averages for specific occupations. The two factors are combined into a single multiplier for the employer to use in calculating premium expense. The rate itself is a proportion of the total payroll.

While workers' compensation is in theory an equitable system designed to protect employees in the workplace, during the 1990's, many calls for reform were heard. Abuse of the system and skyrocketing insurance premiums led many states to re-examine the existing structure.

Workfare: Government-sponsored job-training programs for welfare recipients. Although such programs had existed earlier, the term "workfare" gained currency in the media when Congress produced a welfare-reform package called the Family Support Act (FSA) in 1988. The FSA orders states to collect child-support payments from delinquent fathers and to train and place recipients of AID TO FAMILIES WITH DEPENDENT CHILDREN (AFDC) in jobs. AFDC mothers with children three years of age or older must be trained for and seek work in order to receive welfare. The program has been criticized for channeling poor mothers into poverty-level, dead-end jobs.

Working mothers: Female wage earners with dependent children. The phenomenon of women working is not new; what is new is that greater numbers of women are being financially reimbursed for their contribution to capitalist society. Approximately two in every three mothers were engaged in the paid U.S. labor market in 1990. Dramatic changes have occurred within the last generation: for example, the number of women with children aged six or older who are employed in the labor market rose from 52 percent in 1975 to 75 percent in 1990; and 32 percent of mothers with children under the age of two were employed in 1975, while the figure for 1990 was 52 percent. An even greater proportion of single mothers work for pay. By 1990, approximately 69 percent of all U.S.

single mothers were employed.

Women as a group are paid less than men, earning $0.72 for every $1.00 men earn. They are less likely to be unionized, and fewer women have the opportunity to participate in pension plans. As a result, more women than men either live their entire lives in POVERTY or find themselves poor when they are old. For SINGLE MOTHERS, the risk of poverty is very high. Given that most women receive custody of their children once divorced—and that they cannot depend on support payments alone for sustenance—the proportion of divorced women with children living below the poverty line is very high. These discrepancies are even greater for women of color.

Employed mothers often find themselves with, in effect, two jobs. When they leave their paid jobs, they are often responsible for the care of their children and partners and for housework. Studies on housework reveal that employed mothers contribute an average of twenty-five to thirty hours of domestic labor per week, while men contribute an average of six to eight hours per week. While many employers offer their employees job descriptions, benefits, vacations, and opportunities for advancement, motherhood and housework come with twenty-four-hour responsibilities, no time off, constant challenges, and many mundane activities.

While women's role in the home is central to the production and preparation of the current and next generation of workers for a capitalist economy, it is not generally recognized as "real work." Sociologist Meg Luxton uses the phrase "more than a labor of love" to capture both the essence of women's contribution to their partners and children and the unpaid (and often undervalued) nature of the work.

Employers are slow to recognize the needs of working mothers, including day-care facilities, flexible working hours, geographical mobility for promotion, parental leave, sick leave that includes caring for children or aging parents, storm days when school or other facilities are closed, and the opportunity to attend special school events.

Women report both advantages and disadvantages to combining motherhood and careers. Employed mothers have higher SELF-ESTEEM and suffer less DEPRESSION. In a society that values people according to the size of their paychecks, it is not surprising that women who are members of the labor force feel better about themselves. Yet, there are real costs to be borne by working mothers; fatigue and guilt top the list.

SUGGESTED READING: Meg Luxton's *More Than a*

Labour of Love: Three Generations of Women's Work in the Home (Toronto, Ont.: Women's Press, 1980) gives an overview of the problems faced by working mothers.

World Bank and International Monetary Fund: Financial organizations established by the Bretton Woods (New Hampshire) Agreement in July, 1944, as part of the international order planned by the world's major powers to follow in the wake of World War II. The headquarters of both institutions are in Washington, D.C.

The focus of the World Bank (officially the International Bank for Reconstruction and Development) changed over the years to emphasize technical assistance and loans for agricultural, energy, and transportation projects in the developing nations of Africa, Asia, and the Americas. The bank's emphasis on PRIVATIZATION or denationalization of enterprise in these countries became a source of debate beginning in the 1960's.

The International Monetary Fund endorses loans, with a focus on underdeveloped and indebted countries. To qualify for such loans, a beneficiary country is usually expected to introduce austerity measures that often prove controversial within the country itself.

World Health Organization (WHO): United Nations agency headquartered in Geneva, Switzerland. The WHO's establishment was provided for in the U.N. Charter signed in June, 1945, and ratified by member states in April 1948. The WHO's major mis-

Protesters in Berlin object to the policies of the World Bank and International Monetary Fund. (Reuters/Corbis-Bettmann)

A policeman escorts injured workers from the World Trade Center following the February, 1993, bombing. (Reuters/Corbis-Bettmann)

sion, and defined in its constitution, is "the attainment by all peoples of the highest possible level of health." The organization directs and coordinates international health efforts, assists governments in developing and strengthening health services, provides technical support, assists governments with epidemic diseases, and administers many special programs. Regional headquarters are located in Washington, D.C., Copenhagen, Brazzaville, New Delhi, Manila, and Alexandria.

World Trade Center bombing (1993): U.S. domestic TERRORISM. On Feb. 26, 1993, a powerful bomb exploded in an underground garage of the World Trade Center in New York City, killing six people, injuring more than 650, causing more than a thousand to be treated for smoke inhalation. and virtually closing down the 110-story twin towers, the city's largest building complex.

The blast occurred at 12:18 P.M. on a Friday, leaving a crater two hundred feet long, sixty feet wide, and several stories deep within the garage. The ceiling of the station of a nearby commuter railroad collapsed, trapping dozens under the rubble. The blast crippled the complex's power system, its telephone lines, its television monitors, and its public-address systems, and sent billows of smoke through the ventilating system and up the elevator shafts. All 250 elevators halted when the complex's electricity and gas were shut off in order to protect rescue workers in dangerous areas. Dozens of people were trapped between floors in the elevators. Others groped their way in complete darkness down the smoke-filled stairwells. Twenty people were airlifted from the roof of one of the towers by police helicopter. More than fifty thousand people were eventually evacuated from the buildings.

Using a bit of metal bearing a vehicle identification number (VIN) as a clue, the FEDERAL BUREAU OF INVESTIGATION (FBI) established that the bomb had been a car bomb of a type favored by foreign terrorists. The vehicle carrying the bomb, a van, was traced to a rental agency in New Jersey. On March 4, the FBI made its first arrest when the person who had rented the van came to the agency to claim the refund of a deposit on the vehicle, maintaining that the van had been stolen.

After an intensive search, officials arrested Sheik Omar Abdel Rahman, a blind Muslim cleric who had emigrated to the United States from Egypt in 1991, and charged him with masterminding the bombing. Prosecutors asserted that the World Trade Center inci-

dent was only part of a larger conspiracy to blow up tunnels and major buildings in New York City in an attempt to intimidate the United States into changing its Middle East policies. In January, 1996, Abdel Rahman and nine co-conspirators were convicted and sentenced to terms ranging from twenty-five years to life in prison.

The bombing demonstrated how vulnerable the United States might be to terrorist attacks. The country has virtually no internal travel restrictions or surveillance of its residents, making it nearly impossible for law-enforcement agencies to track suspects before crimes occur. The bombing also brought into question the wisdom of building enormous complexes that might result in great economic losses if they have to be shut down. The damage in the case of the World Trade Center was all the more severe because the complex also houses dozens of New York state agencies, thus restricting the functions of the state government.

The World Trade Center bombing also demonstrated the necessity of international cooperation in containing the spread of terrorism. The incident also, however, foreshadowed the even more destructive bombing of the Oklahoma City Federal Building in April of 1995—an act that was laid at the feet of domestic terrorists.

Wounded Knee, occupation of (1973): Seventy-day standoff between militant members of the AMERICAN INDIAN MOVEMENT (AIM) and federal officials. The standoff occurred after AIM members occupied a number of buildings on the Pine Ridge Indian Reservation in South Dakota.

The American Indian Movement was founded in 1968 to promote public awareness of Native American grievances. In February, 1973, AIM became involved in a dispute between two factions on the Pine Ridge Reservation over control of tribal government. One faction advocated cooperation with the BUREAU OF INDIAN AFFAIRS and its programs. A traditionalist faction wanted less federal government interference in tribal affairs. The traditionalists asked AIM to become involved in the dispute to assure that they would have fair representation in tribal government. On February 27, an armed group of AIM militants seized and occupied by force the church and general store in the tiny village of Wounded Knee.

Wounded Knee held tremendous symbolic significance for Native Americans. It was there, in December

Indian activists stand guard at Wounded Knee in 1973. (UPI/Corbis-Bettmann)

of 1890, that the last "battle" between the U.S. Army and American Indians took place. In reality, it was not a battle but a massacre of two hundred mostly unarmed Sioux men, women, and children. It marked the conclusion of the conquest of the American Indian.

The armed militants at Wounded Knee in 1973 submitted a list of demands to the government. They wanted a change in tribal leadership for Pine Ridge, a federal review of all Indian treaties, and a Senate investigation into the treatment of Indians. They declared that they represented the "Independent Oglala Sioux Nation."

The U.S. Justice Department immediately sent U.S. marshals and other officials to surround the village and force the militants to surrender. In ensuing gun battles, two of the militants were killed, and a marshal was severely injured. The militants had hoped to bring to public attention the plight of Native Americans living on reservations. By 1973, however, the American public had grown weary of the militancy and demonstra-

tions prevalent during the late 1960's and early 1970's. Faced with a hostile public and the unsympathetic administration of President Richard M. NIXON, the militants began negotiations with federal officials.

The AIM militants ended the siege of Wounded Knee on May 8, 1973. They surrendered their weapons after government officials promised they could negotiate their grievances with the government. Indian leaders held one meeting with White House officials; they were then informed that treaties were the business of Congress and that their grievances should be taken up with that body. No further meetings with the White House or with Congress ever took place. Discontent continued for two more years at the Pine Ridge Reservation, culminating in another gun battle in which two Federal Bureau of Investigation agents and one Indian were killed.

While they often deplored the violent means used, many Native Americans felt that the siege at Wounded Knee gave their people a cause to identify with and awakened many Americans to the injustices suffered by Indians. According to AIM leader Dennis Banks, "Wounded Knee was an attempt to help an entire race survive."

Write-offs: Accounting term. Over time, the value of an asset may change. A business may choose to change the value that it assigns to an asset on its books so that the value conforms to estimated value, market value, or appraised value. The process of lowering the book value of an asset in this way is called writing off the asset. A write-off created in this way can be used as a deduction on a firm's income tax. Assets commonly written off include debts that cannot be collected and business machinery that depreciates over time. Recognition of write-offs by tax law means that the law recognizes such expenses as costs of doing business.

Wu, Harry (Wu Hongda; b. Feb. 8, 1937, Shanghai, China): Chinese American activist. As a university student in Beijing, Wu developed a reputation for openly expressing his opinions. After criticizing the Soviet Union in 1960, Wu spent nineteen years in various labor camps. After his release, Wu emigrated to the United States and began to publicize human rights abuses inside China. After secretly returning to mainland China on a number of occasions, Wu was arrested at a remote border crossing in June, 1995.

Harry Wu displays a photograph of a Chinese prison following his release in 1995. (Impact Visuals, Shia Photo)

After being held for sixty-six days, Wu was convicted of espionage and sentenced to fifteen years in jail. Because Wu was a naturalized U.S. citizen, his detention and trial were met with strong protests from American officials, and Wu was expelled from China within hours of his conviction.

Wyatt v. Strickley (1971): U.S. district court case. *Wyatt v. Strickley* was a class action initiated on behalf of Ricky Wyatt and other patients involuntarily confined through noncriminal proceedings at a mental hospital in Tuscaloosa, Ala. The court ruled that the Fourteenth Amendment did not allow the state to confine patients involuntarily for treatment unless there were provisions for scientifically and medically adequate treatment. Determining that adequate treatment was not being provided, the court gave the hospital six months to implement an adequate program. The Supreme Court, however, rejected the "right to treatment" doctrine while limiting involuntary confinement only to dangerous persons in *O'Connor v. Donaldson* (1975).

Y

Yellow journalism: Media reporting marked by sensationalism and emphasis on entertainment. This form of reporting got its name from the color of the ink used by Joseph Pulitzer's *New York World* newspaper in a cartoon called the "Yellow Kid" in the late 1890's.

Yellow journalism reflected the vast changes that occurred in the United States as the economic face of the country began to change from agrarian to industrial, as the frontier closed, and as the ethnic make-up of the country expanded. Yellow journalism also reflected

Tabloids are often cited as modern examples of yellow journalism. (UPI/Corbis-Bettmann)

Russian president Boris Yeltsin with other foreign leaders at a 1996 summit on nuclear security. (Archive Photos, Jacky Naegelen)

increases in literacy, sophistication of printing, technology, and competition among newspapers.

Yeltsin, Boris (b. Feb. 1, 1931, Sverdlovsk province, Russia, U.S.S.R.): Russian political leader. Yeltsin, a Communist party leader in Sverdlovsk and Moscow, broke with the Communist Party of the Soviet Union in 1990 and later led the movement to abolish it. Elected president of the Russian Republic in 1991, Yeltsin led the opposition to the August, 1991, coup against Mikhail GORBACHEV and became an international hero. In the aftermath, he played an important role in the dissolution of the Soviet Union. After winning election as president of the Russian Federation in 1992, Yeltsin first faced opposition from opponents of economic reform, former Communists, and strong nationalists; later, he was accused by other critics of having betrayed democratic reform. In 1993, a showdown between Yeltsin and his parliamentary opponents prompted him to dissolve the parliament; Rus-

sian troops later fired on the parliament building, which had been seized in an abortive coup. In the mid-1990's, Yeltsin's presidency was troubled by internal discord, continuing parliamentary conflict, controversy over his handling of the rebellion in CHECHNYA, rumors of his alcohol dependence, and general ill health.

Yoga: Ancient Hindu science of self-development. Yoga involves commitment to a spiritual, mental, or physical discipline in order to attain unity of soul, mind, and body. Yoga was brought to Western Europe and North America from India in the early twentieth century and since 1960 has been a centerpiece of the holistic health and NEW AGE MOVEMENTS. The most popular disciplines have been Hatha Yoga (physical exercise) and Raja Yoga (meditation), valued partly for their ability to improve health and reduce STRESS. Associated debates include arguments over whether yoga's health benefits are real or imagined and whether Westerners should follow a discipline rooted in a foreign religion.

Yom Kippur War (1973): Arab-Israeli war that began on October 6, 1973 (the Jewish holy day of Yom Kippur), with simultaneous attacks on Israel by Egypt in the Sinai Peninsula and by Iraq and Syria in the Golan Heights. The conflict, which produced heavy fighting, grave losses on all sides, and nuclear alerts in the United States and the Soviet Union, ended in separate cease-fires in November, 1973, and January, 1974, after Israel gained a clear military advantage. The Yom Kippur War, with its high costs and narrowly averted great-power intervention, produced moderating political trends that ultimately led to a 1979 Egyptian-Israeli peace treaty, the Camp David Accords.

Young Offenders Act (1982): Canadian federal legislation. The Young Offenders Act established a separate justice and corrections system for Canadians from twelve to seventeen years of age. The act originally mandated that those convicted of a federal crime in youth court could be held in custody a maximum of three years; in 1994, the term was increased to six years. For extremely serious offenses, young offenders fourteen years of age or older may be transferred to adult court.

Z

Zero Population Growth (ZPG): Organization founded 1968. Since its formation, ZPG has worked to mobilize public support for a sustainable balance of people, natural resources, and the environment, both in the United States and throughout the world, through political LOBBYING, publications, and educational programs.

During the 1960's, many biologists, ecologists, and sociologists claimed that the world's explosive population growth was significantly contributing to increases in pollution and violence as well as to a loss of VALUES and individual privacy. In 1968, Paul R. EHRLICH, a professor of biology at Stanford University and the author of *The Population Bomb*, which was published that year, and others founded Zero Population Growth to persuade Americans to work to halt population growth. By the end of 1969, ZPG had enlisted three thousand members, many of whom were college students, in more than one hundred chapters in thirty states. Supporters promoted population control by working to revise tax laws to discourage large families, reform welfare regulations, and ensure that all methods of birth control, including legalized ABORTION, should be freely available to all Americans. ZPG established a lobby in Washington, D.C., sought to persuade California to create a state commission on population and environment, and began a nationwide educational campaign to convince married couples to limit their families to two children.

In the 1970's and 1980's, the concept of zero population growth became a subject of heated debate in both public and academic circles. In the 1980's, as many as fifty different groups with more than five million members, including the Audubon Society and PLANNED PARENTHOOD, joined ZPG in promoting programs designed to limit the world's population. By the mid-1990's, ZPG had thirty thousand members and an annual budget of about $1,500,000.

Headquartered in Washington, D.C., ZPG continues to work to alter national policies, attitudes, and behavior in order to halt global population growth and to reduce consumption of natural resources. Its proponents argue that the world's increasing population intensifies deforestation, the extinction of plants and animals, and climatic change. Moreover, population growth hampers the functioning of democratic governments, increases urban problems, generates huge amounts of waste, expands competition for scarce resources, and hinders the poor in their attempts to achieve a better life. To accomplish its goals, ZPG monitors and reports on legislative and court activity affecting population issues, analyzes media coverage and interpretation of population matters, sponsors workshops designed to help educators include population studies in their classrooms, and publishes several newsletters to disseminate information on international and domestic population issues.

Critics, most notably economist Julian Simon, author of *The Ultimate Resource* (1981) and *Population Matters* (1990), have accused ZPG and other advocates of population control of attempting to force upon other people their own belief that fewer children should be born into the world. Simon has insisted that interfering with people's freedom to choose how many children they have through fines or forced sterilization contradicts the idea of reproductive freedom that "pro-controllers" claimed to espouse. Given the world's demographic pressures, environmental and social problems, and widespread concerns about natural resources, climate, and POVERTY, the debate over limiting global population growth will undoubtedly continue for many years.

Zero tolerance: Public policy that suggests that society must not tolerate to any degree the breaking of laws. Because crime has steadily increased in many areas of society, "zero tolerance" as an attitude both in and out of the criminal justice system has become a popular response to the general outcry against the rise in the incidence of crime. The term is most commonly applied to antidrug laws that call for severe punishment of even first-time offenders and, often, for the confiscation of vehicles or property used in connection with drug-related offenses.

Zoos and wildlife refuges: Environments managed for the CONSERVATION, protection, or exhibition

President Bill Clinton signs an executive order calling for zero tolerance of drug dealers in public housing. (Archive Photos/Reuters/Rick Wilking)

Zoos and wildlife refuges

of animals. Zoos are relatively small, intensively managed artificial or semi-artificial environments for the purpose of conservation, education, scientific studies, and recreation. Wildlife refuges are larger natural habitats managed for the purpose of protecting wildlife and providing recreation. Both exhibit wildlife in their own way, zoos in a simulated habitat and wildlife refuges in the animals' natural habitat.

Zoos have traditionally been concerned with the exhibition of wildlife for educational and recreational purposes. Conservation and scientific studies have assumed a more important role, however, as more and more species have become endangered. Much of the work at zoos has been extended to conservation and study in the field, including wildlife refuges. This work concerns small-population dynamics, animal behavior, genetics, reintroduction, and other studies of both captive and wild populations.

Zoos are typically considered cultural institutions, like botanical gardens and natural history museums. Some people find the role of zoos as local educational centers and research facilities to be important contributions to society and to wildlife conservation. The

American Zoo and Aquarium Association (AZA) has an accreditation program to ensure that its member institutions meet nationally acceptable standards. Some people, however, believe that the keeping of wildlife outside its natural habitat is not appropriate. Such critics do not believe that zoos should exist or that there is a need for them. They typically argue that captivity violates animals' rights, although these rights have not been established within a legal framework.

Wildlife refuges provide a sanctuary from most human activities, but their animal populations must also be managed, even in the largest refuges. Virtually all animal populations are managed or influenced by human activity to one extent or another as a result of the increasing human population. Thus, these areas have become a different kind of captivity, although they are not often considered as such. Nevertheless, the animals are in their natural habitats; management involves the enhancement of the area to benefit the primary species served by a refuge.

Wildlife refuges conserve a natural area along with its natural resources, including the wildlife. They differ from other natural areas, such as national parks, in that the

Zoos are popular with visitors, but they are often criticized by animal rights advocates. (Susan Hwang)

emphasis is on the wildlife, and the amenities provided for human access are minimal. Refuges may serve a number of functions, such as preserving areas for the breeding, wintering, or feeding of particular species or for the conservation of ENDANGERED SPECIES. They may also include freshwater or marine areas as well as terrestrial habitats. As natural areas shrink and species decline, wildlife refuges (as well as other natural areas) and zoos will likely become increasingly important to the well-being of both wildlife and human society.

BIBLIOGRAPHY
Recent Sources of Interest on Social Issues

AGING

Chopra, Deepak, M.D. *Ageless Body, Timeless Mind.* New York: Harmony Books, 1993.

Doress-Worters, Paula B., and Diana Laskin Siegal. *The New Ourselves, Growing Older: Women Aging with Knowledge and Power.* New York: Simon & Schuster, 1994.

Friedan, Betty. *The Fountain of Age.* New York: Simon & Schuster, 1993.

Hess, Beth B., and Elizabeth W. Markson, eds. *Growing Old in America,* 4th ed. New Brunswick, N.J.: Transaction Publishers, 1991.

Kuhn, Maggie, with Christina Long and Laura Quinn. *No Stone Unturned: The Life and Times of Maggie Kuhn.* New York: Ballantine Books, 1991.

Lucas, Emma. *Elder Abuse and Its Recognition Among Health Service Professionals.* New York: Garland, 1991.

Posner, Richard A. *Aging and Old Age.* Chicago: University of Chicago Press, 1995.

Sheehy, Gail. *New Passages: Mapping Your Life Across Time.* New York: Random House, 1995.

Wicclair, Mark R. *Ethics and the Elderly.* New York: Oxford University Press, 1993.

ANIMAL RIGHTS

Langley, Gill, ed. *Animal Experimentation: The Consensus Changes.* New York: Chapman and Hall, 1989.

McClung, Robert M. Lost Wild America: *The Story of Our Extinct and Vanishing Wildlife.* Hamden, Conn.: Linnet Books, 1993.

Newkirk, Ingrid. *Free the Animals!: The Untold Story of the U.S. Animal Liberation Front and Its Founder, "Valerie."* Chicago: Noble Press, 1992.

Norton, Bryan G., Michael Hutchins, Elizabeth F. Stevens, and Terry L. Maple, eds. *Ethics on the Ark: Zoos, Animal Welfare and Wildlife Conservation.* Washington, D.C.: Smithsonian Institution, 1995.

Regan, Tom. *All That Dwell Therein: Animal Rights and Environmental Ethics.* Berkeley: University of California Press, 1982.

Schaller, George B. *The Last Panda.* Chicago: University of Chicago Press, 1993.

Singer, Peter. *Animal Liberation: A New Ethics for Our Treatment of Animals,* 2d ed. New York: Random House, 1990.

ART

Acker, Ally. *Reel Women.* New York: Continuum, 1991.

Friedman, Lester, ed. *Unspeakable Images: Ethnicity and the American Cinema.* Urbana: University of Illinois Press, 1991.

Lippard, Nancy. *Mixed Blessings: New Art in a Multicultural America.* New York: Pantheon Books, 1990.

Ryan, Michael, and Douglas Kellner. *Camera Politica: The Politics and Ideology of Contemporary Hollywood Film.* Bloomington: Indiana University Press, 1988.

Small, Michael. *Break It Down: The Inside Story from the New Leaders of Rap.* New York: Citadel Press, 1992.

Toop, David. *Rap Attack 2: African Rap To Global Hip Hop,* 2d ed. London: Serpent's Tail, 1992.

White, Timothy. *Rock Lives: Profiles and Interviews.* New York: Henry Holt, 1990.

BUSINESS AND THE ECONOMY

Chappell, Tom. *The Soul of a Business: Managing for Profit and the Common Good.* New York: Bantam Books, 1993.

Henriques, Diana B. *Fidelity's World: The Secret Life and Public Power of the Mutual Fund Giant.* New York: Scribner, 1995.

Kuhn, James W. *Beyond Success: Corporations and Their Critics in the 1990's.* New York: Oxford University Press, 1991.

Lowenstein, Roger. *Buffett: The Making of an American Capitalist.* New York: Random House, 1995.

Novak, Michael. *The Spirit of Democratic Capitalism.* New York: Simon & Schuster, 1982.

Bibliography

Ohmae, Kenichi, ed. *The Evolving Global Economy: Making Sense of the New World Order.* Boston: Harvard Business School, 1995.

Oliver, Melvin L., and Thomas M. Shapiro. *Black Wealth/White Wealth: A New Perspective of Racial Inequality.* New York: Routledge, 1995.

Petzinger, Thomas. *Hard Landing: The Epic Contest for Power and Profits That Plunged the Airlines into Chaos.* New York: Times Business, 1995.

Sampson, Anthony. *Company Man: The Rise and Fall of Corporate Life.* New York: Random House, 1995.

Slater, Robert. *Soros: The Life, Times, and Trading Secrets of the World's Greatest Investor.* New York: Irwin Professional Publishing, 1996.

Weare, Walter B. *Black Business in the New South: A Social History of the North Carolina Mutual Life Insurance Company.* Durham, N.C.: Duke University Press, 1993.

CIVIL RIGHTS

Albert, Peter J., and Ronald Hoffman, eds. *We Shall Overcome: Martin Luther King, Jr., and the Black Freedom Struggle.* New York: Pantheon Books, 1990.

Cone, James H. *Martin and Malcolm and America: A Dream or a Nightmare.* Maryknoll, N.Y.: Orbis Books, 1991.

Harding, Vincent. *There Is a River: The Black Struggle for Freedom in America,* 2d ed. New York: Harcourt Brace Jovanovich, 1992.

King, Martin Luther, Jr. *I Have a Dream: Writings and Speeches That Changed the World,* edited by James Melvin Washington. San Francisco: Harper San Francisco, 1992.

Lederer, Laura, and Richard Delgado, eds. *The Price We Pay: The Case Against Racist Speech, Hate Propaganda, and Pornography.* New York: Hill & Wang, 1995.

Powledge, Fred. *Free at Last? The Civil Rights Movement and the People Who Made It.* Boston: Little, Brown, 1991.

Smolla, Rodney A. *Free Speech in an open Society.* New York: Alfred A. Knopf, 1992.

Sunstein, Cass R. *Democracy and the Problem of Free Speech.* New York: Free Press, 1993.

CONSUMER RIGHTS

Crandall, Robert W., Howard K. Gruenspecht, Theodore E. Keeler, and Lester B. Lowe. *Regulating the Automobile.* Washington, D.C.: Brookings Institution, 1986.

Dadd, Debra Lynn. *Nontoxic and Natural: A Guide for Consumers.* Los Angeles: J. P. Tarcher, 1984.

Drivon, Laurence E. *The Civil War on Consumer Rights.* Berkeley, Calif.: Conari Press, 1990.

Griffin, Kelley. *Ralph Nader Presents More Action for a Change.* New York: Dembner Books, 1987.

Horowitz, David. *The Business of Business: How 100 Businesses Really Work.* New York: Perennial Library, 1989.

Mayer, Robert N. *The Consumer Movement: Guardians of the Marketplace.* Boston: Twayne, 1989.

Nader, Ralph. *Beware.* New York: Law-Arts, 1971.

_____. *Unsafe at Any Speed: The Designed-in Dangers of the American Automobile.* New York: Grossman, 1965.

Nader, Ralph, and William Taylor. *The Big Boys.* New York: Pantheon Books, 1986.

Portnoy, J. Elias. *Let the Seller Beware! The Complete Consumer Guide to Getting Your Money's Worth.* New York: Maxwell Macmillan International, 1990.

Schulte, Fred. *Fleeced!: Telemarketing Rip-Offs and How to Avoid Them.* Amherst, N.Y.: Prometheus Books, 1995.

Whittelsey, Frances Cerra. *Why Women Pay More: How to Avoid Marketplace Perils.* Washington, D.C.: Center for Study of Responsive Law, 1993.

CRIME

Benedict, Helen. *Safe, Strong, and Streetwise: Sexual Safety at Home, on the Street, on Dates, on the Job, at Parties, and More.* Boston: Little, Brown, 1987.

Brownmiller, Susan. *Against Our Will: Men, Women, and Rape.* New York: Fawcett Columbine, 1993.

Cheney, Margaret. *Why: The Serial Killer in America.* Saratoga, Calif.: R & E Publishers, 1992.

Fairstein, Linda A. *Sexual Violence: Our War Against Rape.* New York: William Morrow, 1993.

Ferrell, Jeff, and Clinton R. Sanders. *Cultural Criminology.* Boston: Northeastern University Press, 1995.

Millett, Kate. *The Politics of Cruelty: An Essay on the Literature of Political Imprisonment.* New York: W. W.Norton, 1994.

Phillips, Steven. *No Heroes, No Villains: The Story of a Murder.* New York: Random House, 1977.

Samenow, Stanton E. *Inside the Criminal Mind.* New York: Times Books, 1984.

Terkel, Susan Neiburg, and Janice E. Rench. *Feeling Safe, Feeling Strong: How to Avoid Sexual Abuse and What to Do If It Happens to You.* Minneapolis: Lerner Publications, 1984.

DEATH AND DYING

Edelman, Hope. *Motherless Daughters: The Legacy of Loss.* New York: Delta Trade Paperbacks, 1994.

Kevorkian, Jack. *Prescription—Medicide: The Goodness of Planned Death.* Buffalo, N.Y.: Prometheus Books, 1991.

Kübler-Ross, Elizabeth. *On Death and Dying.* New York: Macmillan, 1969.

Mitford, Jessica. *The American Way of Death.* New York: Simon & Schuster, 1963.

Moody, Raymond A. *Life After Life: The Investigation of a Phenomenon—Survival of Bodily Death.* New York: Bantam Books, 1976.

Moreno, Jonathan D., ed. *Arguing Euthanasia: The Controversy over Mercy Killing, Assisted Suicide, and the "Right to Die."* New York: Simon & Schuster, 1995.

Rachels, James. *The End of Life: Euthanasia and Morality.* New York: Oxford University Press, 1986.

DISABILITY ISSUES

Berkowitz, Edward D. *Disabled Policy: America's Programs for the Handicapped.* Cambridge, England: Cambridge University Press, 1987.

Bickenbach, Jerome E. *Physical Disability and Social Policy.* Toronto: University of Toronto Press, 1993.

Gooding, Caroline. *Disabling Laws, Enabling Acts: Disability Rights in Britain and America.* Boulder, Colo.: Pluto Press, 1994.

Hanson, Marie. *Living Outside Inside: A Disabled Woman's Experience Towards a Social and Political Perspective.* Berkeley, Calif.: Canterbury Press, 1985.

Hockenberry, John. *Moving Violations: War Zones, Wheelchairs, and Declarations of Independence.* New York: Hyperion, 1995.

Lakey, Jane. *Caring About Independence.* London: Policy Studies Institute, 1994.

Morgan, Richard E. *Disabling America: The "Rights Industry" in Our Time.* New York: Basic Books, 1984.

Resources for Rehabilitation. *Resources for People with Disabilities and Chronic Conditions.* Lexington, Mass.: Resources for Rehabilitation, 1991.

EDUCATION

Allen, Walter R., Edgar G. Epps, and Nesha Z. Haniff, eds. *College in Black and White.* Albany: State University of New York Press, 1991.

Berman, Paul, ed. *Debating PC: The Controversy over Political Correctness on College Campuses.* New York: Dell Books, 1992.

Bloom, Allan. *The Closing of the American Mind: How Higher Education Has Failed Democracy and Impoverished the Souls of Today's Students.* New York: Simon & Schuster, 1987.

Dawson, Lallie P. *Bigotry and Violence on American College Campuses.* Washington, D.C.: Commission on Civil Rights, 1990.

Fine, Michelle. *Framing Dropouts.* Albany: State University of New York Press, 1991.

Gates, Henry Louis. *Loose Canons: Notes on the Culture Wars.* New York: Oxford University Press, 1992.

Kozol, Jonathan. *Savage Inequalities: Children in America's Schools.* New York: Crown, 1991.

Rose, Mike. *Possible Lives: The Promise of Public Education in America.* Boston: Houghton Mifflin, 1995.

Routman, Regie. *Transitions: From Literature to Literacy.* Portsmouth, N.H.: Heineman, 1988.

Rubin, Nancy. *Ask Me if I Care: Voices from an American High School.* Berkeley, Calif.: Ten Speed Press, 1994.

Sachar, Emily. *Shut up and Let the Lady Teach: A Teacher's Year in a Public School.* New York: Poseidon Press, 1991.

Sommer, John W. *The Academy in Crisis: The Political Economy of Higher Education.* New Brunswick, N.J.: Transaction Publishers, 1995.

Bibliography

Weis, Lois, and Michelle Fine, eds. *Beyond Silenced Voices: Class, Race, and Gender in United States Schools.* Albany: State University of New York Press, 1993.

ENVIRONMENT

Carson, Rachel. *Silent Spring.* Greenwich, Conn.: Fawcett, 1962.

Cranor, Carl F. *Regulating Toxic Substances: A Philosophy of Science and the Law.* New York: Oxford University Press, 1993.

Cronon, William, ed. *Uncommon Ground: Toward Reinventing Nature.* New York: W. W.Norton, 1995.

Dillard, Annie. *Pilgrim at Tinker Creek.* New York: Harper & Row, 1974.

Freyfogle, Eric T. *Justice and the Earth.* New York: Free Press, 1993.

Gore, Albert, Jr. *Earth in the Balance: Ecology and the Human Spirit.* Boston: Houghton Mifflin, 1992.

Gottlieb, Robert. *Forcing the Spring: The Transformation of the American Environmental Movement.* Washington, D.C.: Island Press, 1993.

Kellert, Stephen R. *The Value of Life: Biological Diversity and Human Society.* Washington, D.C.: Island Press, 1996.

Leopold, Aldo. *A Sand County Almanac: And Sketches Here and There.* New York: Oxford University Press, 1949.

Muir, John. *John Muir: The Eight Wilderness Discovery Books.* Seattle: The Mountaineers, 1992.

FAMILY AND RELATIONSHIPS

Billingsley, Andrew. *Climbing Jacob's Ladder: The Enduring Legacy of African-American Families.* New York: Simon & Schuster, 1992.

Blankenhorn, David. *Fatherless America: Confronting Our Most Urgent Social Problem.* New York: Basic Books, 1995.

Bradshaw, John. *Family Secrets: What You Don't Know Can Hurt You.* New York: Bantam Books, 1995.

Griswold, Robert L. *Fatherhood in America: A History.* New York: Basic Books, 1993.

Hite, Shere. *The Hite Report on the Family: Growing up Under Patriarchy.* New York: Grove Press, 1995.

Scarf, Maggie. *Intimate Worlds: Life Inside the Family.* New York: Random House, 1995.

Trafford, Abigail. *Crazy Time: Surviving Divorce.* New York: Bantam Books, 1984.

Wallerstein, Judith S., and Sandra Blakeslee. *The Good Marriage: How and Why Love Lasts.* Boston: Houghton Mifflin, 1995.

GOVERNMENT AND POLITICS

Baker, James A., III, with Thomas M. De Frank. *The Politics of Diplomacy: Revolution, War and Peace, 1989-1992.* New York: G. P. Putnam's Sons, 1995.

Bashevkin, Sylvia B. *True Patriot Love: The Politics of Canadian Nationalism.* Toronto: Oxford University Press, 1991.

Baum, Lawrence. *The Supreme Court,* 4th ed. Washington, D.C.: Congressional Quarterly Press, 1992.

Cuomo, Mario. *Reason to Believe.* New York: Simon & Schuster, 1995.

Greider, William. *Who Will Tell the People: The Betrayal of American Democracy.* New York: Simon & Schuster, 1992.

Henry, Charles P. *Culture and African American Politics.* Bloomington: Indiana University Press, 1990.

Lamont, Lansing. *Breakup: The Coming End of Canada and the Stakes for America.* New York: W. W.Norton, 1994.

Matalin, Mary, and James Carville. *All's Fair: Love, War, and Running for President.* New York: Random House, 1994.

Rawls, John. *Political Liberalism.* New York: Columbia University Press, 1993.

Schoenbrod, David. *Power Without Responsibility: How Congress Abuses the People Through Delegation.* New Haven, Conn.: Yale University Press, 1993.

Smith, Hedrick. *Rethinking America.* New York: Random House, 1995.

Taylor, Kristin Clark. *The First to Speak: A Woman of Color Inside the Bush White House.* New York: Doubleday, 1993.

Wallis, Jim. *The Soul of Politics: Beyond "Religious Right" and "Secular Left."* San Diego: Harcourt Brace, 1995.

HEALTH AND MEDICINE

Bell, Peter. *Chemical Dependency and the African-American: Counseling Strategies and Community Issues*. Center City, Minn.: Hazelden, 1990.

Boston Women's Health Book Collective. *The New Our Bodies, Ourselves*. New York: Simon & Schuster, 1992.

Bradshaw, John. *Healing the Shame That Binds You*. Deerfield Beach, Fla.: Health Communications, 1988.

Cassell, Eric. J. *The Nature of Suffering and the Goals of Medicine*. New York: Oxford University Press, 1994.

Duh, Samuel V. *Blacks and AIDS: Causes and Origins*. Newbury Park, Calif.: Sage Publications, 1991.

Garret, Laurie. *The Coming Plague: Newly Emerging Diseases in a World Out of Balance*. New York: Farrar, Straus and Giroux, 1994.

Leukefeld, C. G., R. J. Battjes, and Z. Amsel, eds. *AIDS and Intravenous Drug Use: Community Intervention and Prevention*. New York: Hemisphere Publishing, 1990.

Northrup, Christiane, M.D. *Women's Bodies, Women's Wisdom*. New York: Bantam Books, 1994.

Secundy, Marian Gray, ed. *Trials, Tribulations, and Celebrations: African-American Perspectives on Health, Illness, Aging, and Loss*. Yarmouth, Maine: Intercultural Press, 1992.

Shilts, Randy. *And the Band Played On: Politics, People, and the AIDS Epidemic*. New York: Penguin, 1988

IMMIGRATION

Davis, Marilyn P. *Mexican Voices/American Dreams: An Oral History of Mexican Immigration to the United States*. New York: Henry Holt, 1990.

Diaz-Briquets, Sergio, and Sidney Weintraub, eds. *Determinants of Emigration from Mexico, Central America, and the Caribbean*. Boulder, Colo.: Westview Press, 1991.

Fitzpatrick, Joseph P. *Puerto Rican Americans: The Meaning of Migration to the Mainland*, 2d rev. ed. Englewood Cliffs, N.J.: Prentice-Hall, 1987.

Gutiérrez, David G. *Walls and Mirrors: Mexican Americans, Mexican Immigrants, and the Politics of Ethnicity*. Berkeley: University of California Press, 1995.

Haines, David. *Refugees as Immigrants: Cambodians, Laotians, and Vietnamese in America*. Totowa, N.J.: Rowman & Littlefield, 1989.

Reimers, David M. *Still the Golden Door: The Third World Comes to America*, 2d ed. New York: Columbia University Press, 1992.

Salyer, Lucy E. *Laws Harsh as Tigers: Chinese Immigrants and the Shaping of Modern Immigration Law*. Chapel Hill: University of North Carolina Press, 1995.

Siems, Larry, ed. and trans. *Between the Lines: Letters Between Undocumented Mexican and Central American Immigrants and Their Families and Friends*. Tucson: University of Arizona Press, 1992.

INFORMATION, COMPUTERS, MEDIA

Dates, Jannette L., and William Barlow. *Split Image: African Americans in the Mass Media*. Washington, D.C.: Howard University Press, 1990.

Gates, Bill. *The Road Ahead*. New York: Viking, 1995.

Johnson, Deborah G. *Computer Ethics*, 2d ed. Englewood Cliffs, N.J.: Prentice-Hall, 1994.

King, Norman. *Everybody Loves Oprah!: Her Remarkable Life Story*. New York: William Morrow, 1988.

Lichter, S. Robert, Linda S. Lichter, and Stanley Rothman. *Prime Time: How TV Portrays American Culture*. Washington, D.C.: Regnery Publishing, 1994.

Moody, Fred. *I Sing the Body Electronic: A Year with Microsoft on the Multimedia Frontier*. New York: Viking, 1995.

Schement, Jorge Reina, and Terry Curtis. *Tendencies and Tensions of the Information Age: The Production and Distribution of Information in the United States*. New Brunswick, N.J.: Transaction Publishers, 1995.

Schofield, Janet Ward. *Computers and Classroom Culture*. New York: Cambridge University Press, 1995.

Turkle, Sherry. *Life on the Screen: Identity in the Age of the Internet*. New York: Simon & Schuster, 1995.

Twitchell, James B. *Adcult USA: The Triumph of Advertising in American Culture*. New York: Columbia University Press, 1996.

Bibliography

INTERNATIONAL AFFAIRS

Allen, Dana H. *Cold War Illusions: America, Europe, and Soviet Power, 1969-1989*. New York: St. Martin's Press, 1995.

Blumenwitz, Dieter. *This Is Germany: Germany's Legal Status After Unification*. Bonn: Kulturstiftung der Deutschen Vertriebenen, 1994.

Friedman, Robert I. *Sheikh Abdel Rahman, the World Trade Center Bombing, and the CIA*. Westfield, N.J.: Open Media, 1993.

Gregg, Robert W. *About Face?: The United States and the United Nations*. Boulder Colo.: L. Rienner Publishers, 1993.

Hartung, William D. *And Weapons for All: How America's Multibillion Dollar Arms Trade Warps Our Foreign Policy and Subverts Democracy at Home*. New York: HarperCollins, 1994.

Juckes, Tim J. *Opposition in South Africa: The Leadership of Z.K. Matthews, Nelson Mandela, and Stephen Biko*. Westport, Conn.: Praeger, 1995.

Kampfer, John. *Inside Yeltsin's Russia: Corruption, Conflict, Capitalism*. London: Cassell, 1994.

Kissinger, Henry. *Diplomacy*. New York: Simon & Schuster, 1994.

Koh, Harold Hongju. *The National Security Constitution: Sharing Power After the Iran-Contra Affair*. New Haven, Conn.: Yale University Press, 1990.

Mantius, Peter. *Shell Game: A True Story of Banking, Spies, Lies, Politics—and the Arming of Saddam Hussein*. New York: St. Martin's Press, 1995.

Merrill, Christopher. *The Old Bridge: The Third Balkan War and the Age of the Refugee*. Minneapolis: Milkweed Editons, 1995.

Reische, Diana L. *Arafat and the Palestine Liberation Organization*. New York: F. Watts, 1991.

Ridgeway, James, ed. *The Haiti Files: Decoding the Crisis*. Washington D.C.: Essential Books, 1994.

Shaw, Martin. *Global Society and International Relations*. Cambridge, England: Polity Press, 1994.

Slater, Robert. *Rabin of Israel*. New York: St. Martin's Press, 1993.

LAW, ACTS, LEGAL PROCEDURE

Alderman, Ellen, and Caroline Kennedy. *In Our Defense: The Bill of Rights in Action*. New York: William Morrow, 1991.

Cox, Archibald. *The Court and the Constitution*. Boston: Houghton Mifflin, 1987.

Finkelstein, Neil. *The Separation of Québec and the Constitution of Canada*. North York, Ont.: York University Centre for Public Law and Public Policy, 1992.

Irons, Peter. *The Courage of Their Convictions: Sixteen Americans Who Fought Their Way to the Supreme Court*. New York: Free Press, 1988.

Kluger, Richard. *Simple Justice: The History of "Brown v. Board of Education" and Black America's Struggle for Equality*. New York: Vintage, 1977.

Mann, Coramae Richey. *Unequal Justice: A Question of Color*. Bloomington: Indiana University Press, 1993.

Mayer, Jane, and Jill Abramson. *Strange Justice: The Selling of Clarence Thomas*. New York: Plume, 1995.

Prejean, Helen. *Dead Man Walking: An Eyewitness Account of the Death Penalty in the United States*. New York: Random House, 1993.

Rehnquist, William H. *The Supreme Court: How It Was, How It Is*. New York: William Morrow, 1987.

Rowan, Carl T. *Dream Makers, Dream Breakers: The World of Justice Thurgood Marshall*. Boston: Little, Brown, 1993.

Schwartz, Bernard. *The Great Rights of Mankind: A History of the Bill of Rights*. Madison, Wis.: Madison House, 1992.

MILITARY, SECURITY, WAR

Berenbaum, Michael. *The World Must Know: The History of the Holocaust as Told in the United States Holocaust Memorial Museum*. Boston: Little, Brown, 1993.

Builder, Carl H. *The Masks of War: American Military Styles in Strategy and Analysis*. Baltimore: The Johns Hopkins University Press, 1989.

Chalk, Frank, and Kurt Jonassohn. *The History and Sociology of Genocide: Analyses and Case Studies*. New Haven, Conn.: Yale University Press, 1990.

Christopher, Paul. *The Ethics of War and Peace: An Introduction to Legal and Moral Issues*. Englewood Cliffs, N.J.: Prentice-Hall, 1994.

Griffith, Paddy. *The Ultimate Weaponry: The Most Lethal Conventional Firepower in the World*. New York: St. Martin's Press, 1991.

Means, Howard. *Colin Powell: Soldier/Statesman, Statesman/Soldier*. New York: Donald I. Fine, 1992.

Rhodes, Richard. *Dark Sun: The Making of the Hydrogen Bomb*. New York: Simon & Schuster, 1995.

Summers, Harry G., Jr. *The New World Strategy: A Military Policy for America's Future*. New York: Simon & Schuster, 1995.

Van Creveld, Martin L. *Nuclear Proliferation and the Future of Conflict*. New York: The Free Press, 1993.

Woodward, Bob. *The Commanders*. New York: Simon & Schuster, 1991.

POPULATION AND DEMOGRAPHICS

Cote, James E., and Anton L. Allahar. *Generation on Hold: Coming of Age in the Late Twentieth Century*. New York: New York University Press, 1995.

Ehrenreich, Barbara. *Fear of Falling: The Inner Life of the Middle Class*. New York: Pantheon Books, 1989.

Ehrlich, Paul R. *The Population Bomb*. New York: Ballantine Books, 1968.

Ehrlich, Paul R., Anne H. Ehrlich, and Gretchen C. Daily. *The Stork and the Plow: The Equity Answer to the Human Dilemma*. New York: Putnam's, 1995.

Jones, Dionne J., and Stanley F. Battle, eds. *Teenage Pregnancy: Developing Strategies for Change in the Twenty-first Century*. New Brunswick, N.J.: Transaction Publishers, 1990.

Rubenstein, Richard L. *The Age of Triage: Fear and Hope in an Overcrowded World*. Boston: Beacon Press, 1983.

Rushkoff, Douglas, comp. *The GenX Reader*. New York: Ballantine Books, 1994.

POVERTY

Berrick, Jill Duerr. *Faces of Poverty: Portraits of Women and Children on Welfare*. New York: Oxford University Press, 1995.

Bremner, Robert H. *The Discovery of Poverty in the United States*. New Brunswick, N.J.: Transaction Publishers, 1992.

Gordon, Linda. *Pitied but Not Entitled: Single Mothers and the History of Welfare*. Cambridge, Mass.: Harvard University Press, 1995.

Jencks, Christopher. *Rethinking Social Policy: Race, Poverty, and the Underclass*. Cambridge, Mass.: Harvard University Press, 1992.

Katz, Michael B. *The Undeserving Poor: From the War on Poverty to the War on Welfare*. New York: Pantheon Books, 1989.

Kelso, William Alton. *Poverty and the Underclass: Changing Perceptions of the Poor in America*. New York: New York University Press, 1994.

Scott, Hilda. *Working Your Way to the Bottom: The Feminization of Poverty*. Boston: Pandora Press, 1984.

RACE, ETHNICITY, PLURALISM

Bell, Derrick A. *Faces at the Bottom of the Well: The Permanence of Racism*. New York: Basic Books, 1992.

Benjamin, Lois. *The Black Elite*. Chicago: Nelson-Hall, 1991.

Deloria, Vine, Jr. *Behind the Trail of Broken Treaties: An Indian Declaration of Independence*. Austin: University of Texas Press, 1985.

D'Souza, Dinesh. *The End of Racism*. New York: The Free Press, 1995.

Dyson, Michael Eric. *Between God and Gangsta Rap: Bearing Witness to Black Culture*. New York: Oxford University Press, 1996.

Franklin, John Hope. *The Color Line: Legacy for the Twenty-First Century*. Columbia: University of Missouri Press, 1993.

George, Lynell. *No Crystal Stair: African-Americans in the City of Angels*. New York: Verso, 1992.

Gomez-Quiñones, Juan. *Chicano Politics: Reality and Promise, 1940-1990*. Albuquerque: University of New Mexico Press, 1990.

Hacker, Andrew. *Two Nations: Black and White, Separate, Hostile, Unequal*. New York: Charles Scribner's Sons, 1992.

Hill, Anita Faye, and Emma Coleman Jordan, eds. *Race, Gender, and Power in America: The Legacy of the Hill-Thomas Hearing*. New York: Oxford University Press, 1995.

Malcolm X, with Alex Haley. *The Autobiography of Malcolm X*. New York: Grove Press, 1966.

O'Brien, David J., and Stephen S. Fugita. *The Japanese American Experience*. Bloomington: Indiana University Press, 1991.

Bibliography

Perry, Bruce. *Malcolm: The Life of a Man Who Changed Black America*. Barrytown, N.Y.: Station Hill Press, 1991.

Schlesinger, Arthur. *The Disuniting of America*. New York: W. W.Norton, 1992.

West, Cornel. *Race Matters*. Boston: Beacon Press, 1993.

RELIGION AND SPIRITUALITY

Baer, Hans A., and Merrill Singer. *African-American Religion in the Twentieth Century: Varieties of Protest and Accommodation*. Knoxville: University of Tennessee Press, 1992.

Bellah, Robert N., and Frederick E. Greenspahn, eds. *Uncivil Religion: Interreligious Hostility in America*. New York: Crossroad, 1987.

Carmody, Denise Lardner, and John Tully Carmody. *Mysticism: Holiness East and West*. New York: Oxford University Press, 1996.

Hanh, Thich Nhat. *Living Buddha, Living Christ*. New York: Riverhead Books, 1995.

Hirschfelder, Arlene B., and Paulette Molin, comps. *The Encyclopedia of Native American Religions: An Introduction*. New York: Facts on File, 1992.

Johnson, Paul. *A History of Christianity*. New York: Atheneum, 1976.

Keown, Damien. *The Nature of Buddhist Ethics*. New York: St. Martin's Press, 1992.

McGuire, Meredith B. *Religion: The Social Context*, 3d ed. Belmont, Calif.: Wadsworth, 1992.

Newsom, Carol A., and Sharon H. Ringe, eds. *Women's Bible Commentary*. Louisville, Ky.: Westminster/John Knox Press, 1992.

Smith, Jonathan Z., and William Scott Green, eds., with the American Academy of Religion. *The HarperCollins Dictionary of Religion*. San Francisco: Harper, 1995.

REPRODUCTIVE ISSUES

Alpern, Kenneth D., ed. *The Ethics of Reproductive Technology*. New York: Oxford University Press, 1992.

Annas, George J., and Sherman Elias. *Gene Mapping: Using Law and Ethics as Guides*. New York: Oxford University Press, 1992.

Cooper, Susan. *Beyond Infertility: The New Path to Parenthood*. New York: Maxwell Macmillan International, 1994.

Craig, Barbara Hinkson. *Abortion and American Politics*. Chatham, N.J.: Chatham House, 1993.

Ireland, Mardy S. *Reconceiving Motherhood: Separating Motherhood from Female Identity*. New York: Guilford Press, 1993.

Joffe, Carole E. *Doctors of Conscience: The Struggle to Provide Abortion Before and After Roe v. Wade*. Boston: Beacon Press, 1995.

Lauritzen, Paul. *Pursuing Parenthood: Ethical Issues in Assisted Reproduction*. Bloomington: Indiana University Press, 1993.

SCIENCE AND TECHNOLOGY

Coveney, Peter, and Roger Highfield. *Frontiers of Complexity: The Search for Order in a Chaotic World*. New York: Fawcett Columbine, 1995.

Hawking, Stephen W. *A Brief History of Time: From the Big Bang to Black Holes*. New York: Bantam Books, 1988.

McNeill, Paul M. *The Ethics and Politics of Human Experimentation*. Cambridge, England: Cambridge University Press, 1993.

Russo, V.E.A., and D. J. Cove. *Genetic Engineering: Dreams and Nightmares*. New York: W. H. Freeman, 1995.

Sagan, Carl. *Pale Blue Dot: A Vision of the Human Future in Space*. New York: Random House, 1994.

Thorne, Kip S. *Black Holes and Time Warps: Einstein's Outrageous Legacy*. New York: W. W.Norton, 1994.

Wilson, Edward O. *The Diversity of Life*. Cambridge, Mass.: Belknap Press of Harvard University Press, 1992.

SEXUALITY

Cammermeyer, Margarethe. *Serving in Silence*. New York: Penguin, 1994.

Cruikshank, Margaret. *The Gay and Lesbian Liberation Movement*. New York: Routledge, 1992.

D'Emilio, John, and Estelle B. Freedman. *Intimate Matters: A History of Sexuality in America*. New York: Harper & Row, 1988.

Hite, Shere. *The Hite Report: A Nationwide Study of Female Sexuality*. New York: Dell Publishing, 1981.

————. *The Hite Report on Male Sexuality*. New York: Ballantine Books, 1982.

Hudson, Liam, and Bernadine Jacot. *Intimate Relations: The Natural History of Desire*. New Haven, Conn.: Yale University Press, 1995.

Mohr, Richard D. *A More Perfect Union: Why Straight America Must Stand Up for Gay Rights*. Boston: Beacon Press, 1994.

SPORTS

Byers, Walter, with Charles Hammer. *Unsportsmanlike Conduct: Exploiting College Athletes*. Ann Arbor: University of Michigan Press, 1995.

Chadwick, Bruce. *When the Game Was Black and White: The Illustrated History of the Negro Leagues*. New York: Abbeville, 1992.

George, Nelson. *Elevating the Game: Black Men and Basketball*. New York: HarperCollins, 1992.

Guttmann, Allen. *The Olympics: A History of the Modern Games*. Urbana: University of Illinois Press, 1992.

————. *Women's Sports: A History*. New York: Columbia University Press, 1991.

Koppett, Leonard. *Sports Illusion, Sports Reality: A Reporter's View of Sports, Journalism, and Society*. Urbana: University of Illinois Press, 1994.

Levine, Peter. *Ellis Island to Ebbets Field: Sport and the American Jewish Experience*. New York: Oxford University Press, 1992.

Rogers, Susan Fox, ed. *Another Wilderness: New Outdoor Writing by Women*. Seattle: Seal Press, 1994.

VALUES AND ETHICS

Arthur, John. *Morality and Moral Controversies*, 3d ed. Englewood Cliffs, N.J.: Prentice-Hall, 1993.

Bellah, Robert N., et al. *The Good Society*. New York: Alfred A. Knopf, 1991.

Jarrett, James L. *The Teaching of Values: Caring and Appreciation*. New York: Routledge, 1991.

McShea, Robert J. *Morality and Human Nature*. Philadelphia: Temple University Press, 1990.

May, Larry, and Shari Collins Sharratt, eds. *Applied Ethics: A Multicultural Approach*. Englewood Cliffs, N.J.: Prentice-Hall, 1994.

Midgley, Mary. *Can't We Make Moral Judgments?* New York: St. Martin's Press, 1993.

Peck, M. Scott. *The Road Less Traveled*. New York: Simon & Schuster, 1978.

Pojman, Louis P. *Ethics: Discovering Right and Wrong*. Belmont, Calif.: Wadsworth, 1990.

Seligman, Adam B. *The Idea of Civil Society*. Princeton, N.J.: Princeton University Press, 1992.

Sellers, M. N. S., ed. *An Ethical Education: Community and Morality in the Multicultural University*. Providence, R.I.: Berg, 1994.

Shriver, Donald W., Jr. *An Ethic for Enemies: Forgiveness in Politics*. New York: Oxford University Press, 1995.

Wuthnow, Robert. *Learning to Care: Elementary Kindness in an Age of Indifference*. New York: Oxford University Press, 1995.

WOMEN'S ISSUES

Albrecht, Lisa, and Rose M. Brewer. *Bridges of Power: Women's Multicultural Alliances*. Philadelphia: New Society, 1990.

Bataille, Gretchen M., and Kathleen M. Sands. *American Indian Women Telling Their Lives*. Lincoln: University of Nebraska Press, 1984.

Beauvoir, Simone de. *The Second Sex*, translated and edited by H. M. Parshley. New York: Alfred A. Knopf, 1952.

Caraway, Nancie. *Segregated Sisterhood: Racism and the Politics of American Feminism*. Knoxville: University of Tennessee Press, 1991.

Davis, Flora. *Moving the Mountain: The Women's Movement in America Since 1960*. New York: Simon & Schuster, 1991.

Faludi, Susan. *Backlash: The Undeclared War Against American Women*. New York: Crown, 1991.

French, Marilyn. *The War Against Women*. New York: Summit Books, 1992.

Friedan, Betty. *The Feminine Mystique*. New York: Dell Publishing, 1965.

Gilligan, Carol. *In a Different Voice*. Cambridge, Mass.: Harvard University Press, 1982.

Morgan, Robin. *The Word of a Woman: Feminist Dispatches, 1968-1992*. New York: W. W. Norton, 1992.

Morton, Patricia. *Disfigured Images: The Historical Assault on Afro-American Women*. New York: Greenwood Press, 1991.

Bibliography

Steinem, Gloria. *Outrageous Acts and Everyday Rebellions*. New York: Holt, Rinehart and Winston, 1983.

WORK AND LABOR

Castellblanch, Ramon. *Union Support Among Women and Minority Workers*. Berkeley: Center for Labor Research and Education, Institute of Industrial Relations, University of California, Berkeley, 1990.

Danziger, Sheldon, and Peter Gottschalk, eds. *Uneven Tides: Rising of Inequality in America*. New York: Russell Sage Foundation, 1993.

Ewing, David W. *Do It My Way or You're Fired*. New York: John Wiley, 1983.

Griswold DelCastillo, Richard, and Richard A. Garcia. *César Chávez: A Triumph of Spirit*. Norman: University of Oklahoma Press, 1995.

Levitan, Sar, and Isaac Shapiro. *Working but Poor: America's Contradiction*. Baltimore: The Johns Hopkins University Press, 1987.

Moore, Lynda, ed. *Not as Far as You Think: The Realities of Working Women*. Lexington, Mass.: Lexington Books, 1986.

Simon, Paul. *Let's Put America Back to Work*. Chicago: Bonus Books, 1987.

Tannen, Deborah. *Talking from Nine to Five: Women and Men in the Workplace: Language, Sex and Power*. New York: Avon Books, 1994.

Theriault, Reg. *How to Tell When You're Tired: A Brief Examination of Work*. New York: W. W. Norton, 1995.

MEDIAGRAPHY

The following brief list is designed to direct readers to a sampling of notable recent works, in a variety of media, that address social issues in a modern context. Included are literary, cinematic, video, and musical artworks as well as scholarly, critical, and other nonfiction productions. Some of these have been the subject of considerable controversy and have become "issues" in themselves; others offer thought-provoking, unusual, or otherwise useful commentary. All provide valuable perspective on one or more of the major questions engaging the attention of North American culture in the late twentieth century.

BOOKS

Bloom, Allan. *The Closing of the American Mind: How Higher Education Has Failed Democracy and Impoverished the Souls of Today's Students*. New York: Simon & Schuster, 1987. A controversial indictment of the American educational system. Bloom argues that modern American schools promulgate faddish values and produce shallow, passionless graduates.

De Grazia, Edward. *Girls Lean Back Everywhere: The Law of Obscenity and the Assault on Genius*. New York: Random House, 1992. An absorbing analysis of the evolution of twentieth century obscenity laws in the United States. De Grazia's account of the on-going war between artists and censors is illuminating and occasionally riveting.

Erdrich, Louise. *The Bingo Palace*. New York: HarperCollins, 1994. A novel set on an American Indian reservation. Erdrich's book is an absorbing fictional examination of the plight of America's oldest underclass.

Helyar, John. *Lords of the Realm: The* Real *History of Baseball*. New York: Random House, 1994. A fascinating, well-researched economic history of baseball. Helyar's behind-the-scenes glimpses of the machinations of team owners, union representatives, and player agents is essential reading for anyone seeking a real understanding of the business of American sports.

Henry, William A., III. *In Defense of Elitism*. New York; Doubleday, 1994. Henry argues that Americans have stubbornly clung to the myth of egalitarianism. He contests such commonly expressed ideas as the notion that everyone is essentially alike; that self-fulfillment is more important than objective achievement; that everyone has something significant to "contribute"; and that all cultures are equally worthwhile.

Herrnstein, Richard J., and Charles Murray. *The Bell Curve: Intelligence and Class Structure in American Life*. New York: Free Press, 1994. Murray and Herrnstein set off a heated public battle by asserting a link between genetically based intelligence and social class. The most controversial chapters deal with alleged IQ differences between racial groups.

Humphrey, Derek. *Final Exit*. New York: Dell Publishers, 1992. As medical science continues to advance and the expense of medical care skyrockets, the medical community and society at large are confronted by new bioethical dilemmas. Humphrey deals with such issues as whether a physician should keep someone alive regardless of expense and whether medically assisted suicide should be legalized.

Kozol, Jonathan. *Savage Inequalities: Children in America's Schools*. New York: HarperCollins, 1992. Kozol focuses on extremes of wealth and poverty in American schools. He highlights the devastating effects that inequality has on the urban poor and charges that the social policies of the Ronald Reagan and George Bush administrations are largely responsible.

Lukas, Anthony. *Common Ground: A Turbulent Decade in the Lives of Three American Families*. New York: Alfred A. Knopf, 1985. A Pulitzer Prize-winning book that examines three Boston families, one African American, one Irish Catholic, and one Anglo-Saxon Protestant. Lukas traces their disparate experiences in the Boston public school system amid controversies over desegregation and busing.

McDonald, Andrew. *The Turner Diaries*. New York: Random House, 1985. McDonald's fictional account of America in an all-out race war has gained notoriety as one of the "bibles" of the militia movement. Members of militia groups and paramilitary organizations have viewed the book's scenario as a model for what might happen in the United States.

Mediagraphy

Nelson, Jill. *Volunteer Slavery: My Authentic Negro Experience*. Chicago: Noble Press, 1993. Nelson views the experience of African American women as one of double discrimination in which both their race and gender are often held against them. A writer for *The Washington Post*, Nelson depicts black males as often joining forces with white males in an effort to oppress black women.

Nuland, Sherwin B. *How We Die: Reflections on Life's Final Chapter*. New York: Alfred A. Knopf, 1994. Drawing on his own experiences with death among family and patients, Dr. Nuland catalogs the six most common causes of death (heart disease, trauma, cancer, AIDS, Alzheimer's disease, and old age). His work examines what death means to patients, families, and the medical community.

Sale, Kirkpatrick. *The Conquest of Paradise*. New York: Alfred A. Knopf, 1990. A controversial history that depicts the Americas before European colonization as an "Eden of astonishing plenitude" in which people lived in "balanced and fruitful harmony." Sale's work has been criticized as an exercise in revisionist mythmaking.

Shilts, Randy. *And the Band Played On: Politics, People, and the AIDS Epidemic*. New York: St. Martin's Press, 1987. The first major history of the AIDS epidemic. Harshly critical of the government, the press, and the gay community for being slow to respond to the growing crisis.

Staples, Brent. *Parallel Time: Growing up in Black and White*. New York: Pantheon Books, 1994. Staples' memoir is framed around the murder of his younger brother, a twenty-two-year-old drug dealer. A highly personal account of family pain that offers an intimate view of America's race and drug problems.

Stewart, James B. *Den of Thieves*. Portland, Ore.: Touchstone Books, 1992. Stewart examines the freewheeling, deal-making Wall Street of the 1980's, when "financial buccaneers" such as Michael Milken and Ivan Boesky earned fortunes—and prison sentences—in the investment world.

FILMS AND TELEVISION PROGRAMS

The Beavis and Butthead Show: This MTV cartoon series depicts two dysfunctional teenagers whose lives revolve around music videos. The source of controversy when one of its episodes was alleged to have prompted a child viewer to set a fatal fire, the show is frequently cited in discussions of censorship, the moral responsibility of television, and the general decline of culture.

Born on the Fourth of July (1989): Based on the acclaimed autobiography of Ron Kovic, this is one of the better films on the personal fallout of the Vietnam War. Traces Kovic's evolution from idealistic young working-class enlistee into, successively, a proficient soldier, a wheelchair-bound veteran, an antiwar activist, and an advocate for veterans' rights.

Boyz N the Hood (1991): A sober look at gang violence and family strife in South-Central Los Angeles.

The Color Purple (1985): Director Steven Spielberg's adaptation of Alice Walker's novel following the tribulations of an African American woman in the rural South. Although praised by critics, the film triggered protests for its harsh depiction of black men.

Dead Man Walking (1995): A taut examination of the realities of capital punishment, following the developing relationship between a death-row inmate and the nun who acts as his advocate and spiritual adviser. Based on the real-life account published in 1993 by Sister Helen Prejean.

Do the Right Thing (1989): A tragicomic depiction of racial conflict in a multiethnic section of Brooklyn. Director Spike Lee delivers a gritty, realistic look at the causes of urban rage.

Driving Miss Daisy (1989): Prejudice in the South is vividly portrayed in this tender film about an aging Jewish woman and her African American chauffeur. The relationship of the central characters artfully reveals the race-conscious society that shapes them.

Hoop Dreams (1995): An acclaimed documentary chronicling the lives of two talented young inner-city basketball players. A fascinating look at poverty, racism, and the exploitation of athletes.

It's My Party (1996): A thoughtful, poignant film that depicts the "living wake" of a man dying of AIDS who has decided to make peace with everyone he can during a two-day party before he commits suicide.

Kramer vs. Kramer (1979): Exposes the turmoil of a disintegrating family. Divorce, custody battles, and their effects on children are sharply depicted.

The Last Temptation of Christ (1988): Director Martin Scorsese's adaptation of an acclaimed novel portrays Christ as a fully realized human, filled with doubts and temptations. Despite generally positive reviews, the film sparked wide protests from religious groups that decried it as blasphemous.

Mississippi Burning (1988): This harshly realistic drama depicts the FBI's investigation into the 1964 murders of three civil rights workers.

Murphy Brown: This situation comedy became the center of controversy when the show's protagonist chose to bear an out-of-wedlock child, prompting then Vice-President Dan Quayle to cite the series as an example of Hollywood's failure to promote "family values."

Philadelphia (1993): Oscar winner Tom Hanks portrays an up-and-coming lawyer who is the victim of discrimination because he has AIDS. Lauded by critics as a vivid portrayal of the plight of AIDS victims, the film was also protested by gay activists who decried the filmmakers' neglect of gay artists and performers.

Platoon (1986): A riveting and at times poignant look at the Vietnam War, focusing attention on the soldier's point of view of the war as confusing and irrational.

Plutonium Circus (1995): An examination of the post-Cold War dismantling of nuclear weapons at a plant in Amarillo, Texas, where plutonium leaking from the weapons may have contaminated the water supplies of several states. Includes interviews with local officials and business leaders who support the process for its economic benefits.

Profession: Neo-Nazi (1995): A documentary that follows a young neo-Nazi as he travels from Canada to Germany to recruit others to his cause. Along the way, the subject expresses his view that the "Holocaust is a hoax."

Roger and Me (1989): An acclaimed documentary of the havoc wrought on the town of Flint, Michigan by the corporate ruthlessness of General Motors. Director Michael Moore's film was widely praised for its telling, often hilarious moments of insight; Moore also drew criticism, however, for manipulating the film's time frame to emphasize his themes and for including a scene in which a rabbit is clubbed to death and skinned on camera.

The Thin Blue Line (1988): A fascinating examination of the 1976 murder of a Dallas policeman and the ensuing successful efforts by police and prosecutors to convict a probably innocent man of the crime. In 1989, as a direct result of the controversy aroused by the film, the conviction was overturned, and the accused man was released after having spent more than a decade on death row.

POPULAR MUSIC

Body Count, "Cop Killer" (1992): This track from the 1992 album *Body Count* made the group's leader, "gangsta" rapper Ice-T, a household name when police groups threatened to organize a boycott of Time Warner, the record label's parent company. The company eventually dropped the track from the album and asked its other artists to avoid such material, leading to cries of censorship and racism.

Crow, Sheryl. *Sheryl Crow* (1996): This follow-up to the artist's hugely successful 1993 Grammy-winning debut provoked controversy with the track "Love Is a Good Thing," which refers to children killing one another with guns "bought at Wal-Mart discount stores." Wal-Mart refused to stock the album, asserting that it did not sell guns to minors; Crow, however, refused to alter the recording, although the chain's boycott of the album was expected to cost her thousands of sales.

Jackson, Michael, *HIStory* (1995): A poorly received collection of old and new material that stirred controversy with allegedly anti-Semitic lyrics; the album was recalled, and the offending tracks were revised for re-release.

_____, *Thriller* (1982): This enormously successful album (which generated seven top-ten singles) broke the de facto color line on the fledgling music-video network MTV, which had avoided videos by black performers. Jackson's label, CBS Records, threatened to pull its videos unless MTV programmed tracks from Thriller, and the network relented.

Judas Priest, *Stained Class* (1978): In 1986, the parents of two Nevada teenagers sued the veteran heavy-metal band, claiming that subliminal messages contained in the music of this album had driven their sons to shoot themselves; the suit was dismissed in 1990.

Madonna, *Like a Prayer* (1989): The title track and its accompanying video sparked outrage by presenting an eroticized Jesus Christ. After the Vatican issued a censure, public pressure prompted the Pepsi-Cola corporation to cancel the singer's endorsement deal.

Milli Vanilli, *Girl You Know It's True* (1989): This hugely successful release, which generated three

Mediagraphy

number-one hit singles and won a Grammy Award, caused a scandal when it was revealed that the alleged singers were mere photogenic, lip-synching impostors; the revelation prompted lawsuits, fraud charges, and complaints of record-industry cynicism.

Nirvana, *Nevermind* (1991): The album that brought "grunge" music to a broad commercial audience. Lauded by rock critics for its uncompromisingly antiestablishment stance, but controversial for its seeming endorsement of drug use and violence; such charges would resurface with renewed force following the 1994 suicide of bandleader Kurt Cobain.

Osbourne, Ozzy, "Suicide Solution" (1980): A track from Osbourne's *Blizzard of Ozz* album; between 1985 and 1990, the singer was sued three times by different sets of parents who claimed that the song had induced their children to commit suicide (Osbourne prevailed in each suit).

Public Enemy, *It Takes a Nation of Millions to Hold Us Back* (1990): A landmark rap album that sparked debate with its attacks on mainstream media and its praise of controversial Nation of Islam leader Louis Farrakhan as a "prophet"; group members were subsequently accused of anti-Semitism.

2 Live Crew, *As Nasty As They Wanna Be* (1989): 2 Live Crew earned national notoriety when this album was declared obscene by a Florida judge and its sale was subsequently banned in the state; band members were later arrested for performing the songs (the band was acquitted, and the obscenity ruling against the album was subsequently reversed). The ruckus inflamed the debate over "decency" in song lyrics, leading to attacks on the album by Senator Bob Dole, former cabinet secretary William Bennett, and African American women's activist C. Delores Tucker.

Timeline of Major Twentieth Century Court Rulings and Legislation

Cases are U.S. Supreme Court rulings unless otherwise noted

1896	*Plessy v. Ferguson*	Established the "separate but equal" doctrine.
1906	Pure Food and Drug Act	Established consumer-safety standards.
1908	*Muller v. Oregon*	Upheld a maximum-hour law for working women.
1910	Mann Act	Prohibited interstate transportation of women for "immoral purposes."
1911	*Standard Oil Co. v. United States*	Ordered the breakup of Standard Oil.
1914	Clayton Antitrust Act	Expanded and strengthened antitrust laws.
1914	Federal Trade Commission Act	Established the Federal Trade Commission to police unfair business competition.
1914	*Weeks v. United States*	Held warrantless search to be unconstitutional.
1918	Sedition Act	Outlawed forms of seditious speech.
1919	*Abrams v. United States*	Upheld the constitutionality of the 1918 Sedition Act.
1919	Eighteenth Amendment	Outlawed the sale or consumption of alcoholic beverages.
1919	Nineteenth Amendment	Gave women the right to vote.
1919	*Schenck v. United States*	Permitted the prosecution of an antidraft pamphleteer.
1925	*Gitlow v. New York*	Ruled that the First Amendment did not protect advocacy of the violent overthrow of the government.
1927	*Buck v. Bell*	Held that the involuntary sterilization of a mentally handicapped woman was not unconstitutional.
1933	Twentieth Amendment	Repealed the Eighteenth Amendment, ending Prohibition.
1935	National Labor Relations Act	Set up board to settle labor-management conflicts and allowed labor the right to engage in collective bargaining.

Timeline

1935	Social Security Act	Provided retirement income based on withholding from workers' pay.
1936	Robinson-Patman Act	Enumerated illegal types of price discrimination.
1938	Chandler Act	Revised bankruptcy laws.
1938	Fair Labor Standards Act	Established federal minimum-wage and child-labor rules.
1938	Federal Food, Drug, and Cosmetics Act	Amended and expanded the Pure Food and Drug Act.
1939	Hatch Act	Criminalized forms of political corruption.
1940	Smith Act	Required aliens to register with the U.S. government.
1942	Executive Order 9066	Called for the internment of Japanese Americans during World War II.
1943	*Hirabayashi v. United States*	Upheld curfew for Japanese Americans.
1944	G.I. Bill of Rights	Provided educational and economic benefits for World War II veterans.
1944	*Korematsu v. United States*	Upheld internment of Japanese Americans.
1944	*Smith v. Allwright*	Ruled whites-only primaries unconstitutional.
1945	*United States v. Aluminum Company of America*	Ordered the breakup of Alcoa Aluminum.
1947	Taft-Hartley Act	Amended National Labor Relations Act to limit power of trade unions.
1948	Executive Order 9981	Desegregated the U.S. military.
1950	Celler-Kefauver Act	Strengthened the provisions of the Clayton Antitrust Act.
1954	*Brown v. Board of Education of Topeka, Kansas*	Outlawed segregation in public schools.
1954	Espionage and Sabotage Act	Made espionage and sabotage in peacetime capital offenses.
1957	Civil Rights Act	Strengthened federal government's power to enforce voting rights and established Commission on Civil Rights.
1957	*Roth v. United States*	Ruled that the First Amendment did not protect obscene material.

1960	Canadian Bill of Rights	Protected individual rights and liberties.
1960	Civil Rights Act	Increased federal government's power to enforce voting rights laws.
1960	Hazardous Substances Labeling Act	Controlled labeling of household packages of hazardous substances.
1961	*Mapp v. Ohio*	Held that the Fourth Amendment prohibited the use of illegally obtained evidence.
1962	*Engel v. Vitale*	Outlawed prayer in public schools.
1963	*Abington School District v. Schempp*	Forbade public-school prayer and Bible reading.
1963	*Gideon v. Wainwright*	Required that indigent defendants must receive representation.
1964	Civil Rights Act	Forbade discrimination in numerous facets of public life.
1964	*Escobedo v. Illinois*	Reiterated the right to avoid self-incrimination.
1964	*New York Times Co. v. Sullivan*	Ruled that public officials could not sue the press for defamation unless the press acted with malice.
1964	Twenty-fourth Amendment	Outlawed poll taxes and other antivoting measures.
1965	Elementary and Secondary Education Act	Established the right of disabled children to public education.
1965	*Miranda v. Arizona*	Required police to inform suspects of their rights.
1965	National Endowment for the Arts and Humanities Act	Established the National Endowment for the Arts and the National Endowment for the Humanities.
1965	Voting Rights Act	Expanded and protected voting rights, particularly for minorities.
1966	Cigarette Labeling and Advertising Act	Required health warnings on cigarette packages.
1966	*Sheppard v. Maxwell*	Ruled that pretrial publicity violated a defendant's right to a fair trial.
1967	Age Discrimination Act	Prohibited discrimination in hiring and other areas on the basis of age.
1967	Freedom of Information Act	Established public right of access to government records.

Timeline

1967	*In re Gault*	Ruled that juveniles are entitled to due process.
1968	Architectural Barriers Act	Required federally funded buildings to be made accessible to the disabled.
1968	Civil Rights Act	Prohibited racial discrimination in hiring and in public accommodations.
1968	Fair Housing Act	Banned discrimination in sale or rental of housing.
1968	*Jones v. Alfred Mayer Co.*	Ruled that Congress could prohibit private housing discrimination.
1968	Truth-in-Lending Act	Required full disclosure of credit terms in commercial transactions.
1969	Child Protection and Toy Safety Act	Banned many dangerous toys.
1969	*Tinker v. Des Moines*	Upheld students' right to wear armbands to protest Vietnam War.
1970	Occupational Safety and Health Act	Established rules to protect health and safety workers.
1971	*Griggs v. Duke Power Co.*	Ruled that Congress could require job tests to be related to job skills.
1971	*New York Times Co. v. United States*	Ruled that the federal government could not prevent publication of the "Pentagon Papers."
1971	*Swann v. Charlotte-Mecklenburg Board of Education*	Declared forced school busing to be constitutional.
1971	Twenty-first Amendment	Lowered the minimum voting age to eighteen.
1972	*Barker v. Wingo*	Reaffirmed the right to a speedy trial.
1972	Consumer Product Safety Act	Established the Consumer Product Safety Commission.
1972	Education Amendments, Title IX	Prohibited sex discrimination in schools receiving federal money.
1972	*Eisenstadt v. Baird*	Invalidated a state law restricting contraceptive purchases to married couples.
1972	Equal Employment Opportunity Act	Forbade many types of employment-related discrimination.

1972	Equal Rights Amendment	Forbade discrimination on the basis of sex; not ratified.
1972	*Furman v. Georgia*	Struck down most applications of the death penalty.
1972	*Lindsey v. Normet*	Confirmed the right to housing without discrimination.
1973	*Doe v. Bolton*	Invalidated state requirements that abortions be performed only in hospitals.
1973	*Frontiero v. Richardson*	Voided a federal law that apportioned benefits to military defendants differently on the basis of sex.
1973	*Miller v. California*	Set standards for the regulation of obscenity.
1973	Rehabilitation Act	Established federal programs for the disabled.
1973	*Roe v. Wade*	Removed most restrictions on abortion.
1974	*Milliken v. Bradley*	Limited busing for integration across district lines.
1975	Education for All Handicapped Children Act	Expanded the right of disabled children to public education.
1976	*Gregg v. Georgia*	Reaffirmed that the death penalty is not "cruel and unusual punishment."
1976	*Planned Parenthood v. Danforth*	Disallowed parental-notification requirements and other limitations on abortion.
1976	*United States v. American Telephone and Telegraph Co.*	Ordered the breakup of AT&T.
1977	Charter of the French Language	Made French the official language of Québec.
1978	*Regents of the University of California v. Bakke*	Held that college affirmative action programs cannot use race as their sole criterion.
1978	*Village of Skokie v. National Socialist Party*	Affirmed the First Amendment rights of neo-Nazis.
1982	Canadian Charter of Rights and Freedoms	Guaranteed a broad array of fundamental individual rights.
1982	*Plyler v. Doe*	Held that states could not refuse public schooling to illegal aliens.
1983	*Akron v. Akron Center for Reproductive Health*	Struck down restrictions on abortion.

Timeline

1984	Victim and Witness Protection Act	Established protections for victims and witnesses in criminal proceedings.
1984	Voting Accessibility for the Elderly and Handicapped Act	Required voting places to be made accessible to the elderly and disabled.
1986	Air Carriers Access Act	Prohibited airlines from discriminating against the disabled.
1986	*City of Renton v. Playtime Theaters*	Upheld zoning regulations as a means of controlling locations of adult theaters.
1986	Tax Reform Act	Overhauled federal tax laws.
1987	Meech Lake Accord	Canadian constitutional compromise designed to prevent secession of Québec; never ratified.
1988	Civil Rights Restoration Act	Expanded and extended civil rights laws.
1988	*Queen v. Morgenthaler, Smoling, and Scott*	Supreme Court of Canada struck down federal limitations on abortion.
1989	*Brooks, Allen, and Dixon v. Canada Safeway*	Supreme Court of Canada ruled that discrimination on the basis of pregnancy constituted sexual discrimination.
1989	*Daigle v. Tremblay*	Supreme Court of Canada denied a father's effort to intervene in the abortion of his unborn child.
1989	Helms Amendment	Restricted federal arts funding for "obscene" works.
1989	*Richmond v. J. A. Croson Co.*	Placed limitations on affirmative action programs.
1989	*Texas v. Johnson*	Held that burning of the American flag is constitutionally protected speech.
1989	*Wards Cove Packing Company v. Atonio*	Made it more difficult for plaintiffs to prove employer discrimination.
1989	*Webster v. Reproductive Health Services*	Upheld some state restrictions on abortion.
1990	Americans with Disabilities Act	Strengthened civil rights protection for the disabled.
1990	Clean Air Act Amendments	Mandated reductions in air pollution.
1990	*Employment Division v. Smith*	Upheld restrictions on peyote use in religious rituals.
1990	*Maryland v. Craig*	Permitted children to testify via closed-circuit television.

1990	*Osborne v. Ohio*	Held that child pornography is not protected by the First Amendment.
1990	Patient Self-Determination Act	Required health-care providers to inform patients of treatment rights.
1991	Civil Rights Act	Enhanced ability of minorities to sue for job discrimination.
1991	*Harmelin v. Michigan*	Upheld a state law mandating life sentences for drug possession.
1992	*Butler v. the Queen*	Supreme Court of Canada upheld the validity of anti-obscenity laws.
1992	Charlottetown Accord	Constitutional agreement revamping Canada's federal system; never ratified.
1993	Family Medical Leave Act	Mandated time off for workers for infant care or medical emergencies.
1993	*Rodriguez v. British Columbia*	Supreme Court of Canada upheld a ban on medically assisted suicide.
1993	*Shaw v. Reno*	Called for "strict scrutiny" in the drawing of congressional districts.
1993	Violence Against Women Act	Enhanced penalties for gender-motivated crimes.
1993	*Wisconsin v. Mitchell*	Upheld constitutionality of a state hate-crimes statute.
1995	*Adarand Constructors v. Peña*	Held that a broad Department of Transportation affirmative action program was unconstitutional.
1996	Kennedy-Kassebaum Health Act	Made health insurance portable from job to job and curtailed exclusions based on pre-existing conditions.
1996	Personal Responsibility and Work Opportunity Act	Revamped the U.S. welfare system, turning most federal responsibilities over to the states.

ENTRIES BY SUBJECT

Entries by Subject

Entries by Subject

Entries by Subject

Entries by Subject

Entries by Subject

Entries by Subject

Entries by Subject

RELIGION AND SPIRITUALITY.   *See also* Values and ethics

Entries by Subject

ENCYCLOPEDIA
of
SOCIAL ISSUES

INDEX